Battleground Europe
Mediterranean

CRETE
THE AIRBORNE INVASION 1941

D1479316

Battleground series:

With the continued expansion of the Battleground Series a **Battleground Series Club** has been formed to benefit the reader. The purpose of the Club is to keep members informed of new titles and to offer many other reader-benefits. Membership is free and by registering an interest you can help us predict print runs and thus assist us in maintaining the quality and prices at their present levels.

Please call the office on 01226 734555, or send your name and address along with a request for more information to:

Battleground Series Club Pen & Sword Books Ltd,
47 Church Street, Barnsley, South Yorkshire S70 2AS

Battleground Europe
Mediterranean

CRETE
THE AIRBORNE INVASION 1941

Tim Saunders

Pen & Sword
MILITARY

This book is dedicated to
Alain, Philip, Alison and Hazel
of Anglia Battlefield Tours
for whom I conduct tours of
the 1941 Crete Campaign.

First published in Great Britain in 2008 by
Pen & Sword Military
an imprint of
Pen & Sword Books Ltd
47 Church Street
Barnsley
South Yorkshire
S70 2AS

Copyright © Tim Saunders, 2008

ISBN 978 1 84415 558 3

The right of Tim Saunders to be identified as Author of the Work
has been asserted by him in accordance with the Copyright, Designs and
Patents Act 1988.

A CIP catalogue record for this book is
available from the British Library.

All rights reserved. No part of this book may be reproduced or transmitted in any
form or by any means, electronic or mechanical including photocopying, recording or
by any information storage and retrieval system, without permission from the
Publisher in writing.

Typeset in Palatino

Printed and bound in the United Kingdom by CPI

Pen & Sword Books Ltd incorporates the imprints of Pen & Sword Aviation, Pen &
Sword Maritime, Pen & Sword Military, Wharncliffe Local History, Pen and Sword
Select, Pen and Sword Military Classics and Leo Cooper.

For a complete list of Pen & Sword titles, please contact
Pen & Sword Books Limited
47 Church Street, Barnsley, South Yorkshire, S70 2AS, England
E-mail: enquiries@pen-and-sword.co.uk
Website: www.pen-and-sword.co.uk

CONTENTS

Introduction

We left Crete rather hurriedly, as the Bosche decided to share the island with us. Since we were rather snobbish, we decided to let them have it – in more senses than one!   Personal letter - officer 2nd Black Watch

The Cretan Campaign took place a full year after the fall of France and demonstrated that Britain and her Empire partners still lacked the resources to match Axis military power. It was also obvious that they had yet to come to terms with, let alone master, the new style of warfare that the Germans had ushered in over the previous two years. As Churchill said, this learning phase or 'beginning' was not to end until El Alamein, almost eighteen months later.

For the Germans, the campaign was the first and last time that airborne forces were to play more than a subsidiary role in a strategic operation. The result of the Cretan adventure was so costly that Hitler never authorised another major airborne operation. None the less, General Student's distinctive elite were to subsequently fight as highly effective infantry in virtually every theatre where German troops were deployed.

In contrast the British studied the airborne invasion of Crete in detail and comprehensive reports were circulated amongst those responsible for the defence of other Mediterranean objectives and the United Kingdom itself. The lessons of Crete also informed those who were developing Britain's own airborne capability. The recommendations made in these reports were sound but in later years were occasionally forgotten or ignored; where this was so, disaster invariably resulted.

This book covers a short but intense campaign that was full of drama and considerable activity, much of it at a low level of command. In addition, the battle was spread over an area seventy by forty miles and it would be impossible to include every action that was fought in a book of this size. Consequently, within the broad setting of the Cretan Campaign as a whole, I have highlighted the more important actions that for the reader at home or the visitor to the battlefields, give a flavour of what it was like for men of the opposing armies during those twelve days in May 1941.

I have referred to what many would describe as the 'Allies' as the 'Commonwealth' forces in this volume. Technically the Australians provided the Australian Imperial Force but this name does not reflect the changing status of that nation's troops or those of New Zealand or Britain's relationship with their governments. The description

'Commonwealth' most accurately reflects the spirit of the time.

The timings given in this book have all been converted to the time used by the Commonwealth troops by adding an hour to the times quoted by German authorities. Thus, the P Hour for the operation is listed as 0815 hours rather than the German 0715 hours.

As this book is as much a guide to the battlefield, as it is an account of the battle, I have elected to use the modern spelling of place names as they are shown on local signposts in roman script. Over the years, I have found it confusing and the cause of some disorientation when having to cope with a change of spelling (the result of differently accented phonetic translations from Greek into English). Some changes, such as Heraklion or Iraklion, now spelt Iraklio, are obvious but others, typically villages west of the island's capital (Canea or Xania, now Hania), are less obvious. To clarify matters I have standardised the names, but even that is not standard! See table.

Almost finally, many of the photographs were taken by *Fallschirmjäger* and *Gebergsjäger* during the campaign, using their personal Leica cameras. Inexpertly composed, using a film that defies adjustment of contrast and often poorly focussed, the results do, however, give a better flavour of the men and conditions than many official photographs. The majority of the campaign pictures are from German sources, as true to the maxim about withdrawing armies having better things to be doing, few Commonwealth photographs exist. I have saved my last and most important point to last. Visitors must note that although Crete is a part of a modern European Greece, that country as a whole, is in a very sensitive part of the world and that security of military establishments is always high. Two of the locations covered in this book are of particular sensitivity. Iraklio is not only an international airport but an active military airfield, with associated barracks and radar sites. At Maleme the site of the RAF Camp is now a Greek barracks and the airfield is still in commission. Definitely avoid photographing these places. Please heed the advice given in the tour section.

Acknowledgements

I would like to start by acknowledging Anglia Battlefield Tours's part in this book. With a major military customers requiring tours of Crete, I was given the opportunity to both study the campaign in detail and to revisit Crete after several years. During the process of reacquainting myself with the campaign to the depth of detail required, I was able to amass so much material that it was a relatively easy task to assemble it into a *Battleground* book. On the ground, Cretans too numerous to list, helped me to pinpoint the location of events. This was particularly important as, then as now, maps were poor and most of the war diaries that exist were reconstructed after the campaign and, consequently, tend to be rather general than normal in terms of both times and locations. This made placing action more difficult than in other **Battleground** titles. I am therefore extremely grateful for the assistance freely and enthusiastically given by my hosts.

Appreciation must also be recorded for the attitude of both the New Zealand and Australian Government, their military museums and the units concerned, who all encouraged and, more to the point, actively supported my endeavours. My dearest wish is that this book enables more visitors from the Commonwealth not only to enjoy Crete but to visit the scene of some of our nations' most testing times.

Whether at home or on the ground, enjoy the tour.

Tim Saunders
Warminster 2008

Further Reading

Bearing in mind that Crete is a holiday destination the following books could find a welcome space in a suitcase or even be a good read at home:

Officers and Gentlemen (Volume II of the *Sword of Honour* trilogy). Evelyn Waugh – A fictional account based on the author's experience in the Layforce Commandos on Crete.

Ill Met by Moonlight. W Stanley Moss – The contemporaneous diary of the SOE abduction of General Kreipe and the escape through the mountains. Also available in DVD as a drama.

The Cretan Runner. Georre Psychoundakis – Account of the wartime years by an SOE agent/guerrilla covering the Kreipe abduction and numerous other resistance activities.

All are easily found through local bookshops or on-line book sellers.

MODERN NAMES AND THEIR 1941 EQUIVALENT:

Modern	1941	Other Variants
Iraklio	Heraklion	
Hania	Chania	K or Xhania
Maleme	No Change	
Kastelli	Kissamous	Interchangeable today
Rethymno	Retimo	
Galatas	Galatos	
Daratos	Karatos	
Souda	Suda	
Tavronitis		
Agh Pandes	Babali Hani	
Stylos	Stilos	
Pygi	Pyrgos	Pirgos

Chapter One

CRETE AND THE MEDITERRANEAN

With the 'indefinite but inconspicuous postponement' of Operation SEALION, the invasion of Britain, on 17 September 1940, Hitler's attention turned to the defeat of Britain by another strategic route. Wishing to retain the initiative, this resulted in a Peripheral Strategy that aimed to drive Britain into succumbing to German domination before US support became available or the USSR could turn against Germany. The method was for the Axis coalition to attack Britain's vital interests in the Mediterranean, which Grand Admiral Raeder described as 'the pivot of Britain's world empire', and to deny her use of the strategically important Suez Canal. The Mediterranean sea route via Gibraltar and the Suez Canal was indeed the pivotal link in imperial communications with India, Australasia and Eastern Africa. 'Deny this route to British shipping and Britain's position would be untenable', argued advocates of the Peripheral Strategy.

Execution of this German strategy was, however, not straight-forward, as Mussolini, Hitler's leading Axis partner, was keen to carve out a new Italian Empire of his own in the Mediterranean and the Balkans. These interests were to prove to be the undoing of a strategy that was of particular appeal to the *Luftwaffe* and *Kriegsmarine*. Axis politics dictated

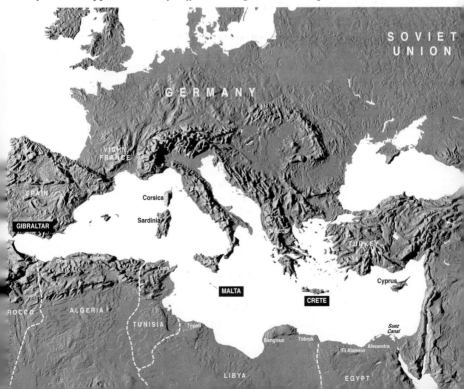

that compromises had to be made. On the one hand, Il Duce resisted offers of German help and involvement, for example. Operation FELIX, the attack on Gibraltar was cancelled, while on the other hand, Hitler vetoed Italian plans to invade Yugoslavia. This country, along with Rumania needed to be firmly in German hands to secure vital raw materials. Particularly important in the latter country were the Ploesti oil fields, which supplied over fifty percent of Germany's fuel.

On 28 October, with Hitler's tacit agreement, the Italian Army crossed the border from their Albanian territory into Greece in a poorly planned and resourced campaign. With a low opinion of the Greeks and their army, Mussolini had erroneously believed that a limited attack, coupled with bombing of Athens, would bring about the disintegration of the small nation: 'By a hard blow at the start, it will be possible to bring about a complete collapse within a few hours.'

Attacking with ten divisions, half the number recommended by his military commanders, the Greeks, despite being riddled with internal divisions, united emotionally and politically against their invader. The bombing failed to break Greek morale and the poorly equipped and trained

The German dictator.

Italian troops were soon bogged down in the mountains as the weather deteriorated. Worse still, the Italians were driven back by a counter offensive. One commentator wrote 'The small, untidy Greek soldier had performed a miracle. What was intended to be a murder now looked like suicide'.

Meanwhile, Hitler's interest in the Peripheral Strategy waned as his attention increasingly focussed on the Soviet Union, gradually relegating German activities in the Mediterranean and on the Channel coast to a deception plan. The uneasy pact between Russia and Germany, which had delivered Soviet complicity in the invasion of Poland and neutrality in the case of France in 1940, was under strain. In the face

The Italian dictator.

of Stalin's growing suspicions and demands, along with an increasing likelihood of an impending transatlantic alliance against the Axis, on 5 December 1940, Hitler finally decided that he would have to march east. As an important preliminary, however, he needed to secure his southern flank by stabilising his hold on the Balkans and completing the elimination of Greece. This would also have the benefit of driving the British back out of bombing range of the Ploesti oil fields. Accordingly, on 13 December 1940, he issued Führer Order 20 for Operation MARITA, the invasion of Greece and occupation of Bulgaria, along with Operation

A German panzer sweep through a portable anti-tank barrier into Greece during operation MARITA.

STRAFE, the invasion of Yugoslavia. Führer Order 21 for Operation BARBAROSSA, the invasion of the Soviet Union, followed on 18 December. It was envisaged that the preliminary Balkan operations would last about four weeks, ending in early April allowing BARBAROSSA to begin in May 1941.

Throughout the autumn of 1940, Hitler actively encouraged the Italians to seize the Greek island of Crete, which with the deployment of the tough and resilient Cretan Division to the Albanian front, the island was virtually undefended. In Axis hands, Crete would in turn be available as a base for Axis air and naval forces to strike at Egypt, support operations in North Africa and dominate much of the eastern Mediterranean. Conversely, in British hands Crete would be an important base from which they could mount long range bombing operations against German interests in the Balkans. The Italians, however, did not take the opportunity to seize the lightly defended island. By the time the advantage of seizing Crete was plain to all, with their invasion of the Greek mainland in trouble, the Italians lacked the resources and will to take on the Royal Navy and invade Crete.

Churchill, a long time advocate of a Peripheral Strategy of his own, was alive to the strategic importance of Crete. Initially, therefore, both the Greek and British governments were reluctant to have a British presence on the island in case such a move provoked the Axis. Troops were put on very

British commanders in the Mediterranean; Cunningham, Longmore and Wavell.

short notice to move to Crete but Britain's resources in the Mediterranean were spread extremely thinly.

Priority for available forces, at a time when the country was seeking to replace the equipment lost during the Dunkirk campaign and fighting the *Luftwaffe* over Britain, was defence of the home base. None the less, Churchill saw the Mediterranean Theatre as not only a threat but also as offering the opportunity to break 'the intolerable shackles of the defensive'. Consequently, even though the cancellation of SEALION was not apparent and the invasion threat persisted into 1941, as Hitler played up his intentions to invade Britain to cover Operation BARBAROSSA; Churchill dispatched not inconsiderable resources to the Mediterranean.

Britain's commander in the Middle East, General Archibald Wavell, concentrated his forces to hold the Italians on the direct approach to Egypt from Libya, while consistently performing a juggling act with the scant remaining forces, as successive threats appeared in his patch, including Sudan in the south, Palestine, Egypt and Cyprus in the centre and Iraq in the east. Professor MacDonald summed up the situation when he wrote 'It was Wavell's misfortune to fight at a time when British industrial capacity was limited and before American resources were fully mobilised against the Axis'.

The most pressing of all the threats was the 350,000 man Italian 'Army of the Nile' and at one time, Wavell had just 36,000 men and seventy-five aircraft available to oppose them. Not only that, the Royal Navy had temporarily lost control of the Mediterranean to the Italian Navy and Air Force, forcing Middle East bound supplies and reinforcements to take the long route around the Cape of Good Hope. Despite this, 76,000 reinforcements arrived from the UK with half as many again coming from India, Australia and New Zealand. With these reinforcements, which were still inadequate for the task, Wavell set about dominating the region and fending off criticism and what he saw as political interference by Churchill.

Wavell's operations included COMPASS (December 40 – February 41), in which Lieutenant General O'Connor struck the Italian incursions in Egypt's Western Desert and drove them back across the Libyan border. During the pursuit west, the Allies captured some 25,000 Italian prisoners, 208 field and medium guns, 23 medium tanks and over 200 other vehicles, along with wells and water distilleries that could produce 40,000 gallons a day – for the cost

A field park of captured Italian guns. A portrait of Mussolini glowers at a couple of victorious Tommies.

Lieutenant General Sir Richard O'Connor, left, and General Sir Archibald Wavell, General Officer Commander-in-Chief. They were responsible for victory over the Italians.

of some 355 casualties. As the advance continued on westwards, General O'Connor advocated finishing the job by pushing on to Tripoli and clearing the Italians out of North Africa. Success in the Western Desert, however, was merely one less thing for Wavell to worry about and he had too few resources, so he could only keep trouble at bay before another problem arose elsewhere. In this case by mid February, maps of North Africa on the walls of his HQ had been replaced by those of Greece.

Informed by decryptions of German Enigma encoded radio traffic, Wavell had received instructions from the Defence Committee to send an expeditionary force to Greece before the Germans invaded the country. By 5 March, preparations for the deployment to Greece were under way stripping resources away from the Western Desert Force that had by now reached Cyrenia in Libya. As we will see, finding men and equipment for Greece further slowed the build-up in Crete.

The Defences of Crete

As already recounted, early moves to secure Crete against the Axis, despite Greece's political alignment with Britain, were thwarted by the simple necessity of not giving the Italians an excuse to invade. All that Middle East Forces could spare anyway was a single Alexandria-based, battalion put on a day's notice to move in the appropriately named Operation SPARROW.

As soon as the Italians invaded mainland Greece on the 28 October, Operation SPARROW was upgraded to two battalions, the leading element of which was at six hours' notice to move by sea. The revised Operation was called ACTION! A decision was also reached to establish a 'second Scapa Flow' in the form of a naval fuelling and arming base at Souda Bay and to protect it with anti-aircraft guns of the Mobile Naval Base Defence Organisation (MNBDO) and up to a brigade of infantry. To assemble shipping and supplies to make use of the best natural harbour in the eastern Mediterranean would take some months. In the meantime 2 York and Lancs, the leading element of ACTION Force, left Alexandria on 31

October 1940, arriving in Crete the following day amidst a bombing raid on nearby Hania.

The reinforcement of the island pleased the Prime Minister, as he 'was convinced of the importance of the occupation of Crete'. With the Greek Government's support, a second wave of reinforcement (2 Black Watch) was dispatched but from the outset it was found that little in the way of resources, food or material of any kind was available for use by the British. This simple factor was a significant brake on the development of the island's defences throughout the six months before the Germans launched their invasion. Consequently, not only was shipping required for men, weapons and equipment but also for continual re-supply convoys, carrying all nature of stores needed to sustain the garrison.

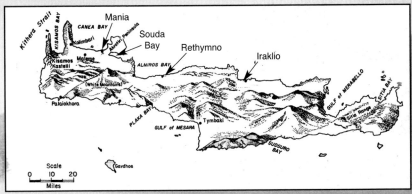

Brigadier Tidbury and a tri-Service staff on an early recce of Crete.

Having established a presence in Crete, Wavell had to continue his regional juggling act and only a trickle of men and resources made their way to the island. Brigadier Tidbury, the first of a series of short duration commanders, each of whose tenure prevented continuity of approach to the defence of the island, reported that in addition to a lack of local resources '... transport and labour were scarce, and road conditions difficult, especially after rain'. Orders were, however, given to prepare infrastructure and stores to support a division-sized garrison in the event of the Greek mainland being overrun.

The problem facing the succession of commanders was not only to maintain an uneasy balance between establishing the necessary logistic infrastructure and building defences but also to define the balance between coastal defence and that of the airfields. The advanced Naval refuelling base at Souda Bay clearly needed both coastal and anti-aircraft defence. The existing airbase at Iraklio and the airfields being developed by the RAF at Maleme, Rethymno and Kastelli needed air defence and being on the coastal strip, defence from amphibious attack as well. With few troops and a lack of resources, neither type of defence could be adequately addressed. The whole issue was, however, bedevilled by narrow single service planning. Facilities would be sited, often without consultation, and then additional ground defences demanded. For example, the RAF at one airfield sited their fuel and ammunition facilities outside the Army's previously agreed defensive perimeter, necessitating time consuming and

A Lewis gun team and Greek gendarmes providing air defence to British capital ships in Souda Bay.

resource intensive adjustments being made at the expense of work elsewhere.

During the period from the Italian invasion of Greece through to the evacuation, the majority of the troops arriving in Crete were from logistic corps and anti-aircraft gunners, with the notable exception of 1 Welch who joined the other two infantry battalions. 1 Welch were eventually to become the CREFORCE reserve. The total of anti-aircraft guns deployed to Crete eventually reached 32 heavy and 36 light guns, against an assessed requirement of 56 and 48 respectively.

Perhaps the greatest shortage of all was in aircraft. The paucity of aircraft with which to defend the airspace over Crete and the surrounding waters, was to cast a very long shadow over the campaign. Those available in the Mediterranean had been forced to fly a 3,000 mile circuitous route across Africa, arriving in Egypt in dire need of refurbishment. The need for strong air forces in Crete (six permanently based fighter squadrons) was, however, recognised but there were simply too few aircraft available to meet all the RAF's tasks. Anyway, due to the lack of resources to build them, there were insufficient airbases in Crete for the required number of aircraft to operate from. As we will see, serious aircraft losses in the campaign in Greece only exacerbated the problem.

The Greek Campaign

With the Italians being driven back behind their start lines in Greece and deep into Libya, it was inevitable that Germany, their Axis partner, would come to their assistance. *Generalleutnant* Rommel took the *Afrika Korps* to Libya and *Feldmarschall* List's Twelfth Army was committed to the Balkans. With intelligence indicating an invasion of Greece, Wavell ordered the deployment of a British Expeditionary Force in early March 1941. W Force, so named after its commander Lieutenant General Henry 'Jumbo' Wilson, consisted of 1st British Armoured Brigade and the ANZAC Corps comprising 6th Australian Division and the New Zealand Division. The force totalled some 58,000 men and was to work with three Greek divisions on the Bulgarian front. The 1942 Ministry of Information pamphlet described the aim:

> The Allied plan was that the three-and-a-half Greek Divisions on the Metaxas line should fight a delaying action, inflicting what damage they could on the Germans, but that the main defensive position should be held by British and Greek forces on a line running along the high ground west of the Axios Valley [Aliakmon]. There had been no conversations with the Yugoslav staff, but the Yugoslavs were expected to hold the passes along their frontier from Bulgaria.

At dawn on 6 April 1941, the Germans invaded Yugoslavia and north-eastern Greece without warning, before General Wilson's W Force had completed its deployment to the Aliakmon position. Resistance by the Greeks did not last long, even though:

> *The Greeks fought with astonishing tenacity and bravery. In spite of the most violent attacks by tanks and shock troops and dive-bombers, the Greeks held on, inflicting very severe losses on the enemy. The forts in the Rupel Pass held out for a week.*

The Southern Yugoslav Army was quickly defeated by the *Waffen* SS divisions, and a second route into Greece through the mountain passes lay open. General Wilson adjusted his deployment to counter the immediate threat, but this weakened the main position still further without making the new left flank strong enough to resist for long. The only sound course was to fall back to a position which was less liable to be turned, and the choice fell on a line from Mount Olympus through the Servia Pass, while the passes at Siatista and Klisoura, connecting the Servia-Monastir road with the valley of the upper Aliakmon, were also to be defended. This was to be only the first withdrawal.

With typical German *Blitzkrieg* momentum and tempo of operations, there was seldom time for one rearward move to be finished before the

Commonwealth troops during the withdrawal in Greece.

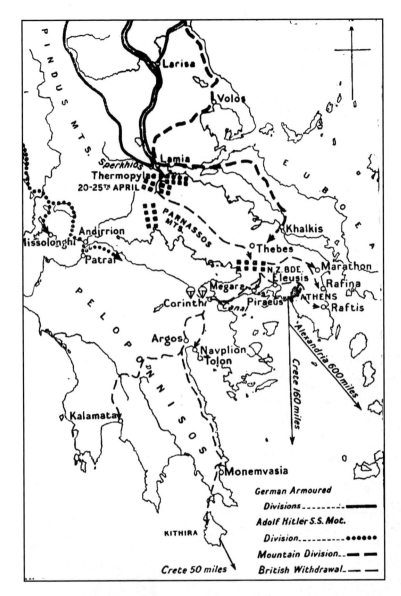

The following labels appear on the map:

PINDUS MTS.

Larisa

Volos

EUBOEA

Sperkhios
Lamia
Thermopylae
20-25TH APRIL

PARNASSOS MTS.

Andirrion
Missolonghi
Patra

PELOPONNISOS

Khalkis

Thebes

Megara
Corinth Canal

N.Z. BDE.
Eleusis
Piraeus
ATHENS

Marathon
Rafina
Raftis

Alexandria 600 miles

Crete 160 miles

Argos
Navplion
Tolon

Kalamata

Monemvasia

KITHIRA

Crete 50 miles

German Armoured
Divisions........... ▬▬▬
Adolf Hitler S.S. Mot.
Division........... ●●●●●●
Mountain Division..▬ ▬
British Withdrawal..▬ ▬

pressure of events imposed another withdrawal. The campaign took on all the characteristics of a rear-guard action, as the Commonwealth and Greek forces were forced south; the British official historian stated that:

> Any hopes of making a prolonged defence on this line were soon dispelled, for the Germans succeeded in crossing the mountains into the upper Aliakmon valley, endangering the Greek armies on the Albanian front and threatening again the left flank of W Force. Lacking the strength

19

A Panzer Mk III in the pass of Thermopylae in April 1941.

with which to restore the situation General Wilson had no choice but to fall
back again - this time to Thermopylae, where the peninsula is only some
thirty miles wide. This ... withdrawal - right across the plain of Thessaly,
meant giving up the principal airfields.

General Wilson believed there seemed to be some chance of making a
useful stand at Thermopylae, no matter what befell the Greek forces. The
Germans, however, could be expected to outflank the position before long.
The two divisions of the ANZAC Corps were insufficient to hold the
determined enemy attacks on the peninsula, as well as defending the vital
points behind them.

At this point, after six months of war 'the Greek political framework
started to crack'. Faced with the inevitability of defeat and the loss of
another army, on 17 April Churchill authorised Wavell to evacuate W Force
from Greece. 'Bombed and strafed by day and night' by *Luftwaffe* aircraft,
Wilson's men withdrew south. The aim was to head south to the
Peloponnese and evacuate as many men as possible. At this point,
however, a disturbing development took place. A German airborne
operation to capture the Corinth Canal Bridge narrowly failed to cut off W
Force's withdrawal. The presence of *Fallschirmjäger* in the Balkans came as
a stark warning to the defenders of Crete.

Corinth and the Evacuation

The bridge over the Corinth Canal represented a choke point on the
Commonwealth line of withdrawal onto the Peloponnese, the capture of

which would trap the majority of W Force, probably leading to the almost total destruction of the divisional sized force still in Greece. Securing the vital bridge would also enable the German armoured spearhead to maintain its momentum without a pause to bridge the canal. Despite its importance, however, the troops allocated to the defence of the key bridge were few but it had been prepared as a reserved demolition.

Seeking a quick and conclusive end to the Greek campaign, Hitler and OKW authorised Operation HANNIBAL in order to cutoff the withdrawing British and Allied force. The task, very similar to the seizure of the Albert Canal bridges the previous May was given to *Fallschirmjäger Regiment (FJR2)* reinforced by a platoon of pioneers (engineers) and a company of medics.

As the attacking *Fallschirmjäger* left the Larissa airfield, which had been only recently been in British hands, General Wilson crossed the Corinth Canal Bridge two hours before dawn on 26 April 1941. At 0700 hours, the *Luftwaffe* began an intensive dive bombing attack on the British anti-aircraft defences within a mile of the bridge. This was followed at 0720 by sustained low-level machine-gun and cannon attack from fighter aircraft; the whole aim being to suppress the air defences and to stun the defenders. At 0740 hours, three DFS-230 gliders landed the German pioneers near the bridge, while over a hundred Ju-52 transport aircraft, some as low as 200 feet, began to drop two battalions of *FJR 2*. Within thirty minutes the force was on the ground. Meanwhile, to interdict Commonwealth reinforcements from Nablion-Argos, 25 miles south of Corinth, German fighters carried out strafing attacks on the Corinth Road.

The *Fallschirmjäger* dropping at either end of the bridge and promptly attacking, overwhelmed the defenders. *Gefreiter* Krug recalled:

Flying on to the canal we came up to some

The Corinth Canal was a deep trench, with few crossing points, and barred access to the Peloponnese.

The Corinth Canal Bridge.

heavy anti-aircraft fire. We landed on very stony and uneven ground, which resulted in unusually heavy drop casualties. Our battalion landed on the north side of the canal and our job was to try to stop the enemy coming from the direction of Athens and to take them prisoner if possible.

The New Zealand Maoris and the Divisional Cavalry Unit (armoured cars/recce) were amongst the defenders:

During the evacuation, the Carrier Platoon was sent back in company with C Squadron of the Divisional Cavalry, to the Corinth Canal as local protection to anti-aircraft guns. Soon after daylight on the 26th it was in hull-down positions overlooking the canal near Corinth. Most of the crews were enjoying a much-needed rest after the all-night drive when a yell, 'They're coming down in parachutes!' sent the carriers into action. In Corporal Hayward's words:

'By this time the parachutists were coming down in dozens and gradually encircling us. At the same time we were being continually and systematically strafed with a string of ME 110s laying down a curtain of fire across the only gap that still remained as a possible escape route towards the hills.'

The sight of the Divisional Cavalry armoured cars already half-way to the hills decided Hayward to make a break through the gap while there was still time. There or four other carriers followed and, after charging through vineyards and over stone walls, got safely away. By this time two carriers had lost their tracks and it was decided to push the others over a cliff and march to an embarkation beach.

The infantry, engineers and the anti-aircraft gunners of the demolition guard, lacking the same mobility were quickly overwhelmed by the *Fallschirmjäger*. *Gefreiter* Krug continued:

We soon had so many prisoners that we didn't know what to do with them! A short time later we were all startled when there was a very loud bang. Looking towards the bridge we saw that it had been blown up and fallen into the canal; some soldiers and a war reporter were killed.

The blowing of the Corinth Canal Bridge.

The Commonwealth demolition guard had, however, fought well to keep the *Fallschirmjäger* at bay and long enough for the Royal Engineers to arm the bridge's demolition charges and blow the vital structure. The Germans were left holding the site, which had cost them 285 casualties but they had the consolation of cutting off 921 Commonwealth troops, mostly from 4 New Zealand Brigade and 1,450 Greeks.

Correctly timing an airborne assault is always difficult and in this case an attack twenty-four or even twelve hours earlier would have delivered a far greater success. The Commonwealth forces were lucky and managed to divert significant numbers to beaches north of the Canal.

Meanwhile, the Evacuation from Greece was under way and lasted from 24 April 1941 through until the end of the month, with the Germans entering Athens on 27 April. A total of 50,732 men were evacuated (including some Greeks and Yugoslavs) of these, 25,000 were evacuated to Crete, along with 10,000 Greeks who mostly escaped from the mainland through a variety of other means. Crete was used initially as a staging post to ensure the shortest possible turn around for ships and aircraft involved in the evacuation. Hence the island had an unexpected influx of troops.

The Greek Campaign cost Britain and her Allies 11,000 men and crucially for Crete, 8,000 trucks were lost, along with most of W Force's heavy equipment, including 400 artillery pieces. In some cases soldiers got away with nothing but the clothes they stood up in. Critically, the RAF lost 209 aircraft of all types in Greece, in a situation where RAF losses were already outstripping the arrival rate of new aircraft. With the *Luftwaffe* operating from bases in mainland Greece the Germans now had air superiority over the Aegean and the northern part of the Libyan Sea, including Crete.

Major General Weston's Report

With events in Greece deteriorating, the importance of Crete finally grew. Consequently, Major General Weston, Royal Marines, was dispatched to Crete on 15 April for a reconnaissance. In his report, he envisaged two separate problems:

> ... the defence of the fleet and air bases in the existing circumstances: and the wider aspect of the defence of the island against invasion, when the situation on the mainland has clearly deteriorated to such an extent that an attack on Crete is clearly imminent.

He believed that the land force should consist of two fresh British brigades and that the number of anti-aircraft guns should be increased to the previously recommended level and with regard to the air force, he believed that a third squadron should be based on the island. No sooner had he returned to Alexandria to make his report than General Weston was ordered to go back to Crete to take over command of the Mobile Naval Base Defence Organisation (MNBDO), which was to defend the port facilities and on 27 April he formally became Commander CREFORCE. Under his command, he had both the MNBDO, which would concentrate on the defence of Souda Bay and Brigadier Chappel's 14 Infantry Brigade, which was deployed around the island's principal airfield at Iraklio.

Even though it was assumed that Crete would be attacked, it was not, however, defences that were General Weston's primary concern on assumption of command but the reception of troops evacuated from Greece. Camps were allocated to the troops but:

> These so called camps were a series of areas marked off ... each provided with a water supply. Officers and men on arrival from Greece were sent to any of their unit who had arrived previously and who had been organised under their officers. Each camp had a commandant who in turn appointed an adjutant. The only cooking utensils were petrol tins; a very large number of men fed out of tin cans, as there were no mess tins, knives, forks or spoons available in large quantities. Each man was as far as possible issued with one set of clothing and one blanket. About 2,000 Australians were without blankets and they averaged in most cases one razor per platoon.

Many of the troops, especially those who had been sunk *en route* from Greece to Crete were without even small arms.

The problem of maintaining the force was worsened by 'useless mouths', chief of which were 15,000 Italian prisoners but on 5 May General Weston was signalling to HQ Middle East that he had another problem:

> There are 10,000 [Commonwealth] *other ranks here without arms and little or no employment other than getting in trouble with the civil population. Can these men be evacuated as soon as possible? Excellent relationship exists between Greeks and ourselves but will be imperilled unless we can get rid of surplus personnel.*

This was agreed but as a low priority and on the eve of the German invasion, 2,000 surplus personnel remained, along with 14,000 prisoners.

Defence Problems and Plans
It was only once the evacuation from Greece was under way that the

Most certainly a public relations photograph showing both Greek and well equipped British soldiers jointly manning a 40mm Bofors anti-aircraft gun.

defence of Crete against invasion began in earnest. Major General Weston assessed the situation as follows:

> The enemy's sea approach to the island is comparatively easy and he can provide air protection for a sea-borne landing. It is difficult for our navy in the face of air superiority to interfere with a seaborne expedition. It is therefore not improbable that he will attempt a sea-borne expedition in conjunction with an airborne attack in the near future.

He concluded that 'Iraklio and its airfield, and Hania, with Maleme airfield and Souda anchorage, must be defended at all costs; the loss of either of these areas would prejudice subsequent relief if German forces landed elsewhere on the island'. With regard to troops to hold his vital terrain, Weston believed:

> For the defence of Iraklio and of the Souda-Hania-Maleme area, at least three brigade groups of four battalions each, and one motor battalion, in addition to the MNBDO for Souda were necessary.

With both amphibious and airborne threats to contend and air superiority in German hands, the Royal Navy were unlikely to be able to stop invasion convoys at sea, the problem of defence was not going to be simple.

At this point, 30 April 1941, Major General Bernard Freyberg VC, commander of the New Zealand Division, whose troops were now the most numerous on the island, was appointed Commander CREFORCE over Major General Weston; much to the latter's chagrin. Almost immediately, he received the following MOST SECRET AND MOST IMMEDIATE signal:

> German attack Crete by simultaneous airborne reinforcements from seaborne expeditions believed imminent. Scale airborne attack estimated 3,000/4,000 parachutists or airborne troops in first sortie. Two or three sorties per day possible from Greece …All above with fighter escort. Bombing attack to be expected some time prior to arrival air and seaborne troops.

Freyberg commented that he could 'scarcely believe his eyes'. This information, which was followed by considerable detail, was the result of ULTRA intelligence. In reply, Freyberg, exercising his charter rights to the New Zealand Government signalled his concerns:

> Feel it my duty to report military situation in Crete. Decision taken in London that Crete must be held at all costs. Have received appreciation on scale of attack from War Office.
>
> In my opinion, Crete can only be held with full support from navy and air force. There is no evidence of naval forces capable of guaranteeing us against seaborne invasion and air forces on island consist of 6 Hurricanes and 17 obsolete aircraft. Troops can and will fight but as a result of campaign in Greece are devoid of any artillery and have insufficient tools for digging, little transport and inadequate war reserves of equipment and

ammunition. Would strongly represent to your Government grave situation in which bulk of NZ Division is placed and recommend you bring pressure to bear on highest plane in London to either supply us with sufficient means to defend island or to review decision Crete must be held. I have of course made my official representation on this matter to C-in-C Middle East.

Major General Freyberg took over General Weston's plans for the defence of Souda, Maleme, Iraklio and Rethymno as 'more or less independent sectors'. Now under command of Brigadier Puttick, the New Zealand Division, consisting of Brigadier Hargest's 5 NZ Brigade (the most complete of the division's formations) which was holding the Maleme/Palatanias area, the remains of 4 NZ Brigade, under Brigadier Inglis, were holding the area between Galatas and Hania, while an *ad hoc* brigade, the 10th, under Colonel Howard Kippenberger were deployed between the coast and Galatas. The Australian 19 Brigade was split into two. Half the brigade, under Brigadier Vasey, were on coastal defence duties at Geogioupoli and the other half under the senior commanding officer, Lieutenant Col Campbell, were holding the coastal airstrip and port at Rethymno. Brigadier Chappel's 14 (British) Brigade, with an Australian battalion under command were to defend the only well developed airfield on the island and hold the nearby port at Iraklio. Major General Weston and the MNBDO was located in the Souda Sector, with about 10,000 men under his command. The CREFORCE reserve was located on the Akrotiri Peninsula, including two Australian battalions. Further details of plans and deployment will be provided in respective chapters and in the order of battle appendix. 6 NZ Brigade had already left for Egypt.

On assuming command Freyberg moved his headquarters from Hania to caves in the Akrotiri Peninsula, just to the east of the town. However, Major General Weston took most of the equipment and staff with him to

Deployment of the New Zealand Division – 20 May 1941.

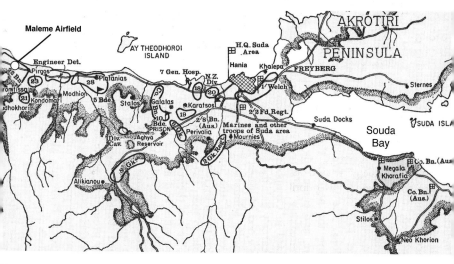

command his own sector and Freyberg, with his own Divisional Signals Regiment having gone ahead to Alexandria, along with most of his staff officers, had to command with an *ad hoc* headquarters at a crucial moment. With changes of command and extemporised HQs, one report stated 'In the six days that I have been here they have moved headquarters, changed the staff, altered the plan twice, and the resultant chaos is beyond description'.

On 3 May General Freyberg issued Operational Instruction No. 10, which gave sector commanders their instructions:

POLICY OF DEFENCE

10. Sector Comds will organise their sectors so that, of the troops allotted to the defence of the aerodromes, one third is disposed on or around the landing ground, and two thirds are kept at such a distance that they will be outside the areas which will be attacked in the first instance.

Major General Bernard Freyberg VC.

11. Possible landing areas other than aerodromes will also be protected in a similar manner on a similar scale.

12. In addition, possible sea landing places will be watched, and if resources permit, held by troops.

13. It is important that each sector should have a sector reserve.

Critically, Freyberg took the words forwarded to him by Wavell's ULTRA controller at face value. The officer who had assessed the original decoded and translated document, put undue emphasis on the amphibious element of the German plans. Consequently, Freyberg's forces were looking in two directions; the beach and the airfields. In the critical Maleme-Hania sector, New Zealand Battalions were strung out in coastal defence positions, where they were to remain fixed until too late, by faulty interpretation of sound intelligence.

The orders issued by Puttick and his subordinate commanders accurately reflected Freyberg's concerns about an amphibious landing and his insistence that his troops mount immediate counter-attacks with all available reserves.

Defenders of Crete

Those British troops, both the infantry battalions and support troops, deployed to Crete between November 1940 and March 1941 tended to be well equipped (by British 1940 standards) but were not necessarily experienced. During the months in Crete before the evacuation of Greece they were largely used as a labour force, with little opportunity for training. Being a low priority, few replacement men or equipment items

A British Merchant Navy officer, a Cretan civilian and a number of Greek soldiers with a mix of British and Greek helmets.

Running but not defeated.

were available for the defence of Crete and a paucity of spare parts led to cannibalisation, particularly of vehicles. The lack of trucks in particular was keenly felt, as the priority of work yo-yoed between defences and building up a logistic infrastructure in the Base Area established between Hania and Souda.

Once it was apparent that the campaign in Greece was going to end with evacuation, need to build up troop levels in Crete was a considerable problem for the resource starved Field Marshal Wavell. While the anti-aircraft guns were mostly complete and accompanied by formed units of gunners, the field artillery equipment he sent was mostly in a parlous state. Of the 100 guns dispatched to Crete, which were a mixture of British, American and captured Italian guns, only 85 were serviceable and only then after some of them, lacking proper sights, were the subject of considerable improvisation. Some of the Gunners who arrived in Crete from the Greek mainland, when presented with 'heaps of junk', could only manage to coax them into action by making sights up from chewing gum and nails.

The twenty-two tanks available were in a similar state of repair, being worn out by their service in the Western Desert. Two of the six heavier MkII Infantry Tanks (Matildas) were deployed to each of the three airfields as a part of their close defence, where much motoring would not be required, while of the sixteen Light Tanks, six also went to Iraklio, while the remainder formed a reserve in the Souda area.

Shipping bringing this heavy equipment to Crete had to run the gauntlet of air attack at sea and dive bombing if caught in daylight still discharging cargo in Souda Bay. Shipping losses were heavy and for example the ship with the Mark IV Light Tanks of 3rd Hussars had difficulty off-loading her cargo at the limited port facilities and was hit only partly discharged. Some tanks and, more importantly, the Light Aid Detachment were still aboard the partly sunk ship, which was sitting on the bottom of the bay when the Germans attacked. The work of the logistic units including Palestinian pioneers was dangerous and extremely arduous in the prevailing conditions.

If General Freyberg had to make do with a skeleton staff and very little equipment, his formations and units were in the same situation. Few had escaped from Greece with even a small proportion of their equipment and even personal weapons were scarce. Such stocks held in the Souda base were soon distributed and what could be scraped together from the remainder of the Middle East Command was soon similarly exhausted.

The 10,000 Greek soldiers on the island were mainly recruits and cadets, poorly armed with a mixture of weapons and equipment. The exception was more experienced and better armed Gendarme units, organised and equipped as infantry. The capability of the Greek soldier and junior commanders had impressed the British in the mountains but the senior element was considered to be 'laughably inefficient'. Training teams of New Zealand officers and senior NCOs were attached and made a difference in the few days available.

Given their partly equipped and trained status most of the Greek units were divided up amongst the brigades and given tasks of holding ground inland. When the attack came, some Greek units performed extremely well, especially where they were actively supported by the local population who armed themselves with captured enemy weapons and fought with a ferocity that shocked the Germans.

Having worked hard to organise CREFORCE and work on the island's defences, Major General Freyberg wrote that 'Feeling hopeful that we could maul any airborne invaders I sent the following cable to General Wavell:

> Have completed plan for the defence of Crete and have just returned from final tour of defences. I feel greatly encouraged by my visit. Everywhere all ranks are fit and morale is high. All defences have been extended and positions wired as much as possible. We have 45 field guns emplaced, with adequate ammunition dumped. Two infantry tanks are at each aerodrome. Carriers and transport still being unloaded and delivered, 2nd Leicesters have arrived and will make Iraklio stronger. I do not wish to be over-confident, but I feel that at least are will give an excellent account. With help of Royal Navy, I trust Crete will be held.'

In summary, the strategic need to defend Crete had been identified in the autumn of 1940 but political and military reasons conspired to ensure that little was done to prepare the island for defence in the months before the evacuation of Greece. At the end of April 1941, Crete was in the front line but Wavell's problems of resources remained and losses of equipment in Greece prevented proper reinforcement. The only significant body of troops available to reinforce Crete were the evacuees from Greece, whose morale was still largely intact but whose commanders had been mesmerised by the speed of their defeat.

COAST DEFENCE.
Close-up 6in. guns Kalibes. All personnel live in Dug-outs under trees,

Air photo of a RM 6 inch gun position near Souda. One of a series taken for a camouflage survey.

Chapter Two

FALLSCHIRMJÄGER AND THE INVASION PLANS

Having suffered the hard school of defeat in 1918, Germany was more open to new ideas to avoid a similar fate again. Key to German tactical doctrine, which came to be referred to as '*Blitzkrieg*', literally translated as 'lightning war', were firepower and speed of movement. *Blitzkrieg* was a development of the tactics that had been so nearly successful in the spring offensives of 1918. Panzers now lighter, faster and more mobile, were combined with mechanised infantry into all arms panzer divisions that once unleashed, were to be closely supported by dive-bombers in the role of flying artillery.

German airborne forces were not a part of the core structure that was built up to support *Blitzkrieg*. However, paratroopers (*Fallschirmjäger*) and other airborne troops epitomised the key *Blitzkrieg* principle of speed and risk, and also demonstrated how the defeated of 1918 were willing to embrace new ideas and technology under the leadership of Adolf Hitler. Military parachuting and air landing of infantry was not an entirely new idea. In 1918 small French raids by two-man demolition teams dropped by parachute behind German lines to attack enemy communications and later the same year, the Allies conducted small-scale re-supply tasks by air during the MICHAEL and Meuse-Argonne campaigns. In the late nineteen twenties Italian paratroopers made mass jumps in North Africa and in 1931 the US Army Air Corps flew a field artillery battery complete with equipment to Panama as a demonstration of 'Hemispheric Defence'. Two years later, in exercising the American preference of the day for air landing rather than parachuting the deployment was repeated but with a full infantry battalion.

It was, however, the Soviets who provided the example that led to the creation of German airborne forces. *General der Flieger Kurt* Student, who became the most famous of the senior *Fallschirmjäger* commanders, described those events:

> *For us Germans, the concept of vertical envelopment received impetus because of two events: First were the Russian manoeuvres in 1934-35, in which large numbers of paratroopers were dropped into open country. The second was in 1936 when Freiherr von Moreau's transport flights flew some of [General] Franco's troops from Morocco to Spain with decisive effect.*

On the basis of these events, both the Army and the *Luftwaffe* set up parachute groups, in order to study and to test airborne operations. The results identified, in theory, three possibilities: One was that the

Fallschirmjäger should be divided up into small units to jump behind the enemy's lines where they could destroy specific targets, which the *Luftwaffe* at the time was technically unable to hit. Another idea was to land directly in the enemy's rear in small units in order to give tactical support to army operations. The third possibility was that *Fallschirmjäger* should carry out their own operations in larger units behind the enemy's front, without being in direct contact with the ground forces.

With the benefit of low-level experiments and with an emerging tactical doctrine, on 29 January 1936, *Reichsmarshall* Göring ordered the formation of what was the nucleus of an airborne force referred to as a Flying or *Flieger* Wing. This name was aimed to conceal the airborne force as a normal *Luftwaffe* 'air wing'. A parachute school was established at Stendal in central Germany.

However, it took the approaching Czech crisis in 1938 to form *7th Fliegerdivision* into an organised combat division. The plan was to deploy a force of three regiments (each equivalent to a British brigade), one of which would be fully parachute trained, with the other two regiments being 'air-landing' troops. *General der Flieger* Kurt Student explained that:

Reichsmarshall **Hermann Göring.**

> *The Wehrmacht provided the 16th Infantry Regiment and handed it over to me, as far as tactics and training were concerned. However, a second regiment could not be provided, and we were helped by an unusual idea: Göring, who knew the SA well, took the leaders and the best men from that organisation and moved them without more ado into the Luftwaffe.*

General der Flieger **Kurt Student.**

Also in this way General Student successfully acquired the necessary men to set up a third regiment within a matter of months. With the infantry strength for a whole division now available, intensive training began but action in Czechoslovakia was averted by the Munich Conference.

The source of much of *7th Fliegerdivision's* manpower being the brown shirted political bully boys of the *Sturm Abteilung* (SA), the Nazi credentials of the *Fallschirmjäger* were high from the beginning. The need for ordinary recruits and replacements further reinforced the fanatically Nazi nature of the organisation by taking the pick of the *Hitlerjugend* movement, until forced to share the cream with the expanding *Waffen SS*. Although a similar political and military elite, the

Fallschirmjäger, however, managed to avoid acquiring a similar reputation to that of the SS.

From a document captured in Crete:

THE TEN COMMANDMENTS OF THE
FALLSCHIRMJÄGER

1. You are the elite of the German Forces. For you, the fight shall be fulfilment. You shall seek it out and train yourself to stand every test.

2. Cultivate true comradeship, for together with your comrades you will triumph or die.

3. Be shy of speech and incorruptible. Men act, women chatter; chatter will bring you to the grave.

4. Calmness and caution, thoroughness and determination, valour and a fanatical spirit of attack will make you superior in the battle.

5. Face to face with the enemy, the most precious thing is ammunition. The man who fires aimlessly merely to reassure himself has no guts. He is a weakling and does not deserve the name of Fallschirmjäger.

6. Never surrender. Your honour lies in victory or death.

7. Only with good weapons can you achieve success. Look after them, therefore, on the principle "First my weapons, then myself".

8. You must grasp the full meaning of each operation so that, even if your leader should fall, you can carry it out coolly and warily.

9. Fight chivalrously against an honourable foe; sharpshooters deserve no quarter.

10. With your eyes open, keyed up to the highest pitch, agile as a greyhound, tough as leather, hard as Krupp steel, you will be the embodiment of a German warrior.

Even without the *Fallschirmjäger* being committed to action, Göring was enthused by the potential of his new arm and large scale airborne exercises followed. With the concepts validated, the *Reichmarshall*, not one to let an opportunity to empire build pass, fully supported plans to develop German airborne forces within the *Luftwaffe*. To that end, in 1939, *22nd Infantariedivision* trained as air landing troops under operational control of the *Luftwaffe*. Meanwhile, Student became not only commander of *7th Fliegerdivision* but also Inspector General of Airborne Forces.

The Division's order of battle, to the envy of airborne forces since that time, was completed by the permanent assignment of both transport and offensive air-support squadrons. Firstly, there were two transport squadrons of Ju 52 aircraft, one squadron of fighter aircraft, one of bombers, and a recce squadron. In addition, to complete the ground ORBAT (order of battle), there was a *Luftwaffe* signal battalion, a strong medical group and other supporting arms necessary for operating in isolation. The division was raised on the expectation that it would fight with light scales, depending heavily on air support. However, as aircraft and equipment were developed, the *Fliegerdivision*'s support weapon elements grew in both number and combat power.

In 1939, *Wehrmacht* scepticism about the utility of the *Fallschirmjäger* relegated Student's elite to a subsidiary role in the invasion of Poland and the weather denied them the one opportunity for a single battalion to demonstrate its capability. Frustrated and with sinking morale, it wasn't until the following year that the *Fallschirmjäger* were to play a leading role in the campaign in the west (FALL GELB) and its immediate forerunner, the invasion of Norway (a single battalion drop in April 1940). In FALL GELB Student's men were to seize the crossings of the Albert Canal and the super fortress at Eben Emael (see **Battleground** *Fort Eben Emael*) by surprise in the opening move of the campaign. Meanwhile, also jumping/landing ahead of the ground forces, the remainder of 7th *Fliegerdivision* and *22nd Infantry Division* would descend on Fortress Holland. Operations were a success but the cost was high in terms of aircraft and men, including Student himself, who was badly wounded. Despite their losses, German airborne forces were planned to play a significant part in Operation SEALION. Perhaps fortunately, the cancellation of the invasion of Britain gave the *Fallschirmjäger* the opportunity to re-equip and retrain.

In early 1941, OKW formally grouped 7th Flieger and 22nd Airlanding Divisions into *XI Fliegerkorps* under command of Student, with *Generalleutnant* Süssmann taking over command of the *Fallschirmjäger*. By the spring, German airborne forces were again more than ready for action and Student was extremely ambitious for his airborne force that had no significant role planned for them in the invasion of Russia. Göring and Student, however, were able to persuade Hitler that the first predominantly

The Ju-52 transport aircraft, known as 'Tante Ju' or Aunt Ju because of its solid construction and reliability.

34

airborne invasion would quickly deliver Crete into his hands. What ultimately sold the idea to Hitler was that the Balkan Campaign could be rounded off without seriously delaying or taking away resources from his main effort, the planned invasion of the Soviet Union – Operation BARBAROSSA.

Gliders

The Germans were severely restricted by the Versailles Treaty in the field of military aircraft, including troop transports. Consequently, as Göring explained in the early 1920s, there was to be an emphasis on the glider as the foundation of the future German *Luftwaffe*; and therefore, by the mid-1930s, sport gliding and glider technology was well established across Germany.

At a political rally in the early thirties, Hitler had been impressed by a spectacular display of formation glider flying and pin-point landing. In 1936 when he met Professor Georgie from the Research Institute of Gliding at the Dramstadt Technical College, the idea of a military utility for gliders came into his mind. Returning to his laboratory and workshop after his meeting with the Füluer, Professor Georgie tasked his flight construction manager Hans Jacobs to look at the possibility of transporting troops by glider.

> *This idea naturally came as a great surprise to me. Up until then we had only developed various types for sport gliding, so it was rather difficult to answer the question. However, my thoughts followed this line: a glider towed up to 6,000 – 9,000 feet can, with an angle of descent of 1 in 18, fly silently for tens of kilometres into enemy territory, all of this in the morning twilight so that the plane cannot be seen. So the idea of deploying the military glider had been born.*

At the beginning of 1937, after some theoretical designs had been produced, orders were issued by the *Reich*'s Aviation Ministry to build a mock-up of an aircraft, which could carry the pilot and up to nine armed and equipped soldiers. This dummy was viewed by representatives of the Ministry, and an order followed immediately for the construction of three prototype aircraft. A military troop-carrying glider was by no means unanimously considered useful (and the *Fallschirmjäger* regarded gliders as unwelcome competition for resources), but the more visionary commanders prevailed. They saw that its foremost advantage was its ability to land troops together as a coherent section ready to fight, rather than an equivalent number of expensively trained paratroops scattered over several hundred yards. Another feature that appealed to the *Luftwaffe* was a glider's ability to make a silent approach.

Work on a military glider began promptly in March 1937 at Dramstadt, based on converting existing designs, and setting up an experimental flight, along with a training command, to gain experience in the *Luftwaffe*'s newest aircraft – the 'Attack Glider'.

Colonel Mrazek described the continuing debate over the usefulness of the glider from a military point of view:

> *A second demonstration was held, this time before the Army General Staff. Ten Junkers (Ju) 52s transporting paratroopers, and ten gliders carrying glidermen towed behind ten more Ju 52s, flew to the airfield at Stendal. There the gliders were cast off, and the paratroopers dropped. The gliders dived steeply and came to rest in close formation, discharging glidermen in units ready to fight. On the other hand, the parachutists, who had the ill luck to encounter a stiff breeze, from which the gliders had actually benefited, landed widely dispersed, in some cases a considerable distance from their ammunition, which had been dropped by parachute. Though this experiment could not, of course, obscure the importance of paratroopers in a future war, it at least proved conclusively that the troop-carrying glider could become a weapon of great value.*

Full production of the DFS-230 Attack Glider began at the Gotha aircraft plant, while the *Luftwaffe* began to train its first 60 military glider pilots on the prototypes and the first production gliders.

DFS-230 Glider

The basis of the DFS-230's design was a meteorological aircraft that was essentially a small engineless transport, which during the redesign process lost its sleek curves and long elegant wings. The result was a short airframe and stubby wings, designed to bear weight and provide sufficient lift for the glider to descend steadily from its release point to its objective. What proved to be impossible was for the loaded aircraft to ride thermals and to remain soaring for protracted periods, as a sport glider would.

A summary of the technical details follows:

Fuselage: Covered with a painted canvas fabric, the DFS 230's fuselage was made up of a framework of steel tubing capable of accommodating a pilot and eight or nine men and equipment, giving a total payload of 2,800 pounds. The aircraft eventually had a position for a light machine gun in a slit in the fuselage on the starboard side.

Undercarriage: The fuselage had wheels for taking off which were normally jettisoned once airborne. These could be retained should the glider be returning to a nicely manicured airfield, but for tactical landings, the DFS-230 would land on a skid fixed below its fuselage.

Wings: With a span of 72 feet and a surface area of 444 square feet, the DFS-230's wings were constructed in traditional glider manner from plywood, which was covered with the same canvas fabric as the fuselage. The DFS-230 had a high wing design braced from the fuselage.

A late version DFS-230 armed with a machine gun.

Here a Stuka flies alongside the DFS-230 glider.

Braking mechanism: For tactical landing the glider relied on friction to bring it to a halt. Eben Emael's assault force, training over winter, tried to enhance the friction by wrapping barbed wire around the skid, but eventually resorted to a saw-toothed braking device. Braking rockets and drogue parachute were fitted to later models of the DFS-230.

Weight: Empty: 2,800 pounds. Laden weight: 4,600 pounds.

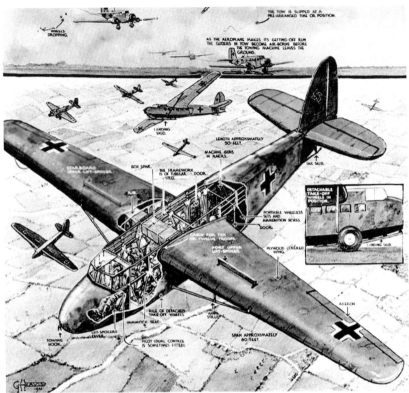

A British wartime sketch showing the construction and layout of the DFS-230.

Flying speed: The optimum speed for towing was 120 miles an hour, with a similar speed for the glide down to the landing zone.

Following the success of the principally glider-borne Albert Canal/Eben Emael operation, an additional unit was formed within *7th Fliegerdivision*, the *Luftlandesturmregiment* (LLSR or Airlanding Assault Regiment). Trained as parachutists and glider troops, their role, as an elite within an elite, was to deliver the vital initial attacks. Landing concentrated in their gliders were able to be in action very quickly. Consequently, they were suitable for *coup de main* operations of the sort they were to perform in Crete in support of Student's main effort.

Invasion Plans

Persuaded of the utility of Student's proposition for an airborne invasion of Crete, between 20 and 25 April 1941, the German High Command (OKW) worked on drafting directives for Operation MERKUR. In a warning order issued on the latter date, overall command of the operation, both ground and air forces, was assigned to *Generaloberst* Lohr, the head of *Luftflotte 4* he was allocated the aircraft of *VIII Fliegerkorps* and the soldiers of *XI Fliegerkorps* for the operation. Five days later, Führer Directive No 20, setting out the aims and objectives of the operation was promulgated.

The aircraft of *Generaloberst* von Richthofen's *VIII Fliegerkorps* were to conduct aerial recce over Crete, mount preliminary attacks on the island's coastal and airfield defences and launch sorties to neutralise anti-aircraft defences during the airborne landing of *XI Fliegerkorps*. Thereafter, *VIII Fliegerkorps* was to provide close air support to the ground forces. Student's *XI Fliegerkorps* was to consist of *7th Fliegerdivision*, under the command of *Generalleutnant* Süssmann and *5th Gerbirgsjägerdivision* (mountain), under the command of *Generalmajor* Ringel, reinforced by *Gerbirgsjägerregiment*

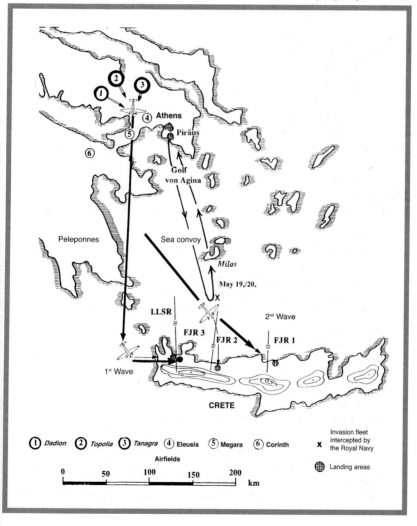

(GJR) 141 from another mountain division. This change in ORBAT, made as late as 8 May, was the result of the airlanding *22nd Infantariedivision* being mal-located for an operation that was being mounted in a tight time scale and in the shadow of preparations for Operation BARBAROSSA. *Generalmajor* Julius Ringle's *5th Gerbirgsdivision*, who had performed well in the invasion of Greece and were readily available. They, however, had no experience of airborne operations and most would be flying into airheads captured by the *Fallschirmjäger*. Other elements of *5th Gerbirgsdivision*, along with some tanks from *5th Panzer Division* would travel to Crete by sea. Naval support for the operation, which included transportation of men and panzers, was the responsibility of Admiral Schuster, with Italian destroyers under command.

Although the operation was to be conducted as quickly as possible, X-Day (the German equivalent of Zero or D-Day; the day an operation begins) still had to be finalised. Setting a date was impossible, as *Generalmajor* Conrad Seibt, *XI Fliegerkorps* chief logistics officer, was experiencing considerable problems supporting the deployment of the *Fliegerkorps* from its bases in the Braunschweig/Stendal area of Germany. Although recently elevated to corps status German airborne forces still lacked corps troops, particularly logistic units. Regrouping von Richthofen's air transport units from preparations for Operation BARBAROSSA also caused delays.

In Operation FLYING DUTCHMAN, *7th Fliegerdivision* left its barracks under heavy security for an undisclosed destination. All *Fallschirmjäger* insignia were to be removed and the division was to travel as ordinary *Luftwaffe* personnel, with all parachute equipment packed away out of sight. As usual the junior officers and men had not been told of their destination but there were rumours based on informed guesses. Measures to ensure that security was maintained included *Hauptmann* Schulz's orders to his *Fallschirmjäger MG Battalion 7*:

> *No member of the battalion is to carry any personal papers or documents with him. Buying and sending postcards as well as using the civilian postal service are strictly forbidden.*
>
> *It is forbidden to sing* Fallschirmjäger *songs. Railway coaches as well as vehicles must bear no identification marks. The special markings identifying our battalion* [the Panther] *must disappear from all vehicles.*

Hauptmann Freiherr von der Hydte commander of *1st Battalion Fallschirmjäger Regiment 3 (I/FJR 3)* described their departure with just a hint of disappointment:

> *During the night the troops and vehicles were entrained. We pulled out of the station in the first grey light of morning towards a rising sun and an unknown destination. We were travelling through suburbs. Houses and streets drifted past the windows. There were quite a lot of people – workers*

Most of the journey was by rail aboard troop trains.

going to their morning shifts in the factories – to be seen in the streets, but nobody took any notice of our train. No one waved. Nobody wished us well. The sight of military transport was all too familiar by the end of the second year of the war. People were much too occupied with their own sorrows and their own jobs to worry about the destinies of those who were carried past them to die. Our departure was an insignificant, anonymous particle of the gigantic war machine.

The majority of the 1,500 mile journey through the Balkans to Athens was to be completed by rail, aboard slow moving troop trains. However, the division's 3,000 trucks and other vehicles were offloaded in Rumania leaving the last torturous 500 miles to the concentration area to be completed by road. The majority of the *Fallschirmjäger* eventually arrived at their designated bivouac sites, near their assigned airfields, between 8 and 12 May. Despite the security measures, *7th Fliegerdivision* reported progress across the Balkans, sent by ENIGMA encoded radio signals, which within eighteen to thirty-six hours were in the hands of Wavell and Freyberg's ULTRA liaison officers.

X-Day, an event closely monitored by the Allies, was eventually settled as 15 May. However, getting all the stores and equipment required for the operation was extremely difficult, against the priority afforded to

BARBAROSSA. The greatest problem facing *Generalmajor* Seibt was aviation fuel. He needed sufficient fuel for three sorties by the transport aircraft but the Corinth Canal was blocked by the wreckage of the bridge blown by the Commonwealth Allies on 26 April and it was not until 17 May that *Kriegsmarine* clearance divers removed sufficient wreckage for the tankers to slip through, with armed troops aboard to 'encourage' the captains. The fuel eventually arrived in drums at the airfield on 19 May, causing a delay in launching the operation of five days.

Ground

Arriving in Greece in the late spring of 1941, the most apparent of the conditions facing the *Fallschirmjäger* was the heat and they only had temperate weather equipment. They were briefed concerning the island of Crete:

> The island of Crete is approximately 240 kilometres (160 miles) long and varies in width from 12 to 50 kilometres (8 to 35 miles). The interior is barren and covered by eroded mountains which, in the western part, rise to an elevation of 2,456 metres (8,100 feet). There are few roads and water is scarce. The south coast descends abruptly towards the sea; the only usable port along this part of the coast is the small harbour of Stahion. There are hardly any north-south communications and the only road to Sphakia which can be used for motor transportation ends abruptly 1,100 metres (3,600 feet) above the town. The sole major traffic artery runs close to the north coast and connects Souda Bay with the towns of Maleme, Hania, Rethymno and Iraklio. Possession of the north coast is vital for an invader approaching from Greece, if only because of terrain conditions. The British, whose supply bases were situated in Egypt, were greatly handicapped by the fact that the only efficient port is in Souda Bay. The topography of the island, therefore, favoured the invader, particularly since the mountainous terrain left no other alternative to the British but to construct their airfields close to the exposed north coast.

Student's Plan

See map on page 39.

The plan that *General der Flieger* Student arrived at was based on an estimate that concurred very closely with the threats identified by British commanders in Crete, from Brigadier Tidbury through to General Weston.

Two versions of the plan were presented; a more cautious plan based on seizing objectives in the Maleme/Hania area, then building up strength, German forces would fan out in a conventional manner to occupy the remainder of the island. However, this plan was too slow for the BARBAROSSA planners to accept and Student was directed to adopt his second plan, a simultaneous descent across the island onto what was thought to be light opposition.

Packing ammunition into colour coded parachute containers.

Folding parachutes and packing weapons containers.

43

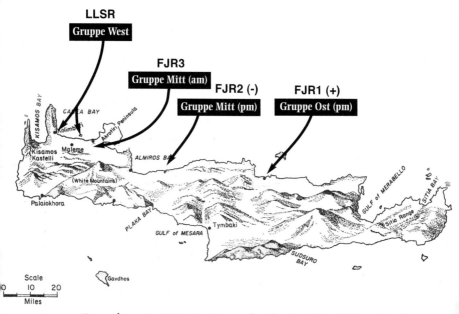

LLSR

Gruppe West

FJR3

Gruppe Mitt (am)

FJR2 (-)

Gruppe Mitt (pm)

FJR1 (+)

Gruppe Ost (pm)

Scale
0   10   20
Miles

From the outset, Student knew that he lacked sufficient aircraft to drop/land *7th Fliegerdivision* in a single lift and that there would have to be two lifts. He identified the need to take at least one of the airfields for the fly-in of the *Gerbirgsjäger* and to defeat the main body of the enemy in the Souda/Hania area. This requirement led him to identify the Maleme airfield and Prison Valley as his main effort in the coming attack and he therefore allocated the LLSR (*Gruppe West*) and *Fallschirmjäger Regiment 3* (half of *Gruppe Mitt*) to this task. The other airfields at Rethymno (remainder of *Gruppe Mitt*), Iraklio (*Gruppe Ost*) and Kastelli, were also important but lacked the necessary proximity for a speedy strike at the strategically important facilities of Hania and Souda. With insufficient aircraft, there would be a morning drop in support of his main effort by *Gruppe West* at Maleme and the half of *Gruppe Mitt* in for Prison Valley. The aircraft would return with a second lift in the afternoon, to drop the second half of *Gruppe Mitt* at Rethymno and *Gruppe Ost* at Iraklio. The *Gerbirgsjäger* would follow, with elements being flown in and others coming by sea, arriving P.M. X-Day and on X+1. *Generalmajor* Ringel later recalled that reading the operation order '…sent a chill down my spine, for it was clear that the operation so laconically described would be a suicide adventure'. The *Fallschirmjäger* were, however, altogether more sanguine about the prospect of executing Student's plan, being a self professed elite and having been virtually excluded from significant operations in the last year. Further details of the German plan will be found in relevant chapters.

Intelligence

It is unusual to consider the intelligence available after examining the plan but Student's plan was arrived at with scant and precious little accurate information on the defences of Crete. Such intelligence as was available had originally been produced in support of Operation MARITA and dated from four months earlier in December 1940. As Crete was not in MARITA's target area this intelligence was very general. Additional information only gradually drifted in from von Richthofen's *VIII Fliegerkorps* once his aircraft

German Estimate	Actual Allied Total
No Greek units on the Island. Greek Government ???	10 Greek units totalling about 11,000 Greek Government present with King of the Hellenes
Italian PWs: 600 officers and 15,000 other ranks	Broadly CORRECT
5,000 men concentrated around Hania	CORRECT – in December 1940 but in May qui: 20,000 evacuees 3,468 fresh reinforcement Total of **41,840**
30 tanks	Broadly CORRECT – 9 x I Tks Tanks and 16 x Lt Tks
30 x heavy AA and 40 x light AA positions.	CORRECT
2 x heavy and 7 x light coastal guns.	Broadly CORRECT
300 other guns.	Over estimate approx 100
10 single engine a/c and 4 twin engine a/c at Maleme	Correct on 17 May. Nil on 20 May
6 aircraft at Iraklio	Nil
Seaplanes at Suda	Nil Visitors only

started operating over Crete in late April. However, as the northern coastal strip where both objectives and Commonwealth troops were concentrated, was covered in olive and citrus groves, this intelligence was limited. The trees gave ample cover to a force whose experience at the hands of the *Luftwaffe* in Greece had taught them to be very aware of the necessity of camouflage and concealment.

The table on page 45 gives the Commonwealth Forces detailed in the intelligence report No. 157/41 by 1c of *7th Fliegerdivision* on 19 May, against those actually on Crete on 20 May 1941:

Statements both verbal and written in orders indicating that more enemy troops than formerly identified in orders may be encountered on the ground, suggest that there may have been, at best, a suppression of information that could have called the operation, vital for the future of the *Fallschirmjäger*, into doubt. At worst this may have been an act of cognitive dissonance, similar to that prior to Arnhem, where facts that did not fit the conceived plan were blanked from the mind of commanders and their staff. One witness, *Hauptmann* Altmann, who was to land in the first wave of gliders, recounts that he was told, as he boarded his glider, that the enemy on Crete totalled not 11,000 but nearer 48,000. The implication of this is that if this officer well down the chain of command knew this at dawn on 20 May, then senior officers must have known the true scale of opposition they faced at least twelve hours earlier and made a conscious decision to commit the *Fallschirmjäger* none the less.

A member of the LLSR dressed and equipped for glider operations. Parachutists wore knee pads and wore their smocks over webbing to avoid snagging parachute rigging lines.

Chapter Three

THE FLY-IN

Arriving in Greece only days before the operation was due to be launched, the *Fallschirmjäger* had little time to acclimatise and prepare their equipment for the coming operation. *Hauptmann* von der Hydte, *I Battalion Fallschirmjägerregiment 3* (I/FJR 3), described the camp set up by his men just to the east of the airbase at Topolia.

Tents were quickly put up, well apart from each other and irregularly dispersed among the trees, and the whole battalion was soon under canvas. Within a few hours of arrival the six hundred young men were already disporting themselves in the evening sun.

The pleasant holiday atmosphere was not to last long before warning orders were issued. While the *Fallschirmjäger* were relaxing in bivouacs at the airfields, Student had moved his headquarters from Berlin and reopened it in Athens on 7 May 1941. Here the detailed plans were made and officers came to be briefed. 'The orderly brought,' said von der Hydte, 'instructions that I should report at eleven o'clock at Hotel Grande Bretagne in Athens for a conference with General Student.'

One look at the hermetically-sealed and shuttered room in the Hotel Grande Bretagne, where the commanders of all the Fallschirmjäger *regiments and battalions were gathered to receive their orders, was sufficient to dispel the secret of our target: a large map of Crete was prominently displayed upon the wall.*

Time for some sightseeing before the off. The Pathenon Athens.

In a quiet but clear and slightly vibrant voice General Student explained the plan of attack. It was his personal plan. He had devised it, had struggled against heavy opposition for its acceptance, and had worked out all the details. One could perceive that this plan had become a part of him, a part of his life. He believed in it and lived for it and in it.

The plan was however bedevilled by a number of practical problems. Chief amongst these was that an adequate number of bases for both transport aircraft and von Richthofen's fighters and fighter bombers could not be

found and aircraft were crammed into the available space. To make matters worse, with the priority firmly on BARBAROSSA, units to man and run the improvised bases were lacking. Again improvisation was needed and the situation was only inadequately resolved by the drafting of *Luftwaffe* reservists and even infantry officers to the task. As we will see, this was to have a significant effect on the conduct of Operation MERKUR.

Availability of operating staff was not the only problem that would impact on the operation. *Oberst* von Heyking explained:

Each of these two landing grounds was made up of flat terrain between mountains. The ground was very sandy and the aircraft wheels sunk in up to the axles. When landing or taking off the aircraft threw up huge dust clouds hundreds of feet into the air, which afterwards fell to the ground very slowly because of the high temperatures and lack of wind in the narrow valley. These difficult conditions would prevent our wing forming up and taking off on the day of the operation.

General der Flieger Wolfram Frhr. von Richthofen.

The wing commander did not think that the operations could be carried out effectively from these two landing grounds. But he received no help from XI Fliegerkorps, *probably because communications were difficult to establish with the other sectors and perhaps because there were no other fields available.*

… When a plane taxied, it caused huge clouds of dust. This was not long in covering the planes and entering the engines. … Means had to be found to get our wing to take off in tight formation and over a short period of time. Two days before the operation, a take-off exercise was planned and seventeen minutes elapsed between one flight taking off and the next getting ready for take off: this was the time needed for the dust clouds to clear.

Confirmation that X-Day would be the 20th came on 18 May and orders were issued to the men the following day, when the purposeful activity of battle preparations began in earnest. Von der Hydte recalled:

As it grew dark we were transported in trucks to the airfield, where we were greeted by the ear-splitting roar of a hundred and twenty air-

Major Schulz *I Battalion Fallschirmjäger Regiment 1* talking to his men before their drop on Iraklio.

transports as they tested their engines in preparation for the take-off. Through clouds of dust we could see red glowing sparks flaring from the exhausts of the machines, and only by this light was it possible to discern the silhouettes of our men. Flashing the pale green beams of their torches in order to indicate their whereabouts, the hundred and twenty officers and NCOs of my battalion tried their best to make themselves heard above the thundering of the engines. The picture reminded me of glow-worms in August.

During the hours which precede a sortie everything seems to become bewitched. Arms containers being hoisted into the racks spill open, aircraft are not where they should be, and the most important machine is liable, for some reason or another, to pack up. But the most extraordinary thing is that despite these numerous hitches the take-off invariably seems to proceed satisfactorily.

Hauptmann von der Hydte decided not to join his men in preparing equipment and aircraft, as 'One can, of course, join one's officers and NCOs, but the only result is that 122, instead of 121, voices are bellowing unintelligibly in the darkness'.

Assembling a mass of strike aircraft and the slower moving transports and glider tugs required daylight, so it was not until dawn on 20 May 1941

A Ju-52 disappears into a dust cloud kicked up by the three engines. This caused severe problems from the beginning.

that the airborne invasion of Crete could begin. This timing dictated the carefully sequenced events of the entire day.

It was a few minutes after 5 a.m. when my aircraft, piloted by the commander of the flight himself, taxied out onto the runway. The first light of dawn scarcely penetrated the red dust, raised by the machines during the night, which hung like a dense fog over the airfield.

The aircraft braked; on our right we could see the shadow of the control-sentry, who would give us the 'All Clear' in a moment or two. Then his torch blinked green. We started to move, the wheels knocking hard on the bumpy ground, faster and faster until suddenly the knocking ceased and gave place to a gentle sensation of gliding as the machine lifted itself from the runway and rose in a wide sweep upwards. Except for the crew, not one of the thirteen men seated in the plane uttered a word. Everyone was preoccupied with his own thoughts. When there is no going back, most men experience a strange sinking feeling, as if their stomachs had remained on the ground.

Suddenly the bright light of the morning sun broke through. The plane had risen beyond the layer of dust and fog.

The results of exercises similar to that conducted by *Oberst* von Heyking allowed the leading aircraft to concentrate into a stream and head south to Crete on time. Despite the difficulties the operation had got off to a reasonable start.

Meanwhile, aboard the aircraft, after a night with very little sleep, the *Fallschirmjägers'* singing quickly gave way to sleep. For the ten men crammed into the light framed DFS-230 glider behind its tug aircraft the rush of the propeller wash was both uncomfortable and noisy. One early casualty was a glider carrying *Generalleutnant* Süssman and elements of his divisional HQ. In the dawn light his slow moving tug and glider combination was crossed by a faster moving bomber shortly after leaving the coastline. Flying into the turbulence caused by the faster aircraft's slipstream, the DFS-230 broke its tow and the pilot was unable to regain control of the collapsing aircraft, which crashed into the island of Agina, with the loss of all ten *Fallschirmjäger* aboard. MERCURE had her first victims.

The aircraft pressed on with the parachute aircraft slowly closing on the slower moving glider tug combinations, who were due to land first at around 0815 hours. Ahead, von Richthofen's aircraft could be seen in action over the objectives, doing their best to suppress enemy flack. In one of the leading aircraft of the LLSR was hero and veteran of Fort Eben Emael, *Oberfeldwebel* Helmut Wenzel:

Crete appears in the distance. Get ready! We stand and hook up the static lines of our parachutes, check each other out and prepare for the drop. I realise we are flying at 180 metres (550 ft); this means it will take some

51

On their way and in good spirits. A stick of thirteen men and at least two containers.

time to float down, thus increasing the risk of being hit in the air! No sooner has this thought crossed my mind when the clocking noise of bullets and little holes in the aircraft tell us that we are already under fire. Events reel off very rapidly as we approach the drop line. The chap behind me is hit and curls up on the floor, probably dead. There is no time to see to him – we have to get out and jump! Heaving out my bicycle first, I jump ahead of my men, holding my camera with one hand, as it will not fit inside my jumping smock any more, my gas mask taking its place.

As I float down, bullets whistle past me and I hear the crackling noise of small-arms fire. The enemy is putting up a hot reception for us and, looking down I can see we are dropping right onto enemy positions.'

The battle for Crete, foretold by ULTRA, had now begun in earnest but would the ambush Churchill hoped for work?

Chapter Four

MALEME

The battle for Maleme is widely seen as the crux of the Cretan campaign; a battle that at several points could have been decided in favour of the Commonwealth. The Maleme airfield, just fifteen miles from the point that the Germans assessed as being the centre of Commonwealth defensive operations (Hania/Souda), was the natural choice of main effort for an airborne force that had to complete its task in the shortest possible time.

The Defenders and their Plans

The New Zealand Division was deployed to the west of Hania covering the beaches, the coastal strip and a likely approach route to the island's capital from Prison Valley. At the western end of the divisional area was the compacted earth airfield at Maleme; the only airfield within striking distance of Hania. This vital area was held by Brigadier Hargest's 5 New Zealand Brigade.

See map on page 26

Aged fifty, James Hargest was typical of the division's senior commanders. At the outbreak of the Great War, he was a member of the New Zealand Territorials, serving with the rank of second lieutenant. He fought in Gallipoli, at Suvla Bay, where he was wounded. In 1916 he served

Men of the New Zealand Division during the division's withdrawal through Greece.

New Zealanders with a Bofors anti-tank rifle in the shelter of an olive tree and surrounded by bamboo.

with 1st Otago Regiment at Armentières, being promoted captain before the Somme, where he was awarded the MC. As the battalion's Second in Command, Major Hargest took part in the Battle of Messines in 1917 and in March 1918 he was given the command of the 2nd Otago Battalion, which he led until he was badly wounded in November.

After the war, he returned to sheep farming and to the New Zealand Territorial Army. Recognised as a distinguished soldier, he was given command of the

Brigadier James Hargest.

Southland Regiment and subsequently of 3 New Zealand Brigade. In 1931 he was elected to the New Zealand Parliament.

In 1939 Hargest again volunteered for service but was not considered fit enough for active service. With political influence, the issue was overcome and he was appointed to command 5 Infantry Brigade and went first to the UK and where the New Zealanders helped hold the 'front line' in southern England during the Battle of Britain. During the winter of 1940/41 the New Zealand Division was transferred to the Middle East.

Having been evacuated from Greece, Hargest and 5 NZ Brigade arrived in Crete on ANZAC Day. According to 21 NZ Battalion's historian, they:

> …*marched inland some three miles to an area in the Perivolia olive plantation, called 'Rest Camp B' to distinguish it from any other area in the same plantation. Instead of tents there were olive trees. Rations came from*

somewhere; cigarettes and matches had been distributed at a point en route
*… The locality was regarded more as a place to live in than a defensive area,
for Crete was then considered to be only a transit camp during the
evacuation of Greece.*

By 1 May, 5 Brigade had been briefed that they were to stay and be a part
of the island's garrison. They marched west to take up positions covering
five miles of the coastal strip between the Tavronitis River and Platanias,
including, towards the western extremity, the Maleme airfield. The
Brigade's three usual battalions were augmented by 28 Maori Battalion and
a composite unit; the Engineer Detachment, made up of New Zealand
Sappers and Ordnance troops, divided into two companies. This enabled
the Brigade to hold not only the airfield and five miles of beach (all of it
suitable for amphibious landing) but to extend two miles inland.

On 11 May, Brigadier Hargest gave his verbal orders at the Court House
in Maleme village and subsequently issued 5 Brigade Operation
Instruction No. 4 to his command.

The area they deployed onto was described as being low ground:

*'… from one and a half to three miles in depth, with the Brigade's inland
boundary along a ridge roughly parallel with the coast, and scoured with
steep-sided valleys. Many of the hills were wooded and the lower land was
covered with olive and citrus groves and occasional fields of corn. Between
the lower land and the almost perpendicular country was an area of terraced
vineyards.'*

Good fields of fire from the tree-cloaked hill were difficult to find but
conversely concealment was good and, as discussed, almost impenetrable
to the air observers' eye or camera. The low ground was similarly clothed

Present day photograph showing one of the good views from Hill 107.

Tavronitis Bridge

Mouth of River

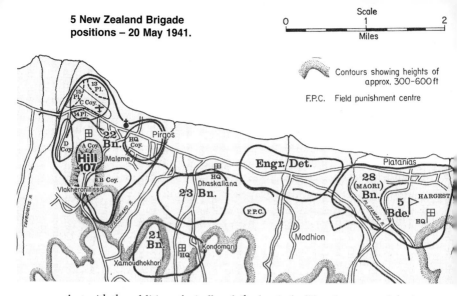

but with the addition of windbreak 'hedges' of tall bamboo around the few diminutive fields. Villages were small and other habitation sparse.

The operation instruction issued on 18 May, confirmed the verbal orders and clarified the roles of the various battalions.

5 Brigade was to 'defend its position at all costs' and, in the event of the enemy making an airborne or seaborne attack on any part of the brigade area between Platanias and the Tavronitis River, its units were 'to counter-attack and destroy him immediately'. The Maori Battalion was to remain in the Platanias area, to patrol the neighbouring beaches and to be 'available for counter attack'. The Engineer Detachments were made responsible for their area and the beaches on their front. Similarly, 21st Battalion was to remain in its position but, since Brigadier Hargest and others recognised the very real danger of an enemy landing in the unoccupied and quite undefended area and beaches to the west of the Tavronitis River, it was to be prepared 'to move and hold line of the river facing West from 22nd Battalion's left flank', and two platoons with a mortar were to take up a holding position along this west flank immediately. 22nd Battalion retained, as its primary task, the static defence of the aerodrome by fire. Its support and reserve companies were to be utilised for 'immediate counter-attack under cover of mortars and M.G. fire'. The instruction added: 'If necessary, support will be called for from 23 Bn and should telephonic means of comn fail here the call will be by "verey" signal (WHITE-GREEN-WHITE).'

Subsequent events make it important that the 23rd's orders be quoted as given:

> *23 Bn will maintain its present position and be prepared to counter-attack if enemy affects a landing (a) on the beach or at Maleme Aerodrome, (b) on area occupied by Det NZ Engineers, West of Platanias.*

This Battalion's role of counter-attack was stressed in both CREFORCE and divisional orders. Brigadier Puttick wrote that 'A good solid battalion' was

56

required for the counter-attack role' in the Maleme area. Consequently, the 23rd, though also dug-in and holding ground, was 'under orders to counter-attack the enemy should he land on the airfield or on the beach to the east of it'.

Preparations

Examples quoted in the following paragraph are generalisable to other battalions across the brigade and indeed the whole division. At first for the 237 men of 21 Battalion, under their Second-in-Command, preparations for the westerly facing defences on Vineyard Ridge were leisurely, for:

As far as the troops were concerned, digging weapon pits ... was an exercise only, for unless the Germans arrived by air or the Navy took a long holiday, they considered there was small chance of using them.

Time passed pleasantly enough. There was a routine stand-to at dusk and dawn, and there were periods when all ranks had to be in their areas. At night one-third of the strength was placed on three hours' sentry duty, and in the daytime there was three hours' training; the balance of the time was spent in preparing battle positions, in swimming parades, and resting. Rations could have been more varied, but the cooks – cooking over open fires in kerosene tins – did their best to vary the invariable bully beef.

With the escape from Greece and return of their commanding officer and thirty-seven men, followed by a further fifty-one, and the presence overhead of an increasing numbers of German aircraft, the pace of life increased noticeably. However, not before relations with the military police deteriorated, as further escapees from Greece were welcomed back:

Naturally enough such events called for suitable celebrations, which in turn necessitated unauthorised trips to Hania for supplies. These out-of-bounds excursions and late returns from lawful leave ...eventually... necessitated the establishment of a Field Punishment Centre. Major Harding was asked to detail an officer to command the centre. Lieutenant Roach's appointment was almost automatic, for four of his depleted platoons were already under sentence owing to a misunderstanding about leave passes.

For shelter and defence the 23rd prepared company defensive positions with limited supplies of tools, mines and wire, the new defences did not compare at all favourably with those the battalion had constructed in Greece. Their historian commented:

Some barbed wire arrived and, since there were no pickets, it was strung from tree to tree or along the vines on the lower slopes. Signals equipment was particularly short. The 23rd possessed only three telephones and just a few hundred yards of signal wire.

The battalion's defences included some captured Italian 75 mm guns but these did not impress, due to the difficulties in communicating with their

Tavronitis Bridge · Line of river · Maleme Airfield

Hill 107 · RAF Camp

Maleme/Pyrgos village

gun position and the Battery's general air of improvisation. In common with other units in 5 Brigade, the Battalion had four Vickers machine guns and a pair of mortars but both weapon types lacked full scales of ammunition and were missing important components.

Such had been the losses amongst the rifle companies in Greece that headquarter companies, with little in the way of administration to do now that most of the battalions' heavy/specialist equipment had been lost, formed a significant part of all four infantry battalions' fighting strength.

Battalion's plans

The Maoris provide us with an example of Brigadier Hargest's assessment of the likely enemy attack and their intent on the arrival in the Brigade area:

The procedure would probably be preliminary bombing and machine gunning to clear areas for paratroopers to land, after which the planes would continue circling and firing to protect the enemy while they organised.

The battalion answer would be action by fire power only until it was certain that any attack was not a feint, whereupon the troops would leave their dug-in positions, deal with the situation, and return again to shelter; reserve platoons were to be concentrated and mobile while all other positions were to be sited for all-round defence; firing was to be controlled as long as possible and only low-flying planes were to be engaged by the troops; trench sentries were to be responsible for operating a system of alarms, as follows:

A series of short whistle blasts—Slit trenches.

Long and short blasts—Battle stations.

White Very lights—Reinforce D and Headquarters Companies' area.

It can be seen from the above that counter-attacks were at the heart of the Brigade plan.

At the centre of the Brigade's position, 'occupying what was to be the unenviable position of honour' was 22 NZ Battalion, commanded by Lieutenant Colonel Andrews, who, like his General Freyberg, had also earned the Victoria Cross during the Great War.

22 New Zealand Battalion's Airfield Defences

Subsequent events required Colonel Andrews to write a full report, which opened with a description of the airfield and the resources available to him for its defence.

The troops concerned with the defence of the 'drome' were as follows but most of these acted under their own commanders:

Two 4-in naval guns with Marine Detachment [Z Coast Battery, RM]

Two 3-in A.A. guns [C HAA Battery, RM]

Ten Bofors guns

Two I Tanks [7 Royal Tank Regiment]

One infantry battalion – weak in strength and weapons – less carriers and with one [Assault Pioneer] platoon away for the defence of the DF [radar] station

Two Platoons of MMGs (4 x Vickers guns)

Four carriers – three manned by drivers from the Welsh Regiment

Fleet Air Arm and RAF detachments (All Planes had been destroyed)

Some 3.7-inch howitzers

A Royal Marine anti-aircraft gun crew prepare for action.

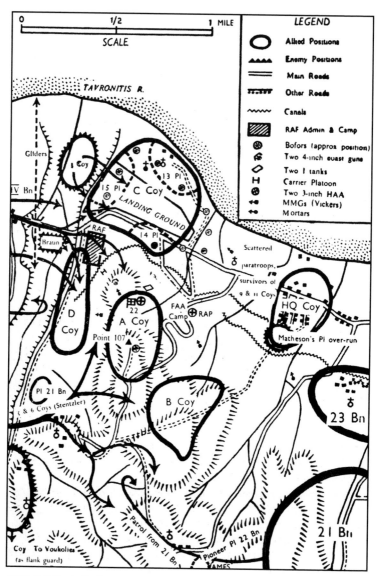

22NZ Battalion's Deployment.

The above force was disposed to cover the drome and prevent landings thereon or on the beach, also landings inland which would move on to the drome. The 4-inch guns were on a spur just south of the aerodrome and could cover the area from the bridge round to Theodora Island. The two 3-in A.A. guns were on the highest point of the ridge south of the drome. The Bofors were distributed round the edge of the aerodrome down on the flat. The two I Tanks were dug in and hidden back against the hills opposite the centre of the drome. One platoon of MMGs was on the ridge overlooking the

60

river bed at the west end of the position with area of fire up and down the
river bed, along the beach both ways and on to the aerodrome itself. The
other platoon was on the right with one section down on the flat just east of
the edge of the drome and able to put fire up and down the beach and on to
the landing area. The other section was back on the spur covering the
ground to the west of Maleme village.

The vital machine guns, despite their good positions had improvised tripods, no spare parts, improvised belts and it is not surprising that Colonel Andrews reported that stoppages were frequent. The 3.7-inch howitzers were well to the east of the battalion area but had an OP on the Hill 107 overlooking the Tavronitis river and ground to the west.

Andrews deployed his rifle companies to cover the aerodrome, river and coastline within his area (see map). The RAF and Fleet Air Arm ground crew and admin staff that remained were centred on the RAF Camp, which in terms of 22 NZ Battalion's defence, was inconveniently placed:

There was another weakness: at the south-west corner of C Company's
position, where this company ended and D Company began near the steel
and wood bridge crossing the Tavronitis River, the RAF had its tented
camp. The camp and the large number of airmen about it made it impossible
for 15 Platoon to tie up thoroughly with the northern platoon of D
Company: one good defence line would have run straight through the
officers' mess – unthinkable!

The Germans eventually came straight through this weak spot, where the airmen '…occupied trenches covering the company holding the river bank and some were to come under my command as a reserve'. The report estimated about forty-three officers and airmen, out of three times that number, played an active part in the defence, the remainder being either unarmed, captured or killed early on.

Another almost criminal weakness in the defences was that 'Mines were laid, but on strict orders from Creforce Headquarters were never primed because they might have blown up friendly Greeks'.

Due to the extent of the airfield area and the reduced strength of his battalion (520 men), Andrews' reserve consisted of a single platoon from the centre company, made up to strength with batmen, HQ clerks and signallers 'who were unable to maintain communication when the show started'.

German Plans – *Gruppe West*

The *Luftlande Sturmregiment* (LLSR), code named COMET, less two companies, was to seize the Maleme area. They were to land following an hour long strike by von Richthofen's bombers and fighter bombers, designed to neutralise both the Commonwealth air and ground defences. Landing by glider or dropping by parachute, the LLSR would be delivered to company LZ/DZs, as was normal German practice, so as to be close to their objectives.

First to land at H-Hour (0814 hours) would be two I Battalion companies plus a platoon in gliders, who would destroy the two obvious anti-aircraft positions on the airfield to the east and west, while the 36-man assault platoon (*Gruppe Brücke*) would glide in and seize the Tavronitis Bridge. This latter commitment of a force to capture a bridge over a river that was by late May, reduced to a trickle, is symptomatic of the German lack of intelligence about Crete and its defences. The First Battalion would be followed by *HQ LLSR* (in gliders), II and III battalions in Ju 52s, who would jump

Generalmajor Meindl.

into company DZs at H+15 and H+45 respectively and seize objectives respectively to the south and east of the airfield. *IV/LLSR*, the heavy weapons battalion would jump with *Generalmajor* Meindl's HQ to the west of the Tavronitis.

The Bombing

During the two weeks running up to the invasion, the *Luftwaffe* had established air superiority over Crete, driven the last RAF aircraft from their bases on the island and begun a programme of bombing targets that they had located along the entire north coast. Shipping in Souda Bay was a particular target. Colonel Andrews described the preliminary bombing:

> For days before the 20th the enemy had regularly bombed and machine-gunned the edges of the drome, the RAF Camp and our positions in the hills. He had stirred up the 3-inch AA guns. He had destroyed all planes on the ground but although we had casualties all weapons were working on the morning of the attack.

On X-Day, in their role as the *Fallschirmjäger's* flying artillery, the *Luftwaffe's* bombers had not only to neutralise the anti-aircraft guns but also soften up the New Zealand defenders before the *LLSR's* aircraft appeared over the Maleme area.

For the defenders, who had mostly only received the vaguest of information, as far as permitted by the security rules for using ULTRA intelligence, the enemy were to be finally expected on 20 May. The day dawned, as usual bright and clear and as the first wave of aircraft came into the attack, General Freyberg in his HQ on the Akrotiri Peninsula grunted into his breakfast that 'They are right on time'.

5 NZ Brigade recorded in their War Diary at 0610 hours, an event, which many thought to be the normal 'daily hate':

Heavy bombing attack on AA defences around airdrome. Three flights of five medium Dornier bombers dropped about 1000 bombs around the perimeter and 22 Bn ridge.

The planes turned back to the north and the men prepared to resume their disrupted breakfast but 'again the air-raid siren sounded from the mysterious Air Ministry Experimental Station [the still secret radar] tucked away up in the hills'. For the infantrymen, however, the approach of the enemy air fleet was felt rather than seen. The New Zealanders could feel the growing throb of hundreds of aircraft through the ground. Just after 0800 hours, 'Cursing men, still hungry, had just taken cover in trench and under trees when twenty-four heavy bombers appeared, the first of an endless fleet, wave upon wave, bombing, strafing, diving'.

One of the two Bofors anti-aircraft positions, manned by Royal Marines of the MNBDO, positioned in the open despite Colonel Andrews'

New Zealanders shelter from the bombing.

protestations to General Weston's HQ, bore the brunt of the attack. Worse still, following a friendly fire incident when an RAF aircraft had been shot down by their own side, the Royal Marine gunners were ordered not to open fire without the authority of an officer and once the bombing began, no officer could reach the guns to order the crews to engage the enemy. Lieutenant Colonel Andrews recorded that:

> From the commencement of the bombing no shot was fired by the 4 inch Naval guns or by the Bofors but the 3 inch [AA] guns remained at their post and were in action against aircraft until put out of action by dive bombers.

The anti-aircraft gunners of the four Bofors, who dared to open fire, were driven into cover by the overwhelming and relentless bombing and strafing attack. Squadron Leader Howell described the attack:

> The ground shuddered like jelly under us. Our eyes and mouths were full of grit. We were shaken till our teeth felt loose and we could hardly see. Debris continued to crash around us and the sides of the trench crumbled. We lost track of time.

For the infantrymen of 22 NZ Battalion in the area surrounding Maleme,

One of the Bofors' positions at the eastern end of the airfield.

the bombing began to build in intensity from 0745, reaching a climax at 0806 hours.

> *Intense machine-gunning of area surrounding aerodrome. Any movement on ground drew intense fire from planes. Aerodrome perimeter was again heavily bombed raising dense clouds of dust, which completely obscured the aerodrome from view.*

Lieutenant Colonel Andrews, in his HQ on the northern extremity of Hill 107, reported that 'This bombing was most intense and the density and size of bombs made the artillery fire of the Somme 1916, Messines 1917 and Passchendaele a mere picnic. I do not wish to experience another one like it'. 22 NZ Battalion recorded that 'men, dazed and numb with the fury of the assault, bled from ears and mouths'. It is estimated that the *Luftwaffe* dropped some 3,000 bombs around the airfield alone.

Colonel Andrews went on to report that the already poor communications were lost, with '... the lines being cut by bombs. One No 18 set to Brigade was functioning in a weak and erratic manner. The artillery FOO lost touch ...'. Under this concentrated attack, the New Zealanders were isolated and driven into cover; consequently, few saw the aircraft bearing the *Fallschirmjäger* approaching Maleme.

The Glider Landings

The thirty DFS-230 gliders bearing 3 and 4 *Kompanies I/LLSR*, under the command of *Oberleutnant* von Plessen and *Oberleutnant* Sarrazin respectively, were at the head of the stream of *Luftwaffe* transports. They and *Gruppe Brücke* arrived early over the landing zones while the bombing was still under way, some time before 0815 hours. Consequently, the gliders swooping down from their release points at 5,000 feet, a mile to the west of the airfield, approaching from the south-west, found it difficult to identify their landing zones amidst the billowing clouds of dust and smoke, which was particularly bad to the east of the airfield. Gliding-in between the Stukas, the pilots sought out places to land.

Major Koch and his headquarters of *I/LLSR* were to land with 4 *Kompanie* in the area most badly affected by smoke and dust on the eastern perimeter but ended up scattered across the RAF Camp and the eastern slopes of Hill 107. Many of the gliders, as they hit the ground,

Major Koch, veteran of the Albert Canal operation in 1940.

were smashed against trees and rocks; their passengers badly injured. Even those *Fallschirmjäger* who had 'good landings', were stunned by the rapid deceleration of their DFS-230s. Three of the gliders that landed in the RAF Camp did so in front of Aircraftsman Comeau's trench. Splintering to a halt

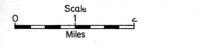

Scale
0   1
Miles

New Zealand positions
German air-landings

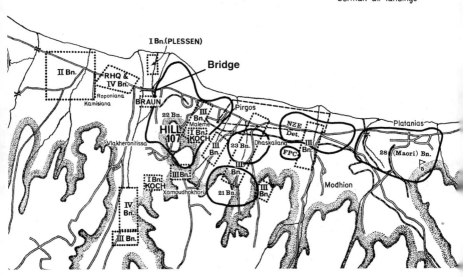

the glider's door opened and a *Fallschirmjäger* staggered out of the wreckage. Comeau recalled that he:

> ... *fired and shot him almost at point blank range. He fell backwards onto a second glider trooper now standing behind him ... The second man was holding his head in his hands. I fired again and he spun round and collapsed, his body blocking the doorway.*

Comeau's rifle jammed at this point and he headed uphill to what he thought was safety, through the rows of olive trees. Major Koch was also wounded in the neck in a similar engagement early in the battle. For the Germans, who had expected the airfield to be lightly held, the strength of the opposition from the dug-in New Zealanders was an unpleasant surprise. So heavy was the enemy's fire and so badly scattered were the gliders that *Oberleutnant* Sarrazin and his surviving men were unable to concentrate into effective groups. However, *Fallschirmjäger* in a glider landing near the two medium machine-gun section on the northern slope of Hill 107 attacked the Vickers gun crews, who lacking small arms with which to defend themselves, were killed and their guns destroyed. This was a stroke of luck for the Germans and was to have a profound effect on subsequent events.

To the west of the airfield, von Plessen's *3 Kompanie* had a better and more concentrated landing, principally in the dry bed of the Tavronitis River. Here they had some cover despite landing virtually under the noses of C Company, 22 NZ Battalion. However, elements of D Company were able to bring fire down on the gliders from the slopes of Hill 107, as they

66

Another view of the glider belonging to *Gruppe Brücke*.

rattled to a halt. The *kompanie* commander, von Plessen was killed along with other junior commanders, as they led their men, storming forward to attack the anti-aircraft guns on the western edge of the airfield near the mouth of the river. Command devolved on their medical officer and ardent Nazi, Dr Weinzl, who, with C Company still suffering from the numbing effect of the bombing, took the anti-aircraft position, in an attack that the gunners had no hope of being able to repel. They had no ammunition for their rifles!

See map page 60

Gruppe Brücke's six gliders with, as in the Eben Emael attack, the pick of the pilots, landed accurately in the river bed at the base of the iron bridge across the stony river bed. Taking possession of the bridge, they drove 18 Platoon of D Company who were charged with covering the eastern end of the bridge, back onto the lower slopes of Hill 107. *Oberleutnant* Braun was, however, killed by a shot to his head and the remainder of *Gruppe Brücke* were pinned down and eventually forced back to the cover of the river bank, as D Company recovered and brought down effective fire. Similarly, *3 Kompanie* were unable to make any headway against the recovering New Zealanders of C Company, whose '15 Platoon, were awaiting a renewed assault on the most westerly tip of the highly prized airfield with rifles and

Gliders on the banks of the Tavronitis River viewed from the bridge.

A glider belonging to *Gruppe Brücke* ended up on the bridge approach banking.

nothing more lethal than … grenades made of jam tins filled with concrete and plugs of gelignite with fuses'.

With most of the glider landed *Fallschirmjäger* scattered, Majors Braun and Koch and many of their junior commanders dead or wounded and their attacks having been halted, the *LLSR*'s initial assault had failed. Crucially, however, they had knocked out one of the anti-aircraft positions and a key element of Colonel Andrews' fire power, two of his Vickers guns covering the airfield and its flanks. The slow moving transport aircraft should be able to approach without impossibly heavy casualties.

Drop of the LLSR at Maleme.

A pair of LLSR soldiers who dropped into an olive grove near Maleme.

The First Parachute Drop

The throb of aero engines grew to a roar as flights of Ju 52s, each carrying a stick of a dozen *Fallschirmjäger* and their equipment containers, started to arrive over the Maleme area around 0830 hours. 22 NZ Battalion's Historian wrote:

> The Luftwaffe crossed the coast a mile or more west of the airfield – out of effective Bofors range – and flew inland at about 500 feet. The two 3-inch anti-aircraft guns on Point 107 could not tackle effectively such low-flying aircraft. The planes turned towards Maleme in a broad swing, skimming low over A and B Companies. The slow troop-carriers do not seem to have been fired at by all of the ten Bofors round the airfield, an angry point with the infantry at the time and later.

However, with the departure of the last Stukas the leading Jus were met with increasing ground fire; some from the anti-aircraft guns and some from small-arms fire. Aircraft were hit and as the *Fallschirmjäger* dived from their aircraft in their spread eagle position, descending on parachute harness linked to a single point on the man's back, many were hit, helpless as they drifted down. A prisoner, originally from Hamburg, belonging to *II/LLSR* told his interrogator that:

> My parachute had scarcely opened when bullets began cracking past me

69

Paratroopers cut down shortly after landing; an all too familiar sight on the first day.

from all directions. It had felt so splendid just before to jump in sunlight over such wonderful countryside, but my feelings suddenly changed. All I could do was to pull my head in and cover my face with my arms.

For the New Zealand Infantry, after enduring the bombing:

Action came as a relief – almost a grim joy – after cowering under cover for a fortnight of air raids, and the remark, 'Just like the duck shooting season!', was widespread at the time.

However, the New Zealanders did not have it all their own way. A member of 22 Battalion recalled that the enemy, as they descended, fired pistols and *Schmeisers* 'indiscriminately certainly, but keeping our heads down'.

First to jump were *II/LLSR*, starting at 0830 hours. However, the battalion dribbled in due to delays caused by dust on the Greek airfields disrupting take-off. Despite their DZs being to the west of the Tavronitis River, many *Fallschirmjäger* were mis-dropped to the east and consequently, suffered heavy casualties during their descent. This dispersal and the inevitable jump casualties caused by the rough ground did much to reduce the combat effectiveness of *II Battalion*. HQ 5 Brigade recorded in its War Diary '0914 Parachutists seen landing west of aerodrome and throughout southern part of our whole front'. With the last company down almost an hour after schedule, it would be some time before *II/LLSR* would be properly in action as a cordinated whole.

Those members of *II/LLSR* who dropped east of Hill 107 were immediately in battle, including some who were unlucky enough to drop in the area of the Field Punishment Centre, which was under command of 23 NZ Bn. The Battalion Provo Sergeant, Sergeant Hulme and the other members of the Field Punishment Centre were at first busy dealing with the *Fallschirmjäger* who were dropping in their area. Lieutenant Roach reported later in the morning that the Germans gave some trouble but 'Sergeant Hulme got cracking – very aggressively. He stood in full view of any German and fired bursts into any suspected places and that closed up the odd burst of fire'. Sometimes alone and sometimes with another – for example, on two occasions he had Private Shatford with him – Hulme went out and dealt with enemy riflemen. Stalking them carefully, he almost invariably got his man. Roach's report shows how much one determined infantryman could dominate an area when it says: 'Hulme used to wander about a lot – from the camp to the road was all his country.' Hulme himself claimed no special credit for the manner in which the Punishment Centre men cleaned up their area but 126 German dead were counted in that general area. Reporting in to 5 Brigade Headquarters on one occasion with some marked maps, Hulme was detailed by Brigadier Hargest to deal with a sniper, whom he stalked and shot.

Sergeant Hulme went on to be one of two New Zealanders to earn the Victoria Cross during the Cretan campaign, as we shall see.

The Second Parachute Drop

Next to jump, now badly delayed, was *III/LLSR*, principally dropping inland from Maleme and Pyrgi. 5 Brigade recorded their arrival at '0950 hours. Second wave commenced dropping'. There follow 'Sitreps' from all the battalions of the brigade reporting paratroopers landing in their area. 23 NZ Battalion reported 'Approx 100 paratroops landing west and 100 in front of position' and the NZ Engineer Detachment reported at '0957, 200 landing in our area'. As before, the drops were dispersed and those *Fallschirmjäger* who landed unwounded, found it hard to locate each other on the ground and were easily taken on by the defenders.

A note follows in the War Diary, 'At this stage it was discovered that every seventh parachute was a container for arms and ammunition to which the descending troops must rally as they were only armed with a pistol'. Many of the colour coded containers, fell into Commonwealth hands. Weapons and ammunition in particular were taken into immediate use to make up for deficiencies in this area. The distinctive rapid fire of *Spandaus* could be heard across the battle area, adding to commanders' confusion, as they expected to hear the slower rhythmic bursts of Bren-gun fire from their positions.

Oberfeldwebel Helmut Wenzel of *9 Kompanie III/LLSR*, who dropped onto Hill 107 recounted:

 I jumped first. At the very moment my parachute opened, I heard

71

The chapel on the crest of Hill 107. The site of the 3-inch AA guns is just behind he chapel.

cracking in the air. Bullets! The English were welcoming us. I was exactly above them and I could see six Tommies standing up firing at me. 'Dogs!' I thought. 'Wait till I land.' I unfastened my thigh straps, which enabled me to get hold of my pistol. Just before I reached the ground I was hit in the chest. The bullet went in above my right shoulder and came out near the carotid artery. Braces, smock and binocular straps were severed, my Leica case also. I landed softly in a vineyard, not thirty metres from the English positions.

I fired my pistol at two Tommies who fell, the others dropped to the ground. That gave me time to get rid of my parachute completely. The enemy was now firing with a machine gun. I lay low in a little depression. My bag and my water bottle stuck out and were riddled with holes. Firing stopped because the Tommies thought I was dead. I crawled away from there. Where was my section? I had to get it together!

Wenzel had dropped onto the eastern side of Hill 107, which was held by A Company, as well as being the position of 22 NZ Battalion's HQ and the 3-inch anti-aircraft guns on the crest. However, thickly covered with olives and vines and with plenty of other isolated groups of both glider and parachute-landed *Fallschirmjäger*, many Germans, such as Wenzel, were able to remain active, even if lightly armed. He continued his account:

Despairing, I got up and shouted –'3rd section, here!' A machine gun immediately fired at me, hitting me in the head. A better shot than at Eben Emael! It went through my helmet, tore my scalp and touched the bone of the skull. I forced myself not to lose consciousness. But my comrades had

72

heard my shouts and four of them closed in on me ... Glóneld did the dressing, and put muck on it to camouflage the white colour. Bullets were whistling all around us and one of them pierced my boot.

Then we attacked with grenades, and forced our opponents to withdraw. That way they would not be able to get near enough to discover how few paratroops they really were facing.

The worst thing for us was being unable to reach our weapon containers! One was nearby; we crawled towards it, but it turned out to contain only the battalion's short wave radio equipment. It did, however, contain a rifle and a Schmeiser. That was something, for up to now we had been fighting with pistols and grenades.

Wenzel and his men spent most of the day lying–up in a defensive circle, in a bomb crater, within sight of the 3-inch anti-aircraft position on the crest of the hill, watching the guns back in action, successfully engage German aircraft after aircraft over the Maleme area. He recalled that during the day, 'The heat was terrible and our clothes were too hot – a kingdom for a water bottle! We chewed vine leaves; they were a bit bitter but they did have moisture. But at no moment did we think of surrendering.' He, like many others, went on to criticise the wisdom of sending troops into battle in equipment designed for use in the inclement weather of northern Europe. Rations too were unsuitable, melting into an unattractive gloop in the heat.

The *Luftwaffe's* fighters, Stukas and bombers overhead were unable to provide much help to the *Fallschirmjäger* fighting the battle around the airfield and Hill 107. Wenzel recorded that '...friends and foe were too close together. Moreover, the enemy used our ground identification signs, flags and some of our weapons. In a short time, they already knew how to use it all. There was no coherent front line'. Nazi flags, found in possession of virtually every *Fallschirmjäger* prisoner, were indeed displayed by the New Zealanders, who found them to be effective protection against attack by enemy aircraft.

See maps pages 60 and 66

Ju-87 dive bombers worked hard to subdue the defences.

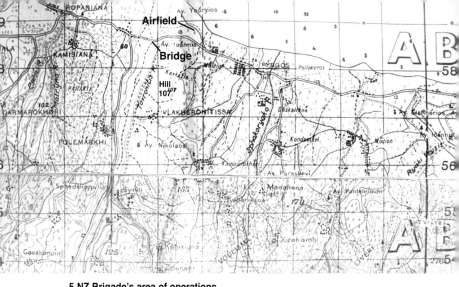

5 NZ Brigade's area of operations

Meanwhile, a part of *11 Kompanie* had been dropped on the coastal strip in Headquarters Company 22 NZ Battalion's area to the west of Pyrgi, where Lieutenant Beaven and three officers and about sixty men, 'mostly administrative staff not previously riflemen' were positioned. Jim Henderson wrote:

> It was at once cut off when several gliders silently swam down between it and Battalion Headquarters, followed by perhaps ten, perhaps twenty, plane-loads of parachutists, plus a small field gun. A second wave of parachutists fell about mid-morning. The invaders suffered severe losses, but the well-equipped survivors rallied to form awkward strongpoints in grape-vines and trees. These strongpoints made movement very difficult indeed.

German paratroopers troops pinned down in the Maleme area.

Contributing to the success was a section commanded by a Great War veteran, Sergeant Jack Pender, a New Zealand REME armourer attached to 22 Battalion. 'Pender... had recently been mounting Browning machine guns out of aircraft... [and] his section had paratroops falling twenty-five yards along the front. Very few of them landed alive.'

Headquarter Company, however, lost an *ad hoc* platoon commanded by Sergeant Major Matheson, which was 'out on a limb to the south', where it was cut-off and overrun. Regimental Quartermaster Sergeant Woods, one of the few survivors recounted:

> Over comes the Hun with Stukas, Junkers and gliders, not mentioning the 109s. By the time the Stukas and 109s had left us the air round about seemed to be alive with Junkers, and believe me the birds that flew out of them were pretty thick. They looked impossible as the odds must have been easily 15 to 1. Shooting was good until enemy grenades got the front trenches, Matheson received a mortal wound, and the platoon position fell.

Private Cowling had been on his way to the company cookhouse for fatigues but was about halfway there when the drops began. Occupying a slit trench, facing towards Matheson's Platoon, he saw:

> ...quite a few paratroops in the area, they were all easy meat... the Transport Platoon were using machine guns. Boy, and weren't they using them too! We later found out they were enemy stuff they had captured.

Actions such as this helped prevent the enemy from advancing west towards Pyrgi village. They were driven to cover in 'small patches among the olives and tried to edge westwards along the coast to the focal point – the all-important airfield'. Headquarters Company continued to hold Pyrgi throughout the day with the help of some unlikely heroes:

> Padre Hurst and a group of 'cooks and bottle-washers', manning a small defensive position and soon using up the few rounds of ammunition they possessed, were joined by Jack Pender, who ... got a German field piece going and he cleaned up a machine-gun nest in a cottage – that was our greatest triumph.

Elsewhere, in 28 Maori Battalion's area, *Fallschirmjäger* were seen at a house by the beach about half a mile west of D Company and Captain Tureia was ordered to send two Maori platoons from D Company to eject them. The battalion's history recorded that:

See map page 66

> By the time they had worked to within 500–600 yards of the objective they were closely attended by several planes circling and gunning as they came round, but the Maoris kept on with fire and movement as practised in England. Logan, on the left, swung his platoon in an arc and closed in. The Germans were in twos and threes around the house and, after seven or eight of their number had been killed, two officers and eight other ranks surrendered. The Maoris' casualties were two slightly wounded, so besides being very gratified at the sight of their captives disliking the attention of

75

their own aircraft, the men felt that a reasonable amount of revenge had been obtained for the men killed in Greece.

The drop on the coastal strip gave rise to accusations of atrocities perpetrated by Commonwealth troops. Not only had some *Fallschirmjäger* been hideously wounded in their uncontrolled descent by dropping into bamboo thickets but had also been caught up in trees and on power lines in this area. Caught in their parachute harness, many men already wounded bled to death, while others were hit attempting to struggle free. Later, the grotesque, blackened and bloated bodies, some repeatedly hit in exchanges of fire during the following days, were eventually seen 'strung up' as their comrades advanced east.

So far, the *Fallschirmjäger's* drop into company DZs on or near their objectives had not helped the *LLSR's* already poor situation. They had suffered very heavy casualties and were dispersed amongst the olive groves that cloaked the area. However, even though prisoners were being rounded up in quantity and groups of *Fallschirmjäger* were being destroyed, the effect on the Kiwis, was marked. There was no neat front line, the situation was confused and 22 NZ Battalion was unsupported and seemingly isolated. The shock of vertical envelopment, was having a profound impact on 5 NZ Brigade's commanders. For the *LLSR*, however, things were about to improve a little.

Generalmajor **Meindl Arrives**

IV/LLSR had jumped into DZs to the west of the Tavronitis River and the Commonwealth defences and dropped out of contact with the enemy, along with Regimental HQ and *Generalmajor* Meindl. Having lost the Vickers section, the 4-inch naval guns could have been useful at this point but D Company's request for fire 'was rejected on the ground that the guns on Hill 107 were sited for targets at sea'. Rapidly appreciating that his plan had miscarried, Meindl set out at a brisk pace towards the Tavronitis Bridge to assess the situation, leaving the *Fallschirmjäger* of *IV Battalion* to follow on with their heavier support weapons. Meindl promptly ordered that the attack be renewed. The remains of 3 and 4 *Kompanies* would attack their previous objectives, the airfield and the RAF Camp, with the latter being supported by both fire and manpower from *Hauptmann* Gericke's *IV Battalion*. Further south, 5 and 6 *Kompanies* of Major Stentzler's *II/LLSR* were to advance into the rear of 22 NZ Battalion's position via a break in the ridge between Hill 107 and the radar (AMES) site.

While the attack was being organised, there was discussion at the *LLSR* HQ beneath the abutments of the Tavronitis Bridge regarding the presence of significant elements of *4/LLSR* in the area of the RAF Camp. Meindl attempting to get a response by waving a swastika flag was hit in the hand by a rifle bullet. Not badly wounded, Meindl stood up so as to be more

Generalmajor Meindl set up his HQ beneath the abutments of the Tavronitis Bridge.

easily seen and was promptly hit in the chest probably by a New Zealander of D Company. Badly wounded Meindl was taken to the Regimental Aid Post that had been established in Tavronitis Village. Thus, the *LLSR* lost a second senior commander within two hours. None the less, a dangerous situation was developing for the New Zealanders in the area of the RAF Camp, which though overlooked by 18 Platoon of D Company, was held by the mixed bag of airmen under Squadron Leader Howell, none of whom had been trained as infantry. A Fleet Air Arm officer interviewed by the Inter Service Enquiry reported with unusual realism:

> *We didn't know where our own people were; we didn't know where the enemy were; many people had no rifles. Many people had rifles and no ammunition …if anyone fired at you, he might be (a) an enemy (b) a friend who thought you were an enemy (c) a friend or an enemy who didn't know who the hell you were (d) someone not firing at you at all.*

Colonel Andrews, despite a situation that was unclear and with the sound of battle, some of it very close to his own HQ, and with a few formal reports of fighting reaching his command post, could not afford to be supine. He reported that he had initially turned down Captain Johnson's request for reinforcements and the I Tanks to secure his C Company position but:

> At approx 1030 hours, the enemy who had landed by the bridge and captured a number of RAF, forced my defences there and pushed up the ridge driving a number of captured airmen in front of them as a screen. This was dealt with, the airmen released and a counter-attack restored the situation down to the road. Again at approx. 1200 hours, the same tactics were used. The airmen were released and a number of enemy killed but the counter-attack was only partially successful. There was further shelling and bombing of the ridge but the positions were not attacked.

During this period the Germans established a vital toehold at the foot of Hill 107 and in the RAF Camp at a heavy cost in casualties. Resistance by small groups of airmen continued among the olive trees, bomb craters, huts and tents, as individuals and groups sniped at the enemy.

The *Fallschirmjäger* found a copy of the Commonwealth codes in the RAF operations centre, from which they were able to gain intelligence, providing them with their first accurate information about the strength and deployment of the force they had taken on. Squadron Leader Howell, realising the danger of losing these documents, was wounded as he attempted to infiltrate back into the camp area.

Meanwhile, away from the RAF Camp, many members of the parachute element of the *LLSR* were also fighting in small groups that only later developed into fighting units of more than nuisance value. Willi Maue of 6 *Kompanie, II/LLSR* was one such man:

> After a rather long march, I came through a little group. I was among those who had escaped and we quickly formed up a group and went over to the attack. Quite a while later, towards midday we recovered the rest of our company in dribs and drabs. Then in the course of the afternoon, the rest of the battalion. Our group of seven men became a fairly strong combat unit which could still function in spite of its losses; we later came across the rest of the company. We were still in a defensive situation with several killed and wounded in our ranks, following very concentrated firing from the enemy artillery which was defending itself against our attacks in a remarkable way.

5 and 6 *Kompanies* had been ordered by Meindl to attack across the saddle at the southern end of Hill 107 but had been unable to advance across the Tavronitis River, having been pinned down by the platoon attached to 22 NZ Battalion to guard against just such a threat. Eventually, however, *II/LLSR* manoeuvred past the blocking platoon, growing in strength as it met up with groups like that of Willi Maue's.

Late Morning and Afternoon

As the morning progressed the *LLSR* became better organised, although with so many commanders killed this was a slow process. The *Fallschirmjäger* maintained pressure on the New Zealand line opposite the

Tavronitis and according to Colonel Andrews:

> At approx. 1330 hours, C Company on the aerodrome carried out a local counter-attack in an endeavour to relieve one of their platoons [15, who were isolated] by the river bed but this was not successful.

The fact that German reinforcements had promptly arrived to decisively check the two C Company platoons, is indicative of increased capability at this stage in the battle. All the while enemy aircraft were overhead attacking anything or anybody in the open. Colonel Andrews commented, '… daylight movement of troops [including runners] was a most hazardous undertaking. Taken in conjunction with the lack of communications an enormous burden is imposed on … commanders'.

C Company, however, received a small but welcome reinforcement, when at:

> About 2 p.m. a spirited lieutenant from an English light anti-aircraft battery led eight men (two 'bomb happy'), survivors from his troop of Bofors guns by the south-east edge of the airfield, into Company Headquarters. They volunteered to join C Company as riflemen and were armed.

By mid afternoon the situation was deteriorating. At 1550, hours '22 Bn reported their left flank had given way but position was believed to be in hand'. This was II/LLSR (Strentzler) beginning to force their way across the saddle at the southern end of Hill 107. It would seem to have been an ideal counter-attack task for elements of 23 NZ Battalion who were nearby and specifically assigned the task. Brigadier Hargest's inaction, even though this message is recorded in his brigade's War Diary, is often excused due to 'poor communications'. He did not implement the 'immediate counter-attack' required in divisional orders or even his own orders. He did, however, agree to support a counter-attack on the western end of the airfield to be mounted at 1700 hours by Colonel Andrews. Captain Johnson recalled:

> At 5 p.m. the long and eagerly awaited order to counter-attack with support of the two tanks arrived from Battalion Headquarters. I had discussed with the tank troop commander the day before just how we would work together. The troop commander, believing the Germans would have no anti-tank weapons capable of hurting a Matilda, feared nothing except enemy soldiers on top of his tanks. He asked that his tanks should be kept sprayed with small-arms fire.
>
> Lieutenant Donald commanded the attackers on foot: 14 Platoon (about 12 below strength) was organised as two sections with a third section of [British and Australian anti-aircraft] gunner volunteers. The tanks left their concealed positions at 5.15 p.m. and moved west past Company Headquarters along the road towards the river in single file about 30 yards apart. The first tank proceeded up to the river, firing as it went, until it stopped in the riverbed.

The appearance of the I Tanks enabled C Company to cross the hitherto fire-swept airfield with hardly a single casualty but with the tanks halted on the bank of the dry river. Lieutenant Sinclair, platoon commander 15 Platoon, in his isolated position west of the airfield, saw the tank 'go down under the big bridge and out a little further west where it came to a halt. The place was seething with enemy plainly visible in the long grass. They seemed uncertain what to do'.

There are various accounts how the tanks came to grief at this point in the battle. One version has it that the leading tank that went into the dry river bed broke down on the rough river bed. However, Captain Johnson wrote that 'Apparently the turret jammed and the crew surrendered'. Lieutenant Sinclair has yet another version: that it was hit by an anti-tank shell in the engine and that '… the crew at pistol point, were forced to service the damaged part but instead ruined it permanently'. The Germans however, used the tank as a pill box and succeeded in getting the 2-pounder in action against D Company on Hill 107. Captain Johnson recalled:

The second tank broken down in the airfield.

The second tank turned about before reaching the bridge and came back past Company Headquarters on the Maleme road. It had not fired a shot and broke down. This left 14 Platoon under withering fire from the front and southern flank. Their position was hopeless. Those who were able withdrew, using the lee side of the tank for shelter. Donald, himself wounded, led only eight or nine men back, most of them wounded, from this brave but disastrous counter-attack. The English [anti-aircraft gunner] officer was killed in this attack after pleading with me to let him take part and lead a section.

Captain Johnson sent a runner to Colonel Andrews' HQ on Hill 107 with the disturbing news that the counter-attack had failed and that:

15 Platoon and the western section of 13 Platoon seemed to have been overcome; 14 Platoon was practically finished, and the cooks, stretcher-bearers, and Company Headquarters staff alone could not hold the inland perimeter of the airfield for long. The company would probably hold out until dark, but reinforcements would be needed then. The CO replied in his last message to get through to Johnson on 20 May: 'Hold on at all costs.'

With C Company having spent itself in under resourced counter-attack and

II/LLSR slowly advancing into the Battalion's area, things were beginning to look bleak for Colonel Andrews' New Zealanders.

Student in Athens

If Colonel Andrews thought that the situation was slipping away from his control, the *LLSR* were reporting to Student that they had failed to capture the airfield. Earlier optimism and self deception born of unrealistic confidence, was replaced by a sense of crisis in Hotel Grande Bretagne, which only worsened as news came in from the other groups further east of a similar lack of success. The option of withdrawal was discussed but faced with a collapse of German airborne forces and loss of his reputation, Student, contrary to the principles of war, decide to reinforce what was arguably a failure at this point. He would concentrate on Maleme, where he perceived a glimmer of success, at the expense of the other groups, who would have to fend for themselves. Orders were given to reinforce *Gruppe West* with both convoys of light shipping and an *ad hoc* battalion of *Fallschirmjäger* who had been left out of battle because of a lack of lift. There was an ideal candidate for commander at hand, *Oberst* Ramcke, who had a reputation as a fighting soldier but had been excluded from active units as he was 'too old' – over forty. He had been brought to Greece only to train and advise *5th Gerbirgsjägerdivision* in air portability but as the sole combat officer of the appropriate rank he was brought to Student's HQ and briefed on the situation. He would jump with every available parachute-trained soldier the following morning.

Attempts to Land

With initial reports being interpreted as success, there early attempts to land Ju-52's at Maleme had already been ordered. Some of those reported by the New Zealanders were no doubt forced landings by damaged aircraft. For example, 28 Maori Battalion reported at 1030 hours that:

> *One troop-carrying plane effected a landing on the beach opposite D Coy lines. It was immediately set on fire presumably by Bren gun fire. These enormous black troop-carrying planes are circling round and round the beach and above the aerodrome seeking landing places.*

At 1500, 5 Brigade recorded that '28 Bn OP reports that troop carrying aircraft had been landing on Maleme aerodrome in ones and twos since mid-day'. These were in fact mainly on the nearby beach but later in the day, C Company, at the western edge of the airfield,

81

were well positioned to deal with what is almost certainly a deliberate attempt at landing on the aerodrome:

> Late in the afternoon two Ju 52s attempted to land on the airfield, but the mauled company was by no means carrion yet. All weapons opened up and the planes, spitting back small-arms fire, swung out to sea.

There were also reports from the Kiwis' OPs during the afternoon that the enemy were landing on the beach to the west of the Tavronitis but these remain unconfirmed. The airfield was clearly not captured and could not receive aircraft flying in heavy elements of *7th Fliegerdivision* and *5th Gerbirgsjägerdivision*. Also delayed by the presence of the Royal Navy in the Aegean was the convoy of Greek caique fishing boats bearing a battalion of *Gerbirgsjägerregiment 100* and anti-aircraft guns. They were supposed to cross from the Greek mainland in daylight, under cover of the *Luftwaffe*, who would keep the Royal Navy away, and land to the west of Tavronitis during the afternoon of X-Day. They would not now arrive until the following afternoon at the earliest.

The Abandonment of Hill 107

As the evening wore on, the aggressive *Fallschirmjäger* maintained pressure from the west and groups that had hitherto been lying-up, started to move around the area and enemy activity levels climbed again. Although under renewed dive bombing, the Kiwi soldiers felt that they were undefeated. However, the sense of isolation from assistance and even encouragement and the pressure to react in a situation of uncertainty was getting to Colonel Andrews. Captain Twig wrote:

See map page 84

> The OC and 2iC showed signs of strain during the day, and I put this down to lack of news and information concerning their own troops and the position in general. I am sure that the bombing or their personal safety did not concern these officers, but the responsibility was great.

Commander of *IV Battalion, Hauptmann* Gericke giving orders for the next attack.

The Battalion's historian offers another factor that was at work on morale in Battalion HQ: 'The counter-attack by 23 Battalion, freely discussed before the invasion, was widely expected, and when it did not come, the feeling of bewilderment and isolation increased.'

At 1925 hours, in response to his situation report describing the failure of C Company's latest attack and his plea for assistance, just two companies, one each from 23 and 28 Battalions, were belatedly dispatched to restore the situation around the airfield. They failed to reach C Company, as they had to brave not only dive bombing and strafing but short sharp fights with isolated groups of *Fallschirmjäger* that they encountered *en route*. According to 22 NZ Battalion's historian:

> ... a company 114 strong from 28 (Maori) Battalion came confidently right to the eastern edge of the airfield and failed by a furlong or so to contact C Company. This would be bitter news to C Company men when they heard some days (or, in some cases, several years) later of the Maoris' thrust. The company now believes the Maoris came to within but 200 yards of Company Headquarters and 14 Platoon, but halted by the knocked-out Bofors guns, and hearing only the shouts and tramplings of noisy German patrols, concluded that the airfield had fallen and pulled back.

This unlucky failure to join up with C Company on the airfield and for the 23 NZ Battalion company to have any impact on the situation around Hill 107 in the gathering darkness, further reinforced Andrews' mood and helped make up his mind. It is hard not to conclude that this is one of those small events that could have tipped the balance of the entire campaign in the Commonwealth's favour.

The situation for Colonel Andrews worsened as the Germans pushed up Hill 107 from the RAF Camp to threaten his HQ. In these circumstances, 'At approx 2100 hrs, I [Andrews] decided to withdraw the remainder of the battalion to B Coy ridge'. Colonel Andrews elaborated on his decision to withdraw:

> In my opinion the strength of the enemy in personnel, machine guns, mortar and SP infantry guns, as well as in the air was greater than one battalion could deal with in such a position. Even if the Brigade counter-attack of two companies could have restored this position that night the place would have become untenable first thing in the morning. On my own, in spite of the excellent fighting qualities shown by the men and in spite of the heavy casualties inflicted, I could not have held on one hour after dawn. I would have been completely surrounded by then and the air attacks and shelling would have completed the work.

This withdrawal, typical of the paucity of communication between 22 NZ Battalion and HQ 5 NZ Brigade, was begun with Brigadier Hargest only receiving the barest of details to which he responded: 'Well, if you must, you must.'

Running to take cover behind a wrecked RAF vehicle. Hill 107 can be seen behind the wreck.

Captain Johnson felt that the withdrawal from the fateful airfield was 'a bitter reward for their day of steadfast defiance'.

A runner went to tell 13 Platoon and returned saying the place was bare. Every man removed his boots and hung them round his neck. Critically wounded men were made as comfortable as possible and left with food and water. The southern wire round 14 Platoon's defences was cut and, in single file, the wounded interspersed here and there, they set off. One man was practically carried, stooped over the back of a friend; another crawled all the way to 21 Battalion on his hands and knees. No stretchers were available; the party could not have carried them in any case, for they had to be prepared to fight their way out. They went past the snoring Germans to the right, through the vineyards separating C Company from A Company, up to A Company's deserted headquarters, on to the road, up the hill past a grounded and ghostly glider...

On reaching B Company Ridge, Colonel Andrews found that the enemy were already advancing around the flanks. He continued:

I may have been able to hold the back ridge that night but I would have been attacked from the left, front and rear in the morning and the holding

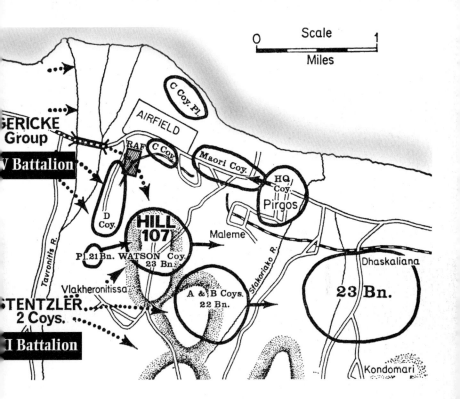

of that ridge did not strengthen the position in row so I decided to withdraw
to 21/23 Bn.

Captain Johnson led his men on '… until, after dawn, they reached a wood
near 21 Battalion's positions. As they fell dead-tired under the trees,
German planes began the morning hate'. Andrews split and positioned the
remains of the A and C Companies he managed to extricate, with 21 and 23
Battalion. Left behind were elements of the battalion who could not be
located in the dark.

On the morning of 21 May, D Company and some men of A Company
were left in possession of Hill 107. The following comment sums up the

**Hill 107 taken from the old Tavronitis Bridge. The new highway bridge is to the right
of the picture.**

view of many D Company Kiwis: 'That night, 16 Platoon was sitting very snug and in control of the position, and in the early morning I was surprised when Tom Campbell contacted me and said we were moving out as we could not contact the rest of the Battalion.'

Also left behind by the withdrawal, although they had heard the battalion passing in the night, was the Assault Pioneer Platoon under Captain Wadey on the AMES Ridge, guarding the radar site. They eventually received word that they should hold on at all costs as the Brigade was to counter-attack the airfield and Hill 107, to the immediate north, that night. Easier said than done! During the morning they tangled with passing groups of Germans. However, in the afternoon, Private Parker:

> *… in an outpost outside the wire, reported enemy flag-waving (ground to air communication), fired, and checked this activity, but soon the bombers turned to pound the mound, a concentrated target with the vehicles, the [radar] masts and the circle of bright new barbed wire.*

Captain Wadey recalled:

> *We received what the battalion had had all the week … the whole hill was heaving in smoke and dust … one of the Stukas seemed to be going to drop right on us … this one carried a bomb, orange in colour, under the belly. I saw it leave the plane and dive for us and knew it was going to be close.*

Student poring over reports and maps.

German casualties after a failed attack.

'This was the end.' The Assault Pioneer Platoon and the RAF detachment withdrew from the AMES ridge.

The Drop on Kastelli

Kastelli twelve miles to the west of Tavronitis, had been included in the list of places to be secured by the *Fallschirmjäger* of the *LLSR* on the morning of 20 May, as it offered a small port to the west of Hania where the amphibious force could land if necessary. Covering the rear of the division, as it advanced eastwards, was also an important consideration. Kastelli had been thought by the Germans not to be strongly held, if at all, but it was in fact garrisoned by 1st Greek Regiment. *Leutnant* Mürbe was tasked with a reinforced platoon of 6 *Kompanie II/LLSR* to:

> *...make a reconnaissance of Kastelli, to take on weak opposition and occupy the town. In the case of the town being heavily defended, we had orders to set ourselves up on a hill to the south of Kastelli and wait for the Regiment's motorised units.*

The arrival of the German aircraft, who circled the area three times before identifying their DZ, was greeted by an immediate mobilisation of not just the Greek soldiers but the local population as well. Old weapons dating back to the Metaxas period and the long Cretan knives were brought out of hiding and into the hands of men and women with a long history of

resistance to invaders. Before the *Fallschirmjäger* had a chance to organise themselves, they were being hunted down in the olive groves. *Leutnant* Mürbe was amongst those killed. Eventually, these who rallied, according to Kurt Pauli, had been 'decimated near the enemy lines after a short but fierce fight', and took cover in a strongly built farmhouse on the main road. With heavy weapons set up, they held the Greeks and Cretans back. The New Zealand advisor to 1st Greek Regiment, Major Bedding, told the commander that the best way to deal with the *Fallschirmjäger* was to keep them contained until thirst, hunger and tiredness forced them to surrender. However, under pressure from the civilians, the Greeks decided to attack at 1330 hours. Despite heavy machine gun fire, the Greeks and Cretans charged the farmhouse, overwhelming the Germans with their sheer weight of numbers.

Fallschirmjäger **killed during the drop.**

The resulting close quarter fight in the farmhouse was brutal and the killing was only just restrained by Major Bedding. The seventeen survivors, of whom four eventually died of their wounds, were taken by school bus to Kastelli bus station, as much for their own protection as for detention. Kurt Pauli complained:

> On the way to town, our equipment and our valuables were taken from us. The civilians in particular mistreated us terribly, hit us and spat at us. Apart from one or two exceptions, the Greek and English soldiers behaved correctly.
>
> We were locked in a little cell in the municipal prison. We were given bread, water and lemons.

This is the first and by no means the only example of Cretan heroism, which prompts the question, why was a formal Home Guard not formed? It would have exploited a source of effective man-power and given protection under the Geneva Convention to the local population who were fighting ferociously in defence of their own land.

Chapter Five

PRISON VALLEY

At the same time that the *Luftlandesturmregiment*'s gliders were swooping down on the Maleme Airfield, *Oberst* Heidrich's *Fallschirmjägerregiment 3* (FJR 3), the leading half of *Gruppe Mitt* (Codenamed ARIS) was beginning its drop into Prison Valley to the south west of Hania. This operation, also in the New Zealand Division's area, would threaten Hania and the Base Area between that town and the port at Souda.

New Zealand Plans
In his appreciation, Brigadier Puttick identified the broad valley between Aghia (Agya) and Hania, as a potential approach to the vital base area of Hania and Souda. Known to the Commonwealth troops as Prison Valley, after the whitewashed prison buildings in the centre of the area, the valley, between two and five miles from the coast, was effectively in the rear of the New Zealand Division as it faced north to the coast and the expected amphibious landing. The immediate area of the enemy drop in the valley was held by Colonel Kippenberger's *ad hoc* 10 New Zealand Brigade, initially known as Oakes Force. This formation consisted of miscellaneous composite units made up from artillerymen, who without guns who were acting as infantry, along with logistic troops who were in a similarly unfamiliar role. Kippenberger's unlikely formation was completed by the allocation of three Greek Regiments.

NEW ZEALAND DIVISION 20 MAY 1941

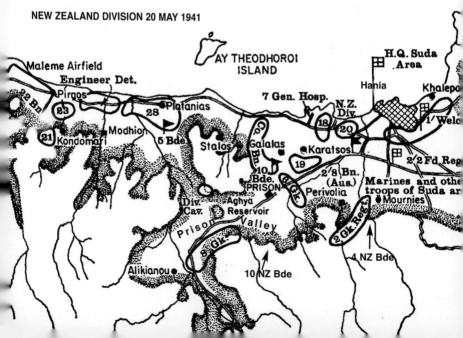

N →

Prison   8 Greek Regiment   Site of reservoir

Looking south-west down Prison Valley from Cemetery Hill.

Colonel Kippenberger.

Just to the east of 10 Brigade was Brigadier Inglis's 4 New Zealand Brigade, which consisted of infantry units of a similar character and state as those of 5 Brigade at Maleme. They had been relieved of a part of their area so that they would be a 'reserve', as earmarked in orders dated 18 May, for 'immediate attack on parachutists'. However, with defensive responsibilities for an area and a vulnerable coastline, they cannot be described as a true reserve, available for immediate deployment. The large area, the difficult ground and the paucity of troops and equipment, forced compromises on General Freyberg and Brigadier Puttick, which eventually and fatally, undermined their counter-attack plans.

The final positions that 10 NZ Brigade adopted were, *per-force*, far from ideal. Problems existed with this sector from the coast, through the Galatas Hills to Prison Valley, even after realignment of New Zealand units and negotiations that

90

brought the Greek units under Kippenberger's command.

Between 6 Greek Regiment and 8 Regiment lay a large gap. Puttick seems to have felt that, since he had no forces to put there, he must rely on the fact that the gap gave access only to very hilly country to the south-east, and that to the east an advance on Hania was barred by 2 Greek Regiment and the units of Souda Force.

Kippenberger had expressed his concern about the isolation of 8 Greek Regiment, so much so that 'it was murder to leave such troops in such a position'. The response he received was that 'in war murder sometimes has to be done'.

German Plans

A captured copy of Heidrich's *FJR 3* operation order, dated 18 May, gives the grouping and mission for the first wave of *Gruppe Mitt*.

> Fallschirmjäger Regiment 3 [FJR 3], *reinforced (less 8 Kompanie) with 1 Kompanie (Hauptmann ALTMANN) and 2 Kompanie (Leutnant GRENZ), Luftlandesturmregiment and 4 Kompanie, Fallschirmjäger ΛΛ MG Battalion attached will clear the area west of HANIA as far as Galatas. South of HANIA as far as the mountains, and eastward as far as the western point of SOUDA BAY, destroying the enemy forces there. It will then capture Hania and put the military and civil authorities out of action.*

The operation order continued to give basic details of the regimental plan:

> *(a)* 1 Kompanie LLSR, *will land at Y-hours* [0815 hours] *on the high ground in the SW part of AKROTIRI Peninsula, east of Hania.* 2 Kompanie LLSR [minus one platoon], *will land at Y-hours in the area between the southern outskirts of HANIA and NE of PERVOLIA.*

The two glider-borne companies' objectives were the heavy (3-inch) anti-aircraft sites that could engage the following flights of Ju 52s carrying the *Fallschirmjäger*. *Leutnant* Grenz would go on to attack a nearby radio site and a 'Supply Dump SE of Hania'. The eventual aim was for 2 *Kompanie* to join Altmann's company to form a *kampfgruppe* on the Akrotiri Peninsula. The plan for the Regiment's main body was:

> *(b) Parachute descents (beginning at Y-Hours+15 minutes).*

See map page 95

> III Bn *and* 4 Kompanie, Fallschirmjäger AA MG Battalion, *between the roads ALIKIANOU-HANIA and HANIA-GALATAS just east and NE of GALATAS foremost elements halting approximately 1 km before the road fork.*

> I Bn *in the area adjoining the road ALIKIANOU-HANIA to the SE foremost elements level with the Supply Dump.*

> Regt HQ, Sigs Pl *and* 14 Kompanie [anti tanks and assault pioneers] *to the NW of the adjoining road – opposite where* I Bn *has dropped.*

II Bn *with* 13 Kompanie [Light Infantry guns] *in the area of* I Bn *and* Regt HQ. *The decision is left with* CO II Bn.

Time taken to complete the parachute drop, approximately one hour.

The tasks of *Fallschirmjägerregiment*'s three battalions can be summarised as follows. *I Battalion* was to drop south of the Aghia-Hania road and secure the drop zones for the remainder of the regiment. They would then advance east between the mountains and the road, towards Tsikalaria and Souda. *III Battalion* was to drop on the high ground between the sea and Prison Valley, to the west of Galatas, clear up Commonwealth troops in the area, including the 'tented camp' on the coast, before advancing on Hania. Major Derpa's *I Battalion* was to be regimental reserve, dropping in the area of the Prison. *7 Fallschirmjäger Pioneer Battalion* was to drop to the west of *Gruppe Mitt* and advance on Alikianos and the prisoner of war camps in the area or, if resistance was strong, adopt a defensive position covering the rear of the regiment.

The Glider Landings

With the warnings of the much greater than anticipated Commonwealth strength that they would be facing, no doubt at the forefront of their minds as they left the Tanagra airfield, *Hauptmann* Gustav Altmann and *Leutnant* Grenz led the *Gruppe* across the Sea of Crete, in a flight that totalled nearly three hours. Altmann's pilots made a navigational error that sent them over twenty miles to the east. Consequently, it was Grenz and his company (minus a platoon), carried in nine DFS 230 gliders, who would be first in action, swooping down on a troop of 3-inch guns from 234 Heavy AA Battery to the south of Hania near the village of Mournies, as the dive bombers departed.

Grenz recalled that he was:

> ... *over our objective on time; however, we were too high (+500 metres). We were obliged to circle over the enemy battery. When we arrived over the coast the AA guns shot at us and their fire became fiercer as we approached the south west of Hania. Two aircraft* [gliders Nos. 3 and 6] *crashed, shot down by the AA guns.*

Miscalculating the height/distance necessary for the DFS 230 to glide directly into its objective had cost Grenz a quarter of his ninety-man force before the battle had even started. Further losses were sustained when Gliders 4 and 8 which came in to land, suffering a further thirteen casualties amongst crew and passengers. It is estimated that almost fifty men of 2/LLSR were about to take on about 180 gunners deployed around the gun pits, trenches, tented camp and buildings.

The gunners, armed only with a few rifles and pistols, were to do their best to hold off the elite German infantry, equipped with machine guns and machine pistols. Despite their losses, the *Fallschirmjäger* were quickly in

One of Grenz's gliders landed reasonably intact.

action. The men in gliders 1 and 5, reinforced by survivors of 4 and 8, swept through the camp and attacked the guns, while the men from gliders 7 and 9 cleared positions to the north-west of the battery towards a crossroads.

According to the Battery War Diary:

> There were only eight rifles on the site, and when five [surviving] gliders came in all round the site, through the dust of the exploding ammunition, little resistance could be offered. The protective LMGs and Lewis guns were stalked and silenced with grenades, three of the gun pits

Other gliders were not so lucky. This glider suffered six dead.

were taken, and finally the command post surrendered when almost all the personnel had been either killed or wounded.

The fight had been short but the *Fallschirmjäger* suffered further casualties, which now totalled three officers and twenty-three ORs killed and one officer and nineteen men wounded or missing. Very soon Grenz and his survivors were being counter-attacked by a force he estimated as numbering seventy men but 'the attack by the English was stopped by *Obergefreiter* Fimberer with his machine pistol'. This was a reserve company of 9th King's Royal Rifle Corps (1st Rangers), supported by the carrier platoon of 1st Welch (1 Welch).

Grenz's force, now totalling twenty-four men rather than the seventy reported by the British, were pinned down and soon had to fight off 'unending English attacks'. Towards 1600 hours, two platoons of Royal Marines and soldiers from 2 Greek Regiment attacked and recaptured the anti-aircraft position, releasing thirty-two prisoners, who soon had their guns operational again.

It had long been clear to Grenz that achieving his secondary missions was not a practical proposition as:

> *Progress towards our objective at the radio station was impossible, our losses were too heavy and the English were attacking non-stop. It was likewise impossible to approach Altmann's* Kompanie; *Hania was occupied. Without any hope of overwhelming this position, I decided to join* FJR 3 *to the south- west.*

Having got away through olive groves, where he was joined by ten mis-dropped *Fallschirmjäger*, Grenz decided,

> *...to head towards the south was the best plan. We could not continue fighting, given the strength of the English forces and we abandoned our arms except machine pistols, grenades and pistols. For five kilometres we crawled in ditches towards the south. ...our scouts came across a position occupied by an English unit's HQ. Seeing the large number of sentries, we could not go around it and I decided to go through this position. If we were noticed, we would make them think we were English. Thanks to my knowledge of their language, I was able to speak to a sentry when we were challenged. While I talked, the* Kompanie *took advantage and disappeared discreetly.*

After further lucky escapes from fire and pursuit based on Grenz's bluffing the remains of 2/LLSR reached German positions in Prison Valley.

Meanwhile, thanks to the navigational errors and attempts to recover from it, *Hauptmann* Altmann's company landed both badly delayed and badly dispersed on the Akrotiri Peninsula. It is clear from the initial reports from HQ CREFORCE that they thought that the dispersed landings were aimed at attacking their position rather than what transpired to be a dummy AA battery. The orders given to *Hauptmann* Altmann were that:

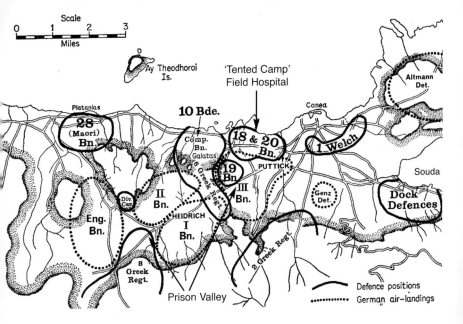

Scale

0 1 2 3
Miles

Ay Theodhoroi Is.

'Tented Camp' Field Hospital

Altmann Det.

Canea

Platanias

10 Bde.

28 (Maori) Bn.

Comp. Bn. Galatas

18 & 20 Bn.

1.Welch

19 Bn.

PUTTICK

Souda

Div. Cav.

II Bn.

III Bn.

Genz Det.

Dock Defences

Eng. Bn.

HEIDRICH

I Bn.

8 Greek Regt.

Prison Valley

Defence positions
German air-landings

1 Kompanie LLSR, *will destroy the enemy AA batteries and any other enemy positions on the high ground in the SW part of the AKROTIRI Peninsula, occupy the Royal Villa and hold the high ground. In the further course of action, the Company will prevent, by fire, enemy attacks from HANIA towards the SE and from SOUDA towards the West, as well as any enemy disembarkation in SOUDA BAY. Observation to be made of developments in the battle in and around SOUDA BAY. Recce to the eastern part of HANIA as far as the coast; optional recce Northward.*

In the event, two of Altmann's gliders were released early and landed well short of their objective, the remainder came under heavy anti-aircraft fire, while most of the others came to grief when landing on the Peninsula's rocky hillside. None the less, the dummy position which had been bombed during the morning, was attacked and 'captured' by one of the scattered groups of *Fallschirmjäger*. The Germans had based their plans on air photographs taken on 30 April and in the succeeding three weeks, as

Australian infantrymen from a composite battalion in the Souda area were amongst those sent to round up Grenz and his men.

further guns arrived and Freyberg reshaped the defences, new sites were chosen. The old site remained in use as a dummy.

Deployed on the Peninsula as a part of CREFORCE reserve, were the 200 men of the Northumberland Hussars, who were dismounted and operating as infantry. Amongst them was Trooper George Ashworth armed with a brand new SMLE rifle. His troop quickly pinned down the survivors of one crashed glider. Having fired a few rounds Ashworth was disconcerted to find streams of oil running down his arms, coming from his rifle. The heat of the firing had melted the protective layer of grease packed between the barrel and the SMLE's wooden furniture. As his troop advanced on the enemy he could hear:

...a German repeatedly screaming 'Shoot me! Shoot me!' I found the source of the shouting in a little grassy hollow, a few yards from his comrades. I don't know how he had got so far, for half his hip was shot away. He had been hit with a heavy calibre bullet of an anti-tank rifle ...A short while before he had been a fine specimen of manhood ...and now here he lay at my feet pleading with me to put an end to his horrible suffering and wasted life.

The real guns on the Akrotiri Peninsula were not destroyed and the survivors of Altmann's Company were rounded up, their only positive contribution being that they served to add confusion in the area around Freyberg's HQ.

Hauptmann von der Hydte, a persistent thorn in the side of the Allies.

The Drop of *Fallschirmjägerregiment 3*

Hauptmann von der Hydte, Commanding Officer of I/FJR 3, dozed in the Ju-52 leading a *Gruppe* of almost fifty aircraft carrying his battalion to battle.

I was roused by my adjutant and started awake, still drowsy, to hear the roar of engines growing louder and louder, as if coming from a great distance. It took me a moment or two to remember where I was and what lay before me.

As the Ju-52s approached the coast of Crete, von der Hydte stepped to the door. Flak greeted the aircraft fire, including from guns that Altmann should have destroyed.

Suddenly, a lot of little white clouds appeared from nowhere and stood poised in the air about us. They looked harmless enough, like puffs of cotton-wool, for the roar of the plane's engines had drowned the sound of the ack-ack shells' detonation.

With the command given, 'Prepare to jump', the *Fallschirmjäger* fastened their hooks on the static line. With the command 'Go', von der Hydte recalled:

Fallschirmjäger jumping from a Ju 52.

I pushed with hands and feet, throwing my arms forward as if trying to clutch the black cross on the wing. And then the slipstream caught me, and I was swirling through space with the air roaring in my ears. A sudden jerk on the webbing, a pressure on the chest which knocked the breath out of my lungs. I looked upwards and saw, spread above me, the wide open, motley hood of my parachute. ...It was like descending in a lift.

His reverie did not last long, as it seemed that he was inexorably descending towards the Aghia Reservoir. But von der Hydte had no way of manoeuvring his parachute and he was left with 'only fear'. 'Then suddenly there came a rough jerk. The drifting, the falling had ceased. I was down to earth again – or at least I was connected to it.' He had come to rest in a fig tree at the very edge of the reservoir. Others were not so lucky and were lost in the lake but unlike

97

All twelve men had to be out as quickly as possible to avoid dispersion on landing.

other units, *I/3FJR* had dropped into the gap in the centre of 10 NZ Brigade's area and casualties were confined to jump injuries consistent with numerous tree landings. The *Fallschirmjäger* were, however, as usual, dispersed around the olive groves and crops in the valley.

II/FJR 3 was not so lucky being dropped north of the area between the prison and Galatas. Their reception by Colonel Kippenberger's men on the Galatas Heights was very hot. *Oberfeldwebel* Karl Neuhoff wrote:

> *The moment we left the planes we were met with extremely heavy small arms fire. From my aircraft we suffered particularly heavy casualties and*

only three men reached the ground unhurt. Those who had jumped first, nearer to Galatas, were practically all killed, either in the air or soon after landing. The survivors rallied to a position near the prison where we became organised, collected equipment, and formed up for an attack up the hill to the north near Galatas.

Meanwhile, *III/Battalion* was dropped on the heights around Galatas and Daratos, with a company jumping further north. This battalion landed amid the New Zealanders and was immediately, as we will see, in trouble. Having lost *Generalleutnant* Sussmann's glider only the remains of Tactical HQ *7th Fliegerdivision* made it to their LZ near the lake and suffered further casualties on landing. They were able to do little to influence events during the first five days of the battle.

I Battalion had several tasks around the area of the DZ:

I Battalion *will immediately take possession of the Supply Dump on the road AGHYA-HANIA NE of the reservoir; if necessary it will clear the dropping zone of the Regiment on both sides of the road and cover the road AGHYA – HANIA approximately level with the reservoir against enemy attacks (with or without AFVs) from the SW.*

This left *Hauptmann* von der Hydte to report to Regimental HQ for further tasking, principally protecting the Regiment's flank east of the prison and to the south of the Agyha–Hania road. The Battalion was to be prepared to:

Move Eastward through the covered ground between the mountains and PERIVOLIA, with its main body (Schwerpunkt) to the right; there it will destroy any remaining enemy troops and will press on up to the path leading NNW from TSIKALARIA. This line will be held by Recce as far as SOUDA BAY.

The battalion commander looking about him could see no one else although he had seen parachutes on every side during the drop,

I was now apparently alone, absolutely alone. I could see no soldiers anywhere, nor even any movement beyond the hundreds of parachutes still in the air.

He set off through the olive groves to a group of white houses on the Hania–Aghya road, which was the Battalion HQ's RV and 'supply dump' mentioned in Regimental orders, which was the objective of 1 *Kompanie.*

Briefly I took my bearings and walked rapidly, as though fleeing from something incomprehensible, in the direction where I expected to find the road. A few hundred yards farther on I saw a hedge of cacti and agaves ahead of me, so I hurried forward, forced my way through the hedge, and found myself standing on a deserted, dusty white road. I could see a whitewashed wall showing through the trees a few hundred yards away. That, I reckoned, would be the prison ...More like a tramp than a soldier at war I walked along the road towards the white wall before me. ...Then suddenly, from the mountains behind me, there came a screech of engines –

The Prison in the 1940s. 10 NZ Brigade were dug in on the Galatas Heights beyond.

not the ponderous roar of a transport 'plane, but a sound more like a siren – followed by a fierce crackle of machine-gun fire. Automatically I hurled myself into the ditch – a deep, concrete ditch bordering a large field of corn – and at that moment a German fighter with all guns blazing swept over within a few feet of where I lay. A stream of bullets threw up fountains of dust on the road, and ricochets sang away into the distance. Then, as suddenly as it had appeared, the apparition passed. The fighter pulled up high and disappeared over the olive groves in the direction of what I took to be Hania. So the first shots to be aimed at me during this attack had been fired by one of my own countrymen! No one could have thought of laying out identification signals so soon after landing, and the fighter-pilot, whose task it was to support our attack, had obviously never imagined that this lackadaisical figure wandering in such unmilitary fashion down the centre of the road could possibly have been the commanding officer of a German battalion.

As he lay 'breathless with fright', in the ditch, 'trying to pull myself together' another terror revealed itself;

I heard, very close to where I lay, a rustling sound in the tall corn, as though someone were dragging himself along the ground. I held my breath and felt for the revolver in the pocket of my jumping-suit; but, before I could pull it out, a pair of brown gloves had parted the corn-plants a few yards away from me and, very cautiously, a German helmet made its appearance. Its owner was one of my sergeants, who also – but much more prudently than I – wished to make his way towards the white walls of the prison.

Reaching the prison, von der Hydte found the 'iron gates open ... and the machine gunners of my battalion covering the road'. They were in 'the highest of spirits; the jump was over, the landing was a success and it seemed that the worst was already behind them'. Elsewhere, the drop of FJR 3 had not been nearly so successful.

100

III Battalion Fallschirmjäger Regiment 3

The drop of Major Heilman's Battalion and the attached MG company, was into New Zealand positions that had not been identified by air recce. Consequently, it was a disaster. It had been intended to drop the battalion on a single DZ north of Galatas but in the event due to the same factors being at work here as at Maleme, namely the bombing, anti-aircraft fire and obscuration, the drop was scattered astride Galatas, less 11 *Kompanie* which was dropped south of the Prison.

The battalion was poorly placed to carry out its orders:

> III Bn. *will immediately make an attack on and occupy the enemy tent encampment West of HANIA immediately South of the 3 finger-like promontories* [9 & 10 Kompanies]; *will block to the East the roads HANIA-ALIKIANOU and HANIA-GALATAS at the road fork, so as to hinder an enemy attack, even with AFVs, from HANIA against the dropping zone of the Regiment.. To the West, GALATAS will be occupied* [11 Kompanie] *and an attack on the dropping zone of the Regiment by any enemy troops which may be around GALATAS is to be prevented. The coastal road to the West must immediately be closed and blocked.*

In the battalion's orders 12 *Kompanie* was tasked to clear Daratos and then move north to support the attack on the 'tented camp'.

As far as the New Zealand defenders of III what was to be *Battalion's* DZ, 19 NZ Battalion, were concerned the 'air armada', arrived 'after a short period of ground strafing across Galatas':

> ... *a large flight of Ju 52s and gliders flew low over its front travelling east. Breakfast forgotten, there was a mad scramble for action positions. Simultaneously parachutists began to drop. The attack had come.*

The first *Fallschirmjäger*, principally from 9 *Kompanie*, began to drop into 19 Battalion's area at 0810 hours. Bombing and machine-gunning had stopped and 'comparative quiet reigned'. The air was, however, 'full of planes and floating figures'.

According to the battalion historian, every man was 'galvanised into action':

> *The awe-inspiring spectacle above was now reduced to terms of targets and the shooting was good. The paratroops jumped at heights varying between 200 and 500 feet; a few parachutes did not open, but the rest in their downward journey looked almost leisurely. Silhouetted against the sky, their leg and arm movements could be clearly seen. They stopped abruptly when a man was struck, and it is safe to say that a large percentage of those who landed in the unit's area were dead when they reached the ground. One falling close to Battalion Headquarters had been hit no fewer than nineteen times. Clearly the 19th's presence had been unsuspected.*

Meanwhile, on Pink Hill Staff Sergeant Tom Alvis of the New Zealand Army Service Corps was among the 'dismayed and hungry bystanders',

Parachutes hanging from trees in 18 NZ Battalion's area.

who 'saw a dead parachutist fall gracefully on to the breakfast tin and send the only hot meal of the day flying'.

The confusion of the first few minutes gave way to 'exhilaration as the realisation dawned that we were having the best of the battle'. The *Fallschirmjäger* around the New Zealanders' immediate area having been 'disposed of', the men started to 'go out after those dropping out of range', mainly *11 Kompanie*, and 'general forays' that would have left the battalion's position without coherent defence had to be discouraged. Consequently, 'organised patrols were sent out to deal with dead ground and areas out of range.' In a letter written in July 1941, Lieutenant Colonel Gray, CO 18 NZ Battalion, deployed to the north of its sister battalion, described the hunting down of the enemy in the area of his HQ:

> I saw a parachute hanging in a tree and detected a movement around the left side of it. Fired quickly with my rifle – every officer in the battalion had a rifle. Then advancing very softly and quickly up to the parachute I looked round the side to see a Hun [German] lying on the ground beside a gaily coloured container fastened to a parachute. He moved, so I shot him at once to make sure, and then moved cautiously from cover to cover.
>
> I shot another hiding behind a tree, and wounded him. He was very frightened, but I told him to lie still and he would be looked after. Took his pistol away and gave it to Dick Phillips who was just on my right. No sooner had I handed it to him than he was shot through the knee. Two Huns

102

about 30 yards away hiding behind a tree were shooting at the two of us.
Two careful ones immediately dispatched them both. There were plenty of
bullets flying around but one had no time to bother about them. I saw
George Andrews sitting on the ground taking careful aim at some cactus
bushes behind us. 'Steady on George,' I said, 'you will be shooting one of
our own chaps.' 'No bloody fear, it's a Hun,' he said, and fired, 'Got him.'

By 1000 hours, reports in the Battalion's War Diary indicated that the
position was clear of enemy. 'Dead paratroops lay dotted all over the
position: some, still in their harness, hung grotesquely from the olive trees.
Due to a failure of recce and intelligence the majority of *III FJR 3* was out
of action almost immediately, losing 155 dead and nine prisoners in 19 NZ
Battalion's area alone.

The shocked and, to the New Zealanders, often surprisingly young and
inexperienced prisoners were an immediate source of information on their
intentions. Wounded officers were found in possession of *FJR 3* and
battalion operation orders, which once translated gave Commonwealth
commanders much useful information. Driver Bill Carson on Pink Hill
recalled other items taken from prisoners:

Our first prisoner had a pistol and three grenades in his hands when he
landed. They climb out of these chutes like lightning. In their water bottles
they carry very strong cold black coffee. They each had with them two days'
rations, which consisted of a poloney, wrapped bread which was remarkably
fresh, dried fruit, and two cakes of milk-chocolate. They also had two cubes
of 'dope', probably some sort of condensed vitamins, which bucked our
chaps up no end when they tried it.

12 Kompanie had, meanwhile, been dropped with *I Battalion* near the prison
and was consequently in good order. They, with the scattered remnants of
III Battalion, did however, have some success. Covering Cemetery Hill,
Prison Valley south-east across the Hania–Aghya road and on to the
Turkish Fort, were the 1,400 men of 6th Greek Regiment, described by the
official historian as:

...armed and although ammunition had arrived some days before and
been distributed to companies, there is some doubt whether it had been
issued to the men. Whether or not it had been issued, however, the length of
the line and lack of training and weakness of armament sufficiently explain
the disaster that quickly overtook the regiment.

Not constrained by the diplomacy necessary in an official history, others
are more explicit with their views on the commander of the regiment.
Captain Basset, Brigade Major of 10 NZ Brigade wrote:

Here I found hundreds of Greeks in flight, rallied and railed at them and
turned them back down the valley; but they showed that they only had three
rounds each which they blazed at high-flying planes. That bloody Colonel
had not issued his ammunition, and his dump was captured at once.

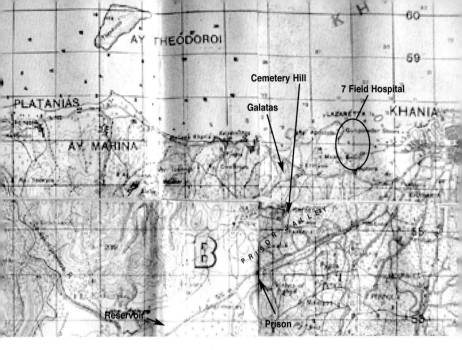

Lieutenant Farran who, as we will see, deployed to the area in his light tank and came across '… Greeks in khaki uniform, who were pleading for ammunition. I gave them a belt of Vickers, but afterwards discovered that it was no good for the calibre of their rifles.'

The result was that, with *I Battalion FJR 3* attacking east along the valley to the south, Cemetery Hill was seized from the Greek soldiers, who in

The view from the Hania - Aghya road towards Cemetery Hill and the positions of 6th Greek Regiment.

addition to their lack of ammunition, had few bayonets and they fell back into Galatas in confusion. Occupying Cemetery Hill, the Germans had a foothold on the Galatas Heights and denied the Allied troops a position from which they could dominate the approach from Prison Valley to Hania. The Galatas and Cemetery Hill area became the focus of fighting throughout the day but, meanwhile, the final company of *III Battalion* was preparing to attack the 'tented camp'.

7 General Hospital

10 Kompanie of *III Battalion*, jumping a little further north, in a gap between the various battalions, assembled in relatively good order and its company commander *Leutnant* Nagel, unaware of the fate of the remainder of the battalion set off, as ordered, to attack the 'tented camp'. This tented camp, in the 'Gunpowder Store' area just to the west of Hania, was in fact 7 General Hospital and the collocated 6 Field Ambulance. The hospital had been set up using the few buildings in the area and numerous tents, a part of which had been sited under the pine trees that cover much of the area. This was not for camouflage but to make the most of the shade. The Hospital was also marked in accordance with the requirements of the Geneva Convention, with large Red Cross air marker panels. The German intelligence analysts were either overwhelmed by the preparation of the invasion in such a short time or coordination between Lohr's and Student's Headquarters was woefully poor.

The attack began with the Hospital being bombed and strafed for an hour and a half, killing or wounding both staff and patients. Assaulting the hospital and Field Ambulance positions at approximately 0930 hours, in two groups, *Leutnant* Nagel's men believing they were attacking a legitimate objective, engaged targets amongst the tents, which tragically included Lieutenant Colonel Plimmet and his second in command, who attempted to remonstrate with the attackers in order to protect their patients. When the adrenalin ebbed from their muscles, the *Fallschirmjäger* realised that they had attacked and captured a medical unit. Puzzled and straying from error into the realm of dubious action, they rounded up prisoners, including walking wounded, 'although a number of bad cases were allowed to remain, the choice probably depending on the temper of the individual parachutist'.

Once the prisoners had been gathered together, a *Fallschirmjäger* officer addressed them in English. He informed them that:

> ... they were now 'prisoners of the German Army' which was master of Crete, that they must obey orders, and provided they did this would be well treated. He told them to take off their steel helmets, as by wearing these the prisoners might be taken for British fighting troops and the Luftwaffe, which was cleaning up the remnants of the defending army, would be liable

to fire on them. He said that they would shortly be moved to the prison area where the headquarters of his particular group was being set up. The harangue concluded, he hurried off, taking some of his men with him.

There was then some delay while *Leutnant* Nagle pondered his next course of action. The New Zealand official historian wonders:

Whether they were able or not to communicate with the rest of their battalion, they must have realised that something was wrong. They were isolated and had probably already begun to feel pressure from 18 Battalion. They had a large body of sick and wounded prisoners on their hands. In this situation their best course was to try and make their way back to the main body near Galatas, taking their prisoners.

About midday, *10 Kompanie* began to shepherd their prisoners towards Galatas. 'But this was also the general direction of 19 Battalion's right flank.' It was, consequently not long before the column was fired on. To the New Zealand infantrymen it appeared that the prisoners, many in hospital pajamas, were being used as shields. In the exchange of fire, 'One of the guards was wounded. Three members of 6 Field Ambulance staff were killed and one wounded.' In the fighting that followed most of Nagle's men were killed, wounded or taken prisoner and 'A few patients were also wounded.' By 1700 hours *10 Kompanie* had been destroyed and the surviving prisoners were all rescued.

Meanwhile, by 1310 hours 16 NZ Battalion had swept through the Hospital area supported by Light Tanks of the 3rd Hussars. A replacement dressing station was soon established, using salvaged medical equipment, in a large culvert under the main coast road. The General Hospital was re-established by medics who had avoided capture, in caves by the shore in the same area. Life-saving operations were carried out all night by two surgeons until the rest of the patients and staff returned. 'By 23 May, faith

The hospital site clearly showing the large red cross.

Some of the medical staff and patients in pyjamas who escaped capture.

in its protection had recovered sufficiently for a Red Cross to be displayed, and the enemy did not molest either ambulance or hospital any further.'

II Battalion – Galatas

Battalion HQ and 5 and 6 *Kompanies* and elements of the Regiment's support companies assembled as planned near the prison. *7 Kompanie*, as requested by its commander, *Leutnant* Neuhoff, had been dropped accurately on the lower slopes of Pink Hill, below the hilltop village of Galatas, which they were to take. *8 Kompanie* did not drop due to insufficient aircraft but would cross the Sea of Crete in the convoy of fishing boats.

It is obvious that the Germans had not appreciated that the hills around Galatas had been put into a state of defence or that Pink Hill was held by the Petrol Company of the Composite Battalion. It was, therefore, a nasty shock for *7 Kompanie* when they came under fire as they jumped. Driver Cyril Crosland was forward of the main position, a member of a patrol manning an outpost. He recalled the chaos when the Germans dropped into Prison Valley around 0815 hours:

On 20 May we were just finishing our breakfast. They were coming over

with big Ju 52 planes with gliders on behind. They let the gliders go. A lot of paratroopers came down in the olive groves around us and were killed. They were in front of us, behind us, beside us. We didn't know where they were. Nobody was telling us what to do. Information was only got by word of mouth. We were busy trying to stay alive, because you didn't know where the Germans were. They were dropping all round us. A lot of them were hung up on trees – killed coming down.

FJR 3 had the best of the drop zones suffering fewer jump casualties than any other regiment. Here a paratrooper retrieves a container filled with small arms.

Despite casualties, *Leutnant* Neuhoff's determined *Fallschirmjäger* collected their weapons from containers and immediately began to advance up Pink Hill. Thus began one of New Zealand's most remarkable stories of a tenacious defence by men who lacked all but the most basic infantry skills. The Petrol Company mainly consisted of soldiers of the Royal New Zealand Army Service Corps, occupying fire trenches hacked out of the rocky soil. Their positions 'were more like bowels than the vertical sided slits described in the infantry training pamphlets'. Their heavy weapons consisted of a Lewis gun and a pair of Bren guns. A rudimentary barbed wire entanglement had been sited fifty yards downhill from the forward positions but no mines were available.

The first Kiwis in action on Pink Hill were at the outpost mentioned above, under Corporal Trevelyan, forward of B Section's area. Trevelyan later reported:

> They landed on three sides of our position and within fifteen minutes were throwing hand grenades at our slit trench. We soon realised that it was useless to remain in this position and decided to retire to our own unit some 300 yards to the rear. If it had not been for the covering fire of Driver Eckersley's Bren gun I am afraid very few if any of us would have come out alive. After reporting to Sergeant Hopley we took up positions with our own B Section.

The first attack on Pink Hill was eventually beaten off but during a pause before the next German attack, Lieutenant Farran of the 3rd Hussars drove

Looking down to the cemetery from Cemetery Hill and the saddle in the ridge where Lieutenant Farran brought his tank into action.

into the battlefield with his troop of Mark IV Light Tanks, having 'marched to the sound of the nearest guns'. Driving through Galatas, handing out ammunition to the Greek soldiers, he 'passed several New Zealand positions who stood up and gave us the thumbs up sign with a grin'. Driving up to the saddle between Pink and Cemetery Hills, he wrote, 'We found ourselves held up by a knife edge road block, barring us from the plain of Aghya'. He had arrived at the front of the battle.

As I was wondering whether I should get out of my tank to remove it, a Schmeiser *fired at me from the cover of the olive trees. I looked around through the visor for a target, but could not see a living soul. And then another machine gun spattered bullets against the turret from the other side of the road. Indiscriminately we raked the trees with fire, pouring long bursts into the black shadows...*

The Germans ... renewed their fire from the olive groves. I felt that it was futile to stay where we were, since we could still see no sign of the enemy and he could obviously see us. I ordered the driver to turn round, but he was so excited by all that had happened that he pulled the tiller too hard, wrenching off a track.

It was fortunate that the lower part of the tank should be concealed by two high banks, so that we were able to repair the track under cover from their fire. But every time we raised our heads a sharp burst from a Schmeiser *rattled against the turret. I think we must have broken all records for repairing a track. We almost fought for the hammer, scrambling over each other in our desire to hurry the matter and pulling off our fingernails in our frantic speed.*

When at last we had got the tank into running order once more, we

109

Oberst **Richard Heidrich.**

drove through the village back towards our leaguer, for I was beginning to have some qualms about my having left without orders.

Dropping at 0900 hours, it was immediately apparent to *Oberst* Richard Heidrich that the Regiment had landed in a broad valley rather than onto a plateau as expected and that the heights to the north echoed with the sounds of *Leutnant* Neuhoff's battle. He realised that, confined to the valley, his command would be destroyed in detail. Consequently, he ordered a renewal of the attack on Pink Hill with the other two companies from Major Heilman's *III Battalion*. Starting at 1000 hours, the attack was supported by the Regiment's mortars firing from base plate locations near the Prison, along with 20mm anti-aircraft guns. With the additional support of fighter bombers, the attack made steady progress driving in the Petrol Company's remaining outposts and pushing back their main positions. The situation was, however, stabilised by the intervention of the Greeks of 6th Regiment, who had earlier fled in panic from Cemetery Hill.

In Galatas the Greeks had earlier been rallied by New Zealander Captain Basset and a British officer attached to the Greek Military Mission, Captain Michael Forester, who 'had come up to see what was happening'. Deciding to 'stay for the party', Forester was placed in command of the four hundred Greeks, who followed this inspirational officer in a timely counter-attack onto the saddle between Cemetery and Pink Hills. This bayonet attack has been variously described as 'mad', 'wild' and 'hair raising', with Forester leading it 'tootling on a tin whistle like the Pied Piper'. Driver Pope wrote:

Captain Michael Forester.

> Out of the trees came Captain Forester of the Buffs, clad in shorts, a long yellow army jersey reaching down almost to the bottom of the shorts, brass polished and gleaming, … He was tall, thin-faced, fair-haired, with no tin hat – the very opposite of a soldier hero… He looked like … a Wodehouse character. It was a most inspiring sight. Forester was at the head of a crowd of disorderly Greeks, including women; one Greek had a shotgun with a serrated-edge bread knife tied on like a bayonet, others had ancient weapons — all sorts. Without hesitation this uncouth group, with Forester

right out in front, went over the top of a parapet and headlong at the crest of the hill. The enemy fled.

The arrival of a force, fired with the light of battle, on their flanks broke the German attack. The *Fallschirmjäger* ran back down the slopes, leaving the ground littered with their casualties. This spectacular attack plugged a gap that the loss of Cemetery Hill had created between Pink Hill and 19 NZ Battalion.

After an opposed drop, and the Greek counter-attack, 7 *Kompanie* had, by late morning, ceased to exist in any meaningful form.

By midday it was plain to *Oberst* Heidrich that he lacked sufficient combat power to overcome the enemy on the Galatas Heights and he signalled Student reporting this and requesting that *FJR 2*, the other half of *Gruppe Mitt*, be diverted from its afternoon drop at Rethymno into Prison Valley. This suggestion was rejected on the grounds that it would have caused confusion even if the orders could have been passed over the rudimentary mainland Greek telephone system.

Meanwhile, the battle settled down into a lull. During this pause the sniper came into his own. Driver Johnson was on the receiving end of this fire:

The deployment of the Composite Battalion around Galatas on 20 May 1941.

> *At approximately 1200 hrs on 20 May, Second Lieutenant Jackson was making his way back to the RAP with a shattered wrist. As he passed my trench which was in an exposed position he fell, and as he fell, a German sniper, who had been causing considerable damage, opened fire on him; although the bullets did not make a direct hit, being of an explosive nature, the shrapnel from same hit Mr Jackson about the right eye and temple. I managed to drag the Lieutenant to the comparative safety of my trench, where I bandaged his wounds and applied a tourniquet. I was not able to get Mr Jackson back to the RAP for some time as the enemy sniper wasn't a new chum with a rifle, and any movement on my part was greeted with a stream of exploding bullets. At approximately 1530 hrs ...we were able to get Mr Jackson out of my trench and on the way back to the RAP, I kept up*

111

Regimental HQ in Prison

Landing ground being prepared

1 Battalion

← Hania

Artillery and mortars

The direction of the attacks mounted by *FJR 3* in Prison Valley. The view from Cemetery Hill looking south west over the prison.

a rapid fire on where I had reason to believe the sniper was, and managed to draw his fire till we were out of his range.

The Afternoon Attack

Colonel Kippenberger had succeeded in clearing the majority of 10 Brigade's area around Galatas but he lacked properly trained infantry to counter-attack Cemetery Hill or to take the battle to the enemy and destroy the *Fallschirmjäger* concentrated around the Prison in the valley below. Messages requesting troops to carry out these attacks were sent to Brigadier Puttick at the New Zealand Division's HQ. Meanwhile, General Freyberg had already released 18th and 19th Battalions from 4 Brigade for deployment in the divisional area, presumably to deliver counter-attacks. The troops, however, remained in position, watching the battle from a distance, as Brigadier Puttick vetoed Kippenberger's requests. It was only reports that the 'Enemy are preparing what appears to be a landing ground 1000 yards to the west of the Prison' that eventually propelled Puttick into action at 1840 hours; a subject to which we will return.

Meanwhile, during the lull in the battle, *Oberst* Heidrich was, even without reinforcement, not ready to concede defeat and set about organising a deliberate attack that was to be supported by the regiment's heavy weapons and of course air strikes by von Richthofen's *Fliegerkorps*. This air support was *ad hoc* and in competition with resource allocation for

Pioneer Battalion

N

Pink Hill

II Battalion's attacks

the afternoon drops at Rethymno and Iraklio.

The new attack opened in the middle of the afternoon with the enemy engaging the Galatas Heights with concentrations of mortar and machine-gun fire. However, the 3-inch mortars of 19 Battalion replied doing 'grand work and locating and destroying many of the enemy weapons'. Sergeant Clark recalled that,

> Our men also used the Hun's own mortars against him, but though these proved to have a greater range than our own, they were not nearly as accurate and required resetting after every round.

The New Zealanders' supporting artillery, F Troop, 28 Battery also provided effective support, having earlier been 'in the thick of the first parachute landing'. Their guns were now in action firing 'over open sights against enemy concentrations across the valley and, despite all difficulties [lack of sights and equipment], gave valuable support to 19 Battalion and other units in the Galatas area'.

Despite the New Zealanders defensive fire, the Germans attacked towards Pink Hill, using the road to Galatas as their axis. The NZASC soldiers, who had reoccupied their original positions, watched the approaching *Fallschirmjäger*, with mixed feelings. 'We had shown them what for in the morning but now they were coming again. This time I knew what to expect and wished I wasn't there but no-one moved, so I stayed. For me, it was one of those moments ... I never looked back again.'

Oberfeldwebel Teichmann wrote of this attack:

> In the afternoon between 1500 and 1600 hours we advanced to attack

113

the hill of Galatas [Pink Hill]. *We proceeded, without opposition, about half-way up the hill. Suddenly, we ran into heavy and very accurate rifle and machine-gun fire. The enemy had held their fire with great discipline and had allowed us to approach well within effective range before opening up. Our casualties were extremely heavy and we were forced to retire leaving many dead behind us. This first attack* [sic] *on Galatas had cost us approximately fifty percent casualties, about half of whom were killed.*

Still lacking infantry under his command, although there was plenty available, Kippenberger was still unable to take this moment of German weakness to counter-attack the *Fallschirmjäger.*

Throughout the day in contrast to the remote Brigadier Hargest at Maleme, Colonel Kippenberger was active on the Galatas battlefield, not just as a cool, encouraging voice at the end of a telephone but as a presence amongst his men, armed with the *Schmeiser* of a *Fallschirmjäger,* that he had himself shot outside his headquarters. The difference in style of the two commanders and, arguably, the result of the day's fighting could not be more explicit.

I Battalion's Advance on Hania

Hauptmann von der Hydte's orders were, it will be recalled, to advance north-east up Prison Valley towards Souda, with *III Battalion* advancing on his left to take Hania. However, with resistance far stronger than anticipated, his advance was to be more limited and circumspect than envisaged. One factor to *I Battalion's* advantage was that 6th Greek Regiment had abandoned Cemetery Hill along with most of its blocking positions that had been established across Prison Valley.

The Valley, about a mile wide, was bisected by the Aghya–Hania Road, which for much of its course ran parallel and just to the north of the dry bed of the Galdiso Stream. The northern slope rose steeply up to Cemetery Hill and the Galatas Heights at an approximate elevation of 200 metres, while to the south, the ground rose more steadily through the foot hills to the White Mountains some fifteen miles distant. These rocky hills were, lower down, cloaked with the usual olive trees and citrus groves, broken up by small fields and paddocks around the small whitewashed hamlets that dotted the hillside. Further up, the slopes were barren and more open. Temperatures were climbing towards thirty centigrade and the *Fallschirmjäger* were wearing the same uniforms as they had used at Narvic, near the Arctic Circle, six weeks earlier.

Beginning their advance during the morning, *Hauptmann* von der Hydte 'had not gone a hundred metres when a machine gun barked in front of us … Single rifle-shots whipped through the air around us. But still we could see nothing'. This was to be the nature of the battle; von der Hydte could see very little and when he was stationary long enough for his

A German heavy mortar crew lending support to the attack.

signallers to net-in their radios, reports from his companies were 'contradictory and obscure'. During the course of the morning, however, his men established positions in the bottom of the Valley just to the east of Pink Hill, while to the right, the *Fallschirmjäger* fanned out up the slope to the south-east. *Battalion HQ* was established in the cover of the bed of the Galdiso Stream where a tributary joined it. While there was cover from fire, there was little shelter from the heat of the mid-day sun.

According to von der Hydte, 'The British seemed slowly to be establishing a line of defence ... but now both sides were gradually organising themselves for battle'. Of concern to the *I Battalion*, however, was that it was apparent that there was a wide gap between his left flank, where *III Battalion* should have been, and the sound of fighting further left around Pink Hill.

In the advance, timed to coincide with the renewed attack on Pink Hill, *2 Kompanie*, while following the Galadiso Stream, located a pair of British guns, in an olive-grove almost certainly belonging to 1st Light Troop, trained on the area of the prison. Von der Hydte wrote:

> With the din of battle drowning the sound of their approach, the [Fallschirmjäger] scouts cautiously worked their way up a steep slope under cover of dense undergrowth until they found themselves overlooking the gun positions from the top of a rocky acclivity. They could hear the

115

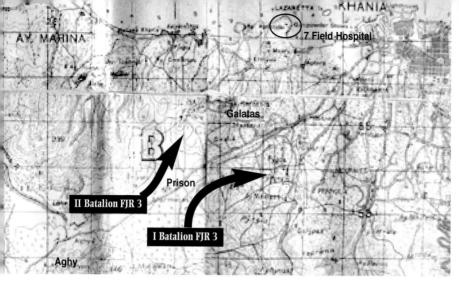

AV. MARINA
KHANIA
7 Field Hospital
Galatas
Prison
II Batalion FJR 3
I Batalion FJR 3
Aghy

British soldiers talking loudly as they made preparations to start firing.
The leader of the scout-party blew his whistle, and his men rushed forward, hurling a couple of grenades as they went. Taken unawares, the crew of the nearest gun fled for cover, and the gun was captured.

The scouting party did not manage to reach the second gun. Its crew, suddenly realising the danger they were in, retaliated with rifles and Schmachineguns, forcing the Germans to take cover. While they fought desperately at such close quarters, a vehicle, ignoring the German fire, drove up. The gun-crew broke cover, rushed to the gun, hitched it up and hanging on to the back of it made good their escape. In their wake they left

Taking cover during the attack.

only two dead and a stack of ammunition.

The *Fallschirmjäger* advanced farther, but had progressed only a short distance before they came under heavy fire from a solitary building, which in more peaceful times probably served as a roadhouse.

The captured gun! Some of the men hauled the gun-carriage round; a lance-corporal loaded it, sighted it on the house through the olive-trees, and fired. The shot was a near miss, and the British nest replied with rapid fire. The next shot hit the roof.

Shouting, the Fallschirmjäger *stormed forward. Only in the fiercest hand-to-hand fighting and by suffering losses themselves they were able to over-come the resistance of the British [sic], and when finally the ruined house fell into their hands not one of the defenders remained unwounded.*

The prisoners were about twenty Greek soldiers, the remnants of 6th Greek Regiment who had remained at their post. Some of them looked sullen, making no attempt to conceal their hatred for us; others seemed frightened, as though sure that their hour had come.

Meanwhile, 1 *Kompanie* were in trouble and was '… suffering losses and had apparently found itself in an unfavourable position opposite strong enemy elements'. This necessitated the intervention of the commanding officer who left Battalion HQ under the command of his Adjutant. Von der Hydte wrote:

I set off with my orderly to try to locate No. 1 Kompanie. … As we neared the firing line, ricocheting bullets sang past our heads and a burst of machine-gun fire caused a spurt of dust to rise from the dry ground barely ten yards ahead of us. Then we saw some soldiers belonging to No. 1 Kompanie. They were strung out in a shallow ditch which ran along the edge of an olive grove facing an open field. We ran the last few yards, threw ourselves down behind some trees, and slipped like seals into the ditch.

The company's position was far from satisfactory. Our men were pinned down by fire from at least two machine guns, none of which had yet been pin-pointed. The road to the left and the deep gully of the Gladiso were also obviously well covered by the British.

The mortar section, accompanied by the commander of No. 4 Kompanie, was not long in arriving, and while the two mortars were being got into position I crawled forward with the company commander to recce the target area.

We had no luck, vainly scanning the olive grove opposite us and the high ground to our left through our binoculars. The British, on the other hand, must have had better eyesight than we, for a shower of bullets spattered the ground immediately in front of us. We wasted no time in crawling back under cover.

Securely pinned down by the enemy and unable to catch a sight of him, the company was obviously in an untenable position. Casualties mounted.

There were cries for assistance on all sides. Someone was calling for stretcher-bearers. A man close by suddenly slumped over his weapon and lay still. Another, with ashen face, dragged himself back under cover of the olive trees to apply a field dressing to his wound.

Suddenly there came a deafening explosion and a shower of earth rose close behind us. British guns were laying down an artillery barrage on our position — and yet we still could not see them.

Von der Hydte eventually spotted movement near an isolated whitewashed house and identified at least a pair of soldiers. *4 Kompanie's* mortars were promptly in action and the Commonwealth shelling ceased as their observers had probably been forced to move. Even though they had a successful engagement the initiative was beginning to slip away from *I Battalion*.

Despite the enemy's fire, I had experienced no feeling of fear until now. I had been annoyed by the firing because it had pinned us down and stopped us advancing, but the thought that I might actually be hit had not struck me. Now, however, that I had seen one of my company commanders lying seriously wounded by the hedge and his second-in-command leaping with a blood-sodden sleeve across the road, I suddenly felt fear crawling into my heart. It literally crawled. I could feel it rising from my stomach towards my heart… In vain I set my teeth to try and steady myself. I clutched the earth, pressing my body against it…

And then the enemy artillery started up again. The shells were landing in the olive grove and shrapnel flew in all directions. I heard a voice behind me: 'One of the mortars has had a direct hit, sir. There are two wounded.'

We were certainly in a spot.

Under effective artillery fire it was clear that *I Battalion* was not going to make progress directly down the valley. Meanwhile, however, *3 Kompanie* were encountering less opposition on the right flank but before von der Hydte could exploit this opportunity:

'Shouting, the *Fallschirmjäger* stormed forward.'

'Panzer!' someone shouted, and the cry was passed from man to man. We could hear the clanking and the rattle of panzer tracks somewhere along the road in front of us. All eyes were strained. And then around the bend about 150 metres away, a small two-man tank cautiously nosed its way into view. Such was our first sight of the enemy. The machine guns which had pinned us down were still invisible to us, but the sight of this tank removed half the terror. The sound of its tracks while it had remained invisible had been infinitely more frightening than its appearance now that it had materialised. It attracted all our fire, like a tin roof under a hail storm; nevertheless it kept coming towards us. It had advanced to within fifty yards when there was a sudden, ear splitting detonation. The little tank swerved violently, pulled up with a jerk in front of a telephone pole, and remained there motionless. Our men continued to fire at it for a while, but slowly they came to realise that it had been knocked out by one of our 37mm shells.

From the timing of around 1600 hours, it would appear that the 'Panzer' was a part of Brigadier Inglis's local counter-attack. It was a 3rd Hussar's Light Tank or possibly one of two New Zealand carriers, which was described as being 'knocked out by heavy machine gun fire, that probed down the valley'. Elements of 4 NZ Brigade had advanced down from the Galatas Heights into the valley and cleared scattered groups of *Fallschirmjäger* and outposts. However, coming up against a solid enemy position, with anti-tank guns and lacking sufficient combat power the force fell back. It had, however, deterred any further advance up Prison Valley to Hania. This is an example of a purely local initiative buying time and having an effect out of proportion to the numbers committed. It is a shame that such counter-attacks were not mounted in 5 Brigade's area or across the boundary into Colonel Kippenbergers area.

Counter-Attack

The arrival of 2/7 and 2/8 Australian Battalion at the north east of Prison Valley from Souda, sealed a potentially dangerous gap in the defences protecting Hania at Perivolia. This finally removed the last reason for Brigadier Puttick not to take offensive action in the Prison Valley area, where it was apparent that his men had gained the upper hand.

At 1830 hours, orders arrived at 19 NZ Battalion for an attack from the west of Galatas to prevent the previously recorded airfield construction work in the bottom of the Valley.

   1. *Enemy are preparing what appears to be a landing ground 1000 yards to the west of the Prison 0553.*

   2. *19 Bn will counter attack this area forthwith, with*

(1)   *[Whole] Bn if situation permits.*

(2)   *Two Coys if Bn Comd considers that one coy should be left in present posn.*

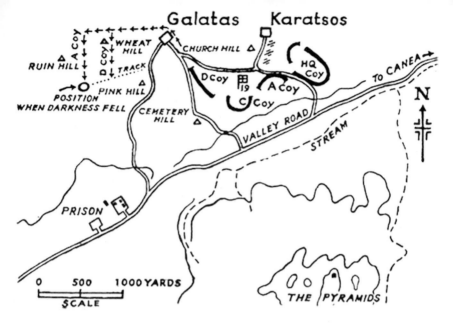

One tp 3 Hussars will come under comd 19 Bn for the operation.

After clearing the landing ground 19 Bn, with under comd 1 tp 3 Hussars will take up a defensive posn covering the landing ground but with bulk of forces north of rd HANIA-AGHYA 0352.

Time of signature 1820 hrs.

Lieutenant Farran and his troop of three Light Tanks, who were to support the attack, arrived at 19 Battalion's HQ to find that they were not entirely popular, being blamed for attracting 'the attentions of the hovering swarm of Messerschmitts'. Shortly afterwards, as reported in the battalion history: 'While arrangements were being discussed, dive-bombers appeared and blitzed the battalion area'. Fortunately, the New Zealanders had worked out one of the enemy's methods of air-to-ground target indication and:

Our troops confused the aircraft by firing Very light signals. Observation during the day had shown that a white light fired from the ground indicated to the plane the locations of German troops, while a red light fired obliquely showed the direction of our positions ... by firing many Very lights simultaneously with theirs it was found that the blitzing lost its intensity owing to the pilots' uncertainty.

Ordering a properly resourced significant counter-attack is easier said than done. The New Zealanders were beset by many 'difficulties and objections that had to be surmounted before the counter-attack could be mounted', against a tight timetable, as it 'was already evening and there were a bare two hours of light left'. There was also a cross country move of about two miles to the objective to consider and, as the return of the attacking force was not envisaged, arrangements for water, rations, and ammunition would have to be made. The thinning out of 19 Battalion's positions would leave an exposed flank in the Galatas defences and they needed replacements. These turned out to be Greeks. These difficulties led to the CO, Major Blackburn, deciding to attack with two companies.

With preparations under way, Lieutenant Farran had some difficulty in locating the Commanding Officer who was found 'out in the forward defence lines potting at a sniper'.

> *I ran along to him with my head ducked, bullets whistling all round, until I noticed that dodging did not quite seem to be the fashion in this part of the world. With a tremendous effort I tried to appear brave and walked up to him. He muttered, 'Just a moment,' out the corner of his mouth, and only turned when he had brought the sniper tumbling from a neighbouring tree. He handed the rifle to his adjutant and said "Well, that's that. That joker has been causing trouble all morning. Now, I suppose you command the tanks".*

The force would cross the start line at 1930 hours and Lieutenant Roy Farran's Troop was to join up with the infantry at Galatas. On his way forward his troop was twice mortared in the gathering darkness.

The two 19 Battalion companies, under the command of Captain

Three Mark IV light tanks of the type used by Lieutenant Farran and 3rd Hussars in Crete.

Pleasants, advanced together with their tanks for an advance of 1,000 yards west of Galatas, passing through the positions of 4 Field Regiment (infantry role in the Composite Battalion), pushed on to the first objective, the point where the force was to wheel south towards the Prison, Lieutenant Farran was leading the way along a track that formed the axis of advance:

> The wire was supposed to have been cut for us, but when we arrived we found that a second tangle stretched across the track. We were already under fire by the time we reached it, so there was no turning back. I charged it head-on and got through; making a gap for the others, though the wire became so tangled up with my bogey wheels that I was to pay for it later. We went along a dark track between the trees, spraying on both sides [with MG fire] as we went. Some fire came back and we ran across a trip wire, which set off a flare. A shower of grenades rolled off our sides, causing no damage. Finally, the track petered out before we had reached our objective.

> I had only been there a few moments when some New Zealanders arrived with bristling bayonets. We waited until they had formed up, intending to at least cover their advance with a barrage of bullets. It was very cold and we sat shivering in the turrets as the New Zealanders slipped like shadows into the ditches.

D Company, on the left, started their southerly advance and immediately ran into opposition. The company's advance came to a halt in the darkness. Meanwhile, in wheeling south to join the battle, A Company on the right, lost contact with one of its platoons – No. 9. After an hour long battle that the battalion history, with studied understatement, described as a 'troublesome engagement in the dark and at close quarters in the olive groves,' the battle died down at 2200 hours, having been called off at about the same time by Colonel Kippenberger, under whom 19 NZ Battalion now came. Casualties had to be evacuated but two enemy 50mm mortars and crews and three machine gun positions were destroyed. Captain Pleasants:

> ...ordered a halt and the three tanks and the two companies laagered for the night. Arrangements were made to continue the attack at first light next morning. The force posted sentries and lay up in the olive groves approximately 800 – 1,000 yards from the prison.

In summary, Kippenberger who had been pressing for the attack for most of the day, finally got an attack but it was too little, too late. An attack by at least one of the two battalions released by Freyberg earlier may well have had a dramatic effect on the fortunes of the Germans. With the *Fallschirmjäger* established in Prison Valley and the New Zealander commanders unwilling to commit their troops in the open where they would suffer the depredations of the *Luftwaffe*, four days of what was described as 'Sitskrieg' began.

Oberst Heidrich had suffered 540 casualties on the first day of the

Armed Cretan civilians.

operation but still had 1,200 men to face the counter-attack he confidently expected would come.

The Cretan Reaction

The reaction by the civilian population to the German invasion was not confined to areas where there were no Commonwealth soldiers; Ted Martin-Smith recounted:

A bit later on, it was a few days after the parachutists arrived, we used to see these old Cretans – most of the young fellas had gone, you see – these old fellas come along and pass through... "Which way are the Germans?" And they'd be out for a day's shooting. Blunderbusses...Carbines, I suppose they could have been. And they'd go back home again at night...

As elsewhere, armed Cretan civilians were active around Galatas. According to the Petrol Company, three armed civilians were brought in for interrogation.

The different languages made questioning a difficult business … but a great grin spread over the face of the leader, and to 'prove' his absolute loyalty, the Cretan plunged a hand into a pocket and proudly produced a couple of ears with the statement "Germanos".

Chapter Six

THE DEFENCE OF RETHYMNO

Brigadier Vasey's 19th Australian Infantry Brigade held the twenty-five miles of the Commonwealth's central or Rethymno sector on the north coast, covering the potential landing beaches of the Almiros Bay at Georgioupoli, in the west and the air strip at Rethymno to the east. This required the Brigade to be split into two. Brigadier Vasey set up his command post at Georgioupoli, with two battalions, while Lieutenant Colonel Campbell was responsible for another two Australian Battalions, 2/1st and 2/11th, and 4th and 5th Greek Regiments along with a Battalion of Greek Gendarmerie at Rethymno.

6th Division of the Australians' Imperial Force, made up entirely of volunteers started to arrive in the Middle East in January 1940 and fought under General O'Connor, against the Italians, in North Africa during his spectacular advance that culminated at Cyrenaica. At this point 6th Australian Division, including 19 Brigade was transferred to General Wilson's Force W in Greece. Here, as a part of I Anzac Corps, they fought well but outnumbered by a more mobile German force that constantly threatened their flanks, they were forced to withdraw to the south for evacuation. Some 8,500 Australians were evacuated to Crete and all but 2,500 who had been transported onwards to Egypt, were on the island when the invasion began. The Australians were concentrated at Georgioupoli and Rethymno but composite units and units of both field and anti-aircraft artillery, were deployed elsewhere, where most needed.

Mention should be made here of the crucial part played by the Australian engineers of Major Torr's 2/2 Field Regiment, who were chief amongst the volunteers who laboured in conditions of extreme danger to unload the vital ships in Souda Bay, when other lesser bodies of men had failed to do their duty. Their labours, as the ferocity of the bombardment built up over the period from the beginning of May, have become almost legendary, as they strove to get the vital stores ashore. The Australian official history records:

> These carried on unloading except when aircraft were directly attacking the ships they were working on. One of their best achievements was to retrieve a number of Bren carriers from a sunken ship with its upper deck several feet under water.

> Their efforts in unloading 15,000 tons of stores from fifteen ships, eight of which were partly sunk or damaged, helped ensure that their comrades at Rethymno had both equipment and ammunition. An allocation, however, of

3,200 rounds per Vickers gun of the two platoons of 2/1 MG Battalion in the Rethymno area and a total of 420 mortar bombs, could not be described as generous. And there was no re-supply available.

Defensive Plans

Lieutenant Colonel Campbell, alerted by intelligence on 16 May that he was likely to be attacked, had three tasks; firstly, the defence of the harbour of Rethymno, secondly, to hold the airstrip some five miles to the east and finally, to prevent a landing across the gravel beaches in his

Lieutenant Colonel Campbell.

area. The airfield was a narrow strip about 1,300 yards long, designed by the RAF for light aircraft but was more than capable of taking the robust Ju 52 aircraft. The port, though small, would have facilitated the off loading of heavy equipment and stores from the amphibious force.

Rethymno was to be held by eight hundred well armed and well disciplined Greek gendarmes, while the remainder of the Australian force would be concentrated three miles further east between Platanias and the airfield. Deployed on a three mile front Campbell's force of 1,250 Australians and 2,300 Greeks of whom the latter were described as 'conscripts of about three weeks training', made use of the range of low hills that overlooked the main Coast Road and the airfield on the coastal plain, which varied between 100 and 800 yards wide. The ridge and the coastal plain were cut by water courses, which, following their service in North Africa, the Australians referred to as wadis. The most significant of

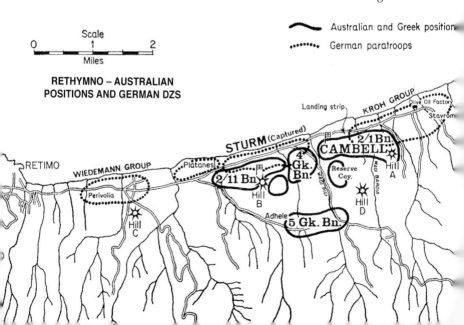

Scale
0   1   2
Miles

RETHYMNO – AUSTRALIAN POSITIONS AND GERMAN DZS

⌢ Australian and Greek position
⋯⋯ German paratroops

these were Wadi Pigi, which flowed from a village of that name, and a wadi unnamed on the map that was named Wadi Bardia, after an Australian victory in Libya earlier in the year. Other wadis were identified by a single letter. The most significant hills were also given nick names; Hills A to D (see accompanying map). These terraced hills were favourable for defence, with vineyards and the ubiquitous olive groves giving cover against air recce. Where forced to dig in more exposed positions, the Australians dug trenches in the shadows at the back of terraces, even tunnelling into them for extra protection.

The two Australian battalions with the strongest of the Greek regiments, the 4th Regiment, in between, lined these hills, while in depth, each Australian battalion maintained a company in reserve. 5th Greek Regiment was Campbell's force reserve, located in the village of Adhele, in a valley that separated the coastal ridge from the hills, which rose up to the mountains further to the south. The two 7 RTR Matildas allocated to the Rethymno sector were concealed in a wadi under olive trees, ready to counter-attack onto the airstrip.

Positioned amongst the forward troops were the machine guns of 2/1 MG Battalion and a battery of 2/3 Field Regiment Royal Australian Artillery, equipped with some eight guns of mixed types and calibres (100mm and 75mm). Also able to engage the enemy, with indirect fire, were two 3-inch mortars per battalion. There were no anti-aircraft guns at Rethymno.

Few defence stores were available to strengthen their position but the airfield had been earlier surrounded by barbed wire. In May there was only barbed wire sufficient to wire parts of Hills A and B. Despite the evacuation from Greece, the lack of defence stores and a less than generous allocation of ammunition, Lieutenant Colonel Campbell recorded that his veteran soldiers' 'morale was high and they were eager for a fight'.

Enemy Forces and Plans

The Germans experienced similar problems, as elsewhere, in locating the Commonwealth positions at Rethymno. For example, an air photo taken from 10,000 feet, dated 8 May, was recovered from a crashed *Luftwaffe* aircraft, on which a single company position was marked. The position was promptly abandoned and the company redeployed. By the time of the last enemy recce flight on 18 May, little had been added to the intelligence picture. Consequently, the Germans believed that there would be negligible opposition to the drop of the second half of *Gruppe Mitte* on the afternoon of X-Day. The force destined for Rethymno was the smallest of the four drops, consisting of two battalions of *Oberst* Alfred Sturm's *Fallschirmjägerregiment 2 (FJR 2)*, who were supported by a *2 Machine Gun Kompanie* and a Heavy Weapons Detachment equipped with mortars, light

RETIMO WIEDEMANN GROUP Platanes 2/11 Bn 4 Gk. Bn. 2/1 Bn. Landing strip KROH GROUP Olive Oil Factory Stavrome CAMPBELL
Perivolia Hill B Reserve Coy. Hill A
Hill C Adhele 5 Gk. Bn Hill D
WADI PIGI WADI BARDIA

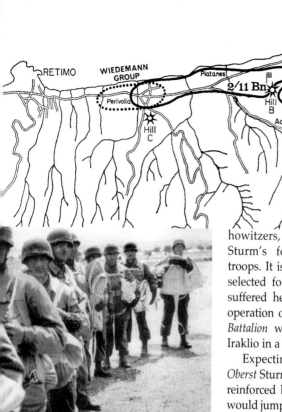

Fallschirmjäger of *FJR 2* muster with life jackets in Greece.

howitzers, and anti-tank guns. In all, Sturm's force numbered about 1,600 troops. It is probable that *FJR 2* had been selected for this 'easy task' as they had suffered heavy casualties in the Corinth operation only a month earlier. *FJR 2's II Battalion* was attached to *Gruppe Ost* at Iraklio in a flanking role.

Expecting little serious opposition, *Oberst* Sturm's plan was simple; *I Battalion*, reinforced by the machine gun company, would jump east of the airstrip and capture it. *III Battalion* with artillery, would land well to the west, between the Platanes River and Perivolia, and seize Rethymno. Sturm with his HQ staff and a reserve rifle company would drop in the centre, to the west of the airstrip, and act as a reserve. Having taken their initial objectives, *FJR 2* was to leave a force to secure both port and airstrip and to advance west on Souda Bay, where the remainder of *Gruppe Mitte* would be in action.

The Second Wave Arrives

Although Colonel Campbell did not receive notice that the invasion had begun, he and the rest of the Australians at Rethymno saw fourteen 'German aircraft, each towing a glider, passed over us flying from east to west towards Souda Bay at 3,000 feet'. This force was almost certainly Altmann's *Kompanie* of the *LLSR* (see Chapter 5) who had made a navigational error. Alerted that the invasion was on and hearing the distant rumble of battle, all they could do was wait.

Meanwhile, in Athens, with indications that all was not well with the first lift at Maleme and in Prison Valley, Student at his HQ in the Hotel

Left: A German column marches through Greece. The Germans had been obliged to come to the aid of the Italians when Greek and later, British troops, resisted Mussolini's invasion.

Below: A German Henschel HS 126 reconnaisance plane flies over the Greek capitol, Athens.

German map for Operation MERCURY.

MOST SECRET

M. FORM No. 1479
TO BE KEPT UNDER LOCK AND KEY AND NEVER TO BE REMOVED FROM THE OFFICE
THIS FORM IS TO BE USED FOR AIR INTELLIGENCE MESSAGES ONLY

	GR. No.			OFFICE SERIAL No.
		TIME OF RECEIPT	TIME OF DESPATCH	SYSTEM

...R'S No.

ARMY.

SEA-TRANSPORT OF FLAK UNITS, FURTHER ARMY ELEMENTS AND
...PLIES.

...ANGEMENTS MADE WITH 12TH ARMY:-

THE 12TH ARMY HAS BEEN ORDERED BY SUPREME COMMAND
THE ARMY TO DETAIL THE 3RD MOUNTAIN REGIMENT (3 GER.
...GT.) FOR THIS OPERATION. FURTHER ELEMENTS OF PANZER
...TEILUNGEN, MOTOR-CYCLISTS (KRAD-SCHUETZEN), ANTI-TANK
...ITS (PANZERJAEGER), ENGINEERS, AND FLAK ARE STILL TO BE
...TAILED BY SUPREME COMMAND OF ARMY.

...ITS OF THE ARMY DETAILED FOR THIS OPERATION WILL BE PLACED
...NDER FLIEGERKORPS (ROMAN) XI AND WILL BE TRANSFERRED IN GOOD TIME
...HE ADVANCED LANDING-GROUNDS OR EMBARCATION-PORTS RESPECTIVELY.
...ILITARY UNITS ARRIVING BY SEA-TRANSPORT WILL NOT BE PLACED UNDER
...FLIEGERKORPS (ROMAN) XI UNTIL THEIR ARRIVAL IN CRETE.

...ARRANGEMENTS MADE WITH ADMIRAL SOUTH EAST:-

ADMIRAL SOUTH-EAST WILL UNDERTAKE PROTECTIVE DUTIES WITH
UNITS OF THE ITALIAN FLEET (TORPEDO-BOAT FLOTILLAS, MINE
...SWEEPERS (RAEUMBOOTE), SUBMARINE-CHASERS, AND IF NECESSARY
...U-BOATS), AND WILL CARRY OUT THE SEA-TRANSPORT WITH ITALIAN
...AND GERMAN TRANSPORT-VESSELS.

MOST SECRET

M. FORM No. 1479
TO BE KEPT UNDER LOCK AND KEY AND NEVER TO BE REMOVED FROM THE OFFICE
THIS FORM IS TO BE USED FOR AIR INTELLIGENCE MESSAGES ONLY

	GR. No.			OFFICE SERIAL No.
		TIME OF RECEIPT	TIME OF DESPATCH	SYSTEM

...R'S No.

5) CLOSE CO-OPERATION BETWEEN THE BRANCHES OF THE ARMED FORC...
CONCERNED HAS BEEN SECURED BY THE EXCHANGE OF LIAISON
OFFICERS, CLOSE PROXIMITY OF BATTLE HEADQUARTERS, AND THE
CONTINUOUS ISSUE OF ORDERS FOR OPERATIONS AND SUPPLY.

(A)

THE ABOVE WAS PASSED TO CAIRO AND CRETE FOR NAVY ARMY AIR AT
2340/6/5 GMT IN THE FOLLOWING FORM:-

O.L.2167.

PREPARATIONS FOR OPERATION AGAINST CRETE PROBABLY COMPLETE
ON ONE SEVEN MAY. SEQUENCE OF OPERATIONS FROM ZERO DAY ONWARD
WILL BE PARACHUTE LANDING OF SEVENTH FLIEGER DIVISION PLUS
CORPS TROOPS ELEVENTH FLIEGERKORPS TO SEIZE MALEME CANDIA
AND RETIMO. THEN DIVE BOMBERS AND FIGHTERS WILL MOVE TO
MALEME AND CANDIA. NEXT AIR LANDING OF REMAINDER OF
ELEVENTH FLIEGERKORPS INCLUDING HEADQUARTERS AND
SUBORDINATED ARMY UNITS. THEN FLAK UNITS FURTHER TROOPS
AND SUPPLIES. THIRD MOUNTAIN REGIMENT FROM TWELFTH ARMY
DETAILED, ELEMENTS OF ARMOURED UNITS MOTOR CYCLISTS ANTI-TANK
UNITS TO BE DETAILED BY SUPREME COMMAND ARMY AND ALL
TO BE UNDER ELEVENTH FLIEGERKORPS. ADMIRAL SOUTH EAST WILL...

MOST SECRET

M. FORM No. 1479
TO BE KEPT UNDER LOCK AND KEY AND NEVER TO BE REMOVED FROM THE OFFICE
THIS FORM IS TO BE USED FOR AIR INTELLIGENCE MESSAGES ONLY

	GR. No.			OFFICE SERIAL No.
		TIME OF RECEIPT	TIME OF DESPATCH	SYSTEM

...R'S No.

PROVIDE PROTECTION WITH ITALIAN TORPEDO BOAT
FLOTILLAS MINESWEEPERS SUBMARINE CHASERS AND POSSIBLY U-BOATS.
SEA TRANSPORT BY GERMAN AND ITALIAN VESSELS. OPERATION TO
BE PRECEDED BEFORE ZERO DAY BY SHARP ATTACK ON ROYAL AIR FORCE
MILITARY CAMPS AND ANTI-AIRCRAFT POSITIONS.

R/A/W   HD/DPL   0418/7/5/41.

RD AM 0418/7/5/41. IM
RD BG   " GL

C.
In view of the gt importance of
this I also like the actual text
transmitted in MOST SECRET
together with warnings about
absolute secrecy.
W...
7. 5

British intercepts of German Enigma Ultra messages decoded at Bletchley Park, Buckinghamshire, which outlined the plan for the airborne invasion of Crete. Forewarned, General Freyberg's men were able to inflict heavy casualties on Hitler's parachute troops.

Right: Italian propaganda poster quoting Mussolini's boast that he would destroy the Greeks.

Bottom left: sight-seeing after the fall of Crete.

Bottom right: postcard extolling victory over the Allies in Crete by the German mountain troops, who were airlifted in during the battle.

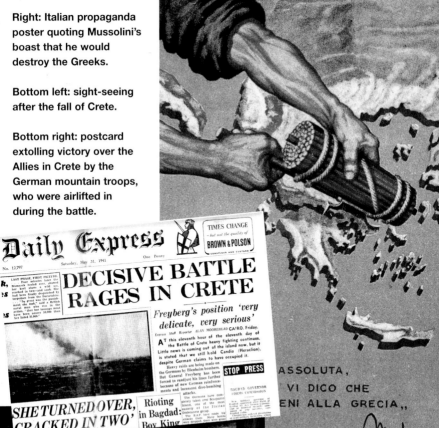

Daily Express

TIMES CHANGE
— but not the quality of
BROWN & POLSON
CORNFLOUR AND CUSTARD

No. 12,797   Saturday, May 31, 1941   One Penny

DECISIVE BATTLE RAGES IN CRETE

Freyberg's position 'very delicate, very serious'

Express Staff Reporter ALAN MOOREHEAD CAIRO, Friday.

AT this eleventh hour of the eleventh day of the Battle of Crete heavy fighting continues. Little news is coming out of the island now, but it is stated that we still hold Candia (Heraclion), despite German claims to have occupied it.

Heavy raids are being made on the Germans by Blenheim bombers. But General Freyberg has been forced to readjust his lines further because of new German reinforcements and increased dive-bombing attacks.

STOP PRESS

BAGDAD GOVERNOR FORMS COMMISSION

'SHE TURNED OVER, CRACKED IN TWO'

Rioting in Bagdad: Boy King

ASSOLUTA,
VI DICO CHE
ENI ALLA GRECIA,,

Mussolini

Hurra die Gams!

Men of the *2/FJR 3.* pose for a photographer after the fighting for Crete was over.

Looking south from Hill 107.

The Iraklion battlefield looking east towards East Ridge (IBW) and Ames Ridge beyond.

Above: The 'Little Saucer'; one of the few oasis on the road that winds its way up into the arid mountains.

Right: The memorial on the quayside at Hora Safakion.

Generalmajor Meindl set up his HQ beneath the abutments of this bridge.

The author on Tavronitis bridge.

Grande Bretagne, was not yet ready to change his plans. However, there was a problem closer to him that he was not yet aware of. The difficulties of dust experienced during the initial take off were now multiplying, as aircraft returned for refuelling and repair. Also many were damaged and some crashed on landing blocking the strips. Other factors now came into play to further disrupt a process that was already drifting away from schedule. The time allocated for maintenance and refuelling was always optimistic but aircrew casualties, battle damage repairs and the time needed to refill aircraft from large oil drums further slowed the turn around. Attempts were made to warn Student and von Richthofen's fighter bombers about the delay but again, the overloaded Greek telecoms circuits failed and the messages did not get through. As a result the second lift was to be dropped without the benefit of a coordinated stunning, aerial bombardment.

On schedule the fighter bombers appeared. Colonel Campbell recorded that '... this occurred at 1600 hours, when ten [sic twenty] aircraft bombed and strafed the airstrip and vicinity ... because of the excellent concealment and cover, the German attack did negligible damage' in their fifteen minute attack. The raw recruits of 4th Greek Regiment, however, started to abandon their positions, even though they were not directly attacked. The Australian official history records:

> Australian NCOs were sent from the left of the 2/1st and right of the 2/11th, and they steadied the Greeks, led them forward to their original front line and stayed with them there. One of these N.C.Os, Corporal Smallwood, not only led the Greeks back to their positions but later took forward a large patrol of them to the main road capturing some twenty prisoners.

The first of the 161 Ju-52s bearing the *Fallschirmjäger*, however, were not seen approaching from seaward until 1700 hours, having been delayed by the clouds of dust that shrouded the Greek airfields, which could not even be damped down by the best efforts of the fire tenders. The delay and ineffectual bombing meant that the Australians were fully prepared to receive the *Fallschirmjäger*. They count the approaching aircraft:

> ...twenty-four troop-carrying aircraft appeared. They came from the north towards Refuge Point, some miles to the east, then turned west, flying parallel to the coast, slowly, at about 400 feet. Other groups of troop carriers followed until 161 had been counted.

As the aircraft approached steady and straight, heading for their drop zones, the Australians opened fire with rifles, as they lacked anti-aircraft guns. The German pilots found themselves in cones of rising small-arms fire. Rudolf Adler, a member of *HQ FJR 2*, described the experience of being aboard one of the leading aircraft:

> We spotted the island and the aircraft went down [to dropping

37mm anti-tank gun being secured under the belly of a Ju 52.

Ju-52s of the second lift heading south.

height]. *AA fire started. Events rushed by. Bullets were ripping through the body of the aircraft at head height. The first three jumpers fell on the floor of the aircraft. We approached the door; it was blocked by the bodies of the dead and our bundles. Everybody was shouting 'Out! Out!'*

The engine started coughing; there was black smoke. Impossible to think but the instinct for survival was there... I don't remember how I left the aircraft.

Private Lofty McKie manning a battle trench on Hill A wrote:

I turned the Bren on the men coming down, they landed all round our position right on top of us... I got many of the first wave, as they were so close you couldn't miss!

The Australians, however, were not having it all their own way, Lew Lind recalled that the *Fallschirmjäger* had, '...their knees hunched up close to their chins and they were firing Tommy guns clamped between their knees'. On the receiving end of the return fire, Karl Schuldt of *III Battalion* commented that 'It was hell! We hadn't even touched down before suffering our first casualties'.

Of the Ju-52s that took part in the drop, seven and two other ground attack aircraft were shot down, most of them crashing in flames near Perivolia at the western end of their run. 'Other aircraft were on fire as they flew homewards.' The drop was again dispersed and many of the 1,380 *Fallschirmjäger* who were dropped found themselves in the wrong place. Rudolf Adler explains:

Because of the enemy fire, the Fallschirmjäger *left their aircraft earlier than planned and missed their drop zone, the weapon containers dropped into enemy-held territory and we jumped directly over their lines. Hours later, I found the first three of my surviving comrades.*

Most serious miss drop was experienced by Major Kroh, commander of *III Battalion* who was mis-dropped, with a complete company, three miles to the east of his objective; the airfield, 'on ground so rocky that many men were disabled while landing'.

Drop of *Fallschirmjägerregiment 2*

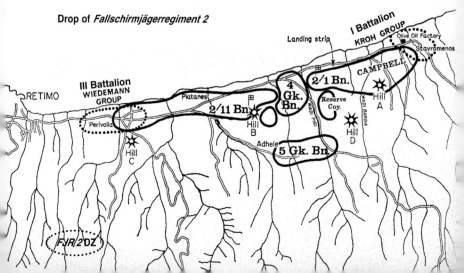

Fallschirmjäger descending on Rethymno in the late afternoon of 20 May.

The Battle for Hill A

On Hill A, the battle began as the enemy dropped amongst the Australians. From his vantage point to the rear on Hill D Colonel Campbell saw that 'Troops from both sides were inextricably mingled in many places'. Lieutenant Dieppe was on Hill A:

> I saw one of our 2/1 MG Battalion machine guns being enveloped by a parachute. At the same time one parachutist landed almost on top of me, and immediately surrendered. He was shaking like a leaf... I saw a parachutist throwing a stick grenade while still in the air.

There followed, what the Australian official history describes as 'a bitter series of fights between sections or platoons of Australians on the one hand and, on the other, such groups of paratroops who survived long enough to organise and go into action'. The ground cover provided by vines and terraces gave the *Fallschirmjäger* the chance to regroup and attack. Meanwhile, Major Kroh had dashed west with his company from the area of Refuge Point, and, on the way, collected the remnants of *2 Kompanie MG*

Battalion 7 along with elements of *10* and *12 Kompanies* of *III Battalion* who had been mis-dropped east of the airfield. Assembling his force, Major Kroh joined his men in the attack with a bare minimum of orders to the troops he had collected *en route*. The official historian describes the attack by *I Battalion* on the guns of D Troop sited on the forward edge of Hill A:

> On the east of the line paratroops landed on top of one platoon of infantry [7 Platoon], the 75mm guns, and the two Vickers guns, under Lieutenant Cleaver. Crew after crew of the Vickers guns were shot down, and the guns were finally put out of action by a German mortar bomb. The surviving gunners of the 75s, who had no small arms except three pistols, withdrew to the battery headquarters farther up the ridge, carrying their breech-blocks with them. There they fought on; using some captured weapons, and held their positions until a concerted German attack about nine P.M.

This German attack, despite its unpromising beginnings in the shambles of the drop, succeeded in partly taking Hill A; the Australians' vital ground. But 9 Platoon held its ground and the remainder of A Company was able to withdraw and establish a line just to the rear of their old positions.

Another group of Australian gunners, 2nd Field Troop, behind the crest of Hill A, were at an unaccustomed close proximity to the enemy. Gunner Snowy Wilson recalled that, as the Germans approached to within a yard or two of their position:

> As one paratrooper leapt forward to fire his machine gun into the gun pit, the Australians, having little else to defend themselves with, fired the

A Company 2/1 Battalion's Positions on Hill A

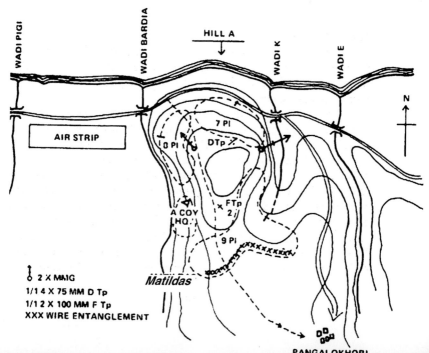

Present-day photograph of Hill A viewed from the west.

100mm gun at point blank range, the man vanished in a puff of smoke and flame.

The cost of taking Hill A had however been high, as explained in an official German account: 'These elements found themselves among strongly occupied enemy positions and, fighting in small groups against superior forces, were mostly destroyed.'

Rather than awaiting events like so many commanders elsewhere, Colonel Campbell deployed two platoons, via Wadi Bardia, from his central company, which was not engaged, in order to prevent a German advance east from Hill A, down onto the airfield. Also dispatched were Lieutenant George Simpson's two 7 RTR Matildas. Motoring out from their hide in Wadi Pigi with the task of advancing around Hill A to its east side to support A Company, the tanks approached the airfield. The leading Matilda promptly bellied on the edge of a drainage ditch on the north side of the airfield. Lieutenant Simpson dismounted but was promptly killed by a burst of *Spandau fire*. The second Matilda succeeded in getting around to the east of Hill A and after firing a few shots, slid into Wadi 'K', which was eight to ten feet deep. The surviving tank crewmen remained with their immobile vehicles but were unable to provide support for the rest of the day.

In order to contain the Germans on Hill A, Colonel Campbell also regrouped a platoon with A Company, with the task of clearing the vineyards on the north-west side of the feature. According to the official historian 'This platoon reached Captain Channell's headquarters about 6.30 but was unable to advance across the north-west slopes, where

134

paratroops were now firing from excellent cover among the vines and terraces'.

Meanwhile, in the Australian centre, the few *Fallschirmjäger* who landed in front of 4th Greek Regiment were soon dead or taken prisoner.

Hill B

In the left part of the Rethymno Sector Major Sandover's 2/11th Battalion immediately dealt with the *Fallschirmjäger* who dropped within the perimeter of their barbed wire surrounded defensive position. One member of the battalion who wished to remain anonymous, showed the author where he was in action.

I had been shooting at Germans coming down within a hundred yards of us. Easy stuff but as they landed, the survivors, more than I expected, were like sheep on their backs. Some of us got out of our trenches, bayonets fixed, and went for them. The first I stuck with fear and revenge for Greece. With that done, we waited as more came down. One paratrooper coming straight down on us, shot a pistol at me, and my cobber shot back but he missed. I was waiting with my bayonet when the bastard landed.

Later when they were all down, we cleared our area, cornered an officer and a couple of men. We had a brief fire fight but having left our trenches with just the spare ammunition in my pocket, we were out of ammunition. They had their opportunity to run and they took it, running down hill towards our wire. We followed and with them unable to go any further, we

Fallschirmjäger attacking uphill using the rocky terraces as cover.

N ←

Looking east from Hill B towards the forward positions of 4 Greek Regiment.

N ←

Hill B from the area where many *Fallschirmjäger* landed.

finished them off, trapped against our wire.

I felt good for a while but that was the first and last time I used my bayonet in five years of war.

With his position cleared of enemy, Major Sandover went over to the offensive to deal with isolated groups of enemy below him. The majority of his battalion were ordered to sweep forward and by nightfall the line of the coast road was almost clear but in places, the *Fallschirmjäger* were still holding out. In growing darkness Australian casualties started to increase, as the balance of advantage swung to the concealed Germans.

Consequently, Major Sandover ordered his men back to their position with the wired perimeter. He, however, deployed patrols to dominate his area and try and prevent the Germans who were reported to be moving west from reaching Rethymno.

By dark, 2/11 Bn had captured eighty-four *Fallschirmjäger* and were busy redistributing a 'mass of captured arms' to his equipment starved infantrymen. Major Sandover, a German speaker, was busy questioning the prisoners, who in the shock of capture, told him that no more *Fallschirmjäger* would be dropped at Rethymno. Later, he translated a document detailing the arrangement of coloured air panels designed for the *Fallschirmjäger* to communicate with aircraft. The following day 2/11 Battalion laid out the signal requesting a re-supply of mortar bombs. Most satisfyingly, a Ju 52 duly delivered the bombs, which were soon in use in captured mortars. Throughout the battle the Australians were supplied with a variety of weapons and equipment by the Germans! *See translated order on next page.*

As night fell at Rethymno, another element of Operation MERCURE had failed badly. A small force had dropped expecting little opposition and found themselves against veteran Australian infantry led by an active commander who was willing to take the battle to the enemy. The operation had failed so badly that the normally ebullient and active *Oberst* Sturm, according to Rudolf Adler '… was tired and incapable of giving orders'. Sturm was also unable to report his failure to Student, who drew his own conclusions from the ominous silence. Colonel Campbell, however, without any knowledge of the situation elsewhere, was eventually able to get through on the radio to HQ CREFORCE, with a request for reinforcement. About midnight, a reply was received from Freyberg regretting his inability to send reinforcements and wishing Campbell luck.

The Second Day

During the night, the Germans had overwhelmed one of A Company's remaining isolated outposts forward on Hill A and had pushed down onto the airfield where they captured the crews of the two stranded tanks. However, '…most of these Germans withdrew by dawn, but about forty remained behind the bank at the back of the beach'.

Overnight the Australians prepared counter-attacks that were to begin at dawn. 2/11 Battalion were to complete the clearance of the area in front of their positions and those of the Greeks, while 2/1 were to retake Hill A. The battalions would be supported by Greek troops from 5th and 4th Regiments respectively.

Captain Channell's plan was for platoons to advance around the flanks of the hill while the main attack, in the centre, was to be delivered on to Hill A. Lieutenant Dieppe described how on the crest of the feature:

At 0525 sharp we moved out silently in one straight line, at walking

137

Following visual signals will be used during the operation MERCURY :—

ALL SIGNALS WHITE OR YELLOW

(1)   H.Q. East Group.
                 H.Q. Centre Group.
                 H.Q. West Group.
(NOT Swastika flag.)

(2)   H.Q.

(3)   No enemy.

(4)   Enemy resistance. Pointer indicates situation of enemy.

(5)   Extreme emergency ! Signal only to be given on order of a battalion or higher commander.

(6)   Spot where supplies are to be dropped.

If the exact point of danger from the enemy is known, the distance may be indicated as follows :—

      Enemy resistance at 1,200 metres.

      Enemy resistance at 1,300 metres, and so on.

In so far as these signals are different from those laid down in regulations, they will take the place of regulation signals for the operation MERCURY.

For all other V/S for communication between aircraft and troops on the ground previous orders will be followed.

Responsible for correctness of copy.
Signature : GERBERSZUGE (?)
Lt.

Low altitude resupply flights by Ju 52s.

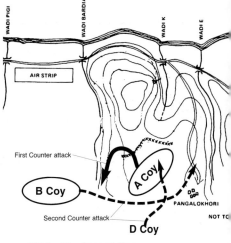

Hill A – The Second Day.

pace, towards the enemy positions. After an advance of approximately 90 metres, the darkness was broken by heavy enemy machine gun fire... the enemy started using mortars.

It appeared that, expecting the attack, the Germans promptly engaged the Australians advancing along the crest of the ridge with well registered mortar fire. Elsewhere the attackers and defenders were soon locked in a confused battle amongst the terraces and the vines. Private Lofty McKie wrote:

As I was snaking through the vineyard, I turned to see who was snaking along behind me. It was a Jerry! They must have been trying to reinforce along the same line we were attacking on. The German had a Tommy gun but he didn't seem able to pull the trigger. I was...

The Australian's attack ground to a halt despite Captain Channell personally leading the attack, in which he, as recorded in his MC citation, 'was wounded but continued to lead his men against heavy opposing fire; finally destroying a German MG Post...' A Company, however, now had a toe hold on the south west corner of Hill A.

Back at his HQ on Hill D, Colonel Campbell received a telephone message that 'Position on Hill A very desperate'. With line communication tenuous, Campbell knew that to influence the battle he had to be at the front. Collecting Captain Moriarty's D Company as he passed, he headed for Hill A. At HQ A Company, he found Captain Channell lying wounded and that his right (east) flank was 'hanging in the air'.

B Company was immediately redeployed from its position near the airfield, up Wadi Baria, and across to the right rear on the ridge. The Greeks would be deployed further south on the right flank. With the immediate situation under control, Colonel Campbell returned to his HQ, which had found to have been forced by mortar fire to move south by 200 yards onto the rear slope of Hill D.

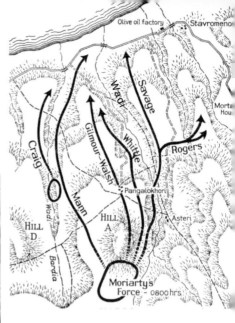

The German 81mm mortar, as used by both sides at Rethymno.

Colonel Campbell now collected all the men he could find; cooks, signallers, gunners, etc., for a counter-attack with D Company and returned with them to Hill A, arriving in time to witness a Dornier drop six bombs on the *Fallschirmjäger* on the neck of Hill A. This act of fratricide killed sixteen men and the Australians seized the opportunity to exploit the confusion. Sergeant Roffey recorded that:

> One or two [bombs] dropped on the particular gun we were interested in. In the ensuing confusion in went my platoon. What a sight presented to us. Three or four half-dead Germans were making feeble motions of begging us for cigarettes.

At approximately 0800 hours, Captain Moriarty, with his own company, the remains of A Company and the 'cooks and bottle washers', launched the counter-attack on to Hill A. Organised into four groups who, making use of their detailed knowledge of the ground, their aim was to outflank the enemy by first moving down Wadi K. Lieutenant Rogers with four platoons (including the pioneers and the carrier crews) made good progress, clearing successive *Fallschirmjäger* positions as they went taking twenty-five prisoners. Rogers' main body '... then turned east ... and moved on to the hill east of A, while one of his platoons under Lieutenant Savage advanced north to the road'. Meanwhile, on the other flank Lieutenant Craig had started to clear down Wadi Bardia, where going was slower but 'he took a good bag of prisoners'.

With the enemy outflanked and only too aware of this, the remainder of Captain Moriarty's force, pressing home their advantage, cleared the vine clad terraces. Four platoons delivered the attack, two each under Lieutenants Whittle and Gilmour-Walsh, supported by a fifth on their left flank, commanded by Lieutenant Mann. The attack progressed well and the Germans fell back abandoning their wounded. Lieutenant Mann's group alone took thirty-four prisoners. The number of prisoners was actually becoming a problem for the Australians by mid morning on 21 May.

To add to colonel Camphell's administrative woes, the withdrawing Germans, perforce, left behind their medical officers, staff and patients, who were all taken prisoner, but as recorded by Campbell, 'were at once treated as equal to our own wounded and ambulance staff'. The German medics and patients were moved to join a company of 2/7 Field Ambulance at Adhele, where during the next nine days the medics of the opposing armies worked together. 'The Germans were well supplied with medical equipment and medicines, and the cooperative arrangement benefited the wounded from both sides.'

The German MERCURE report records that on 21 May Major Kroh had been 'attacked again, his flank was enveloped and he was forced to retire east to the Olive Oil Factory where he reorganised and beat off repeated attacks'. The Olive Oil Factory, which the *Fallschirmjäger* proceeded to fortify, was about a mile east of Hill A, near Stavromenos and was the focus of the action on this flank during the remainder of the battle. A supply drop zone was established by the *Fallschirmjäger* near another factory on a hill five miles to the east and a detachment was deployed to defend it against 'Greek troops and guerrillas' who were active there and wherever else the Germans ventured inland.

With the Germans withdrawing from the coastal strip in front of 2/1 Battalion and the Reserve Greek Battalion being in position south of Stavromenos as arranged, Colonel Campbell concluded that at this stage the 'the crisis on Hill A seemed to be over along with the immediate threat to the airstrip'.

Perivolia

Operations by 2/11 Battalion, on 21 May, from their positions on Hill B, concentrated on dealing with the remaining pockets of resistance by *III Battalion* down on the coastal plain. Sweeps through the vines and olive groves, often with the help of local Cretans, increased the New Zealanders' haul of prisoners. Amongst them was *Oberst* Sturm, along with his headquarters. Staff officer Rudolf Adler recalled that day:

The view west from Hill B.

It was dawn and tanks [carriers] were advancing slowly followed by infantry in light khaki. We stayed in our shelter. The group leader, a Feldwebel from the Staff who was unknown to us took up position with his MG and I took up position with my rifle at the window of the hut. The enemy was attacking from the mountains. The machine gun started firing, only a few bursts as we did not have a lot of ammunition. The tanks and infantry retreated. A few more bursts from our MG. The enemy was 300 metres away.

Two hours later; the mortars started again. We looked for shelter in a little house and behind some walls. There were many inside the vineyards and they saved my life several times... The mortar fire lasted two hours without doing us any damage, a miracle! We could hear the Tommies advancing rapidly with their tanks and infantry, imagine 15 men against 500. Our courageous machine gunners were firing at point-blank range. The enemy was firing at us from all sides. Our gunner got a bullet right in the head and died immediately. My friend Siegfried was wounded by a bullet which passed through his pelvis. I took off my shirt and tied it to my rifle. I left my position and surrendered.

The Tommies approached us with their weapons in their hands. They took our weapons and an officer invited us to sit down on the ground, took out cigarettes and offered them to us. I can still see today his hand trembling when he lit our cigarettes.

As the prisoners were marched to the rear it was observed,

Many of our comrades were dead still hanging from their parachutes. They were all black and swollen because of the heat. It was the worst thing I have ever seen.

142

The grotesque condition of the bodies, the fact that they had been looted by both soldiers and locals, all capped by the work of the crows, led to persistent accusations of the barbaric mutilation of the dead.

Amongst the prisoners was the shocked *Oberst* Sturm. He was taken for questioning by Major Sandover which was:

> ... *a very unpleasant interview ... He was far older than I was and he couldn't speak English but I could talk German and I had his operation order which he didn't like and he'd lost his brush and comb set and he was a very frightened man! And he didn't like me at all. He wasn't very cooperative. He wanted to see whose Operation Order I had and I wouldn't show him. Because of course you are not allowed to take an Operation Order into battle ...*[and] *one of his officers had disobeyed this rule.*

By the end of day two of the invasion, the remnants of the *III Battalion* had withdrawn west until they came into contact with the Greek Gendarmes probing out from Rethymno and, stuck between the two forces, went into defences in the village of Perivolia. With *I Battalion* similarly confined in the Olive Oil Factory, *FJR 2* was fighting for its survival in two separate locations.

Subsequent Days – Perevolia

Space does not permit a blow by blow account of all that happened at Perivolia and the area around the Church of St. George where the *Fallschirmjäger* established well sited strongpoints, in the surrounding buildings. From these positions, they had good fields of fire over ground across which the Australians and Greeks would have to attack. 2/11 Battalion, however, lacked the combat power to overcome the Germans in Perevolia.

On 22 May, Colonel Campbell aimed to destroy the *Fallschirmjäger* to his west and open the road to Souda Bay. Consequently, he ordered the 2/11 Battalion to attack Perivolia. In the absence of artillery that was effective against enemy in buildings, a part of the plan included an attempt to use enemy ground signals to call for German aircraft to bomb their own infantry around St George's! Captain Honner laid out the panels and enemy aircraft soon obliged. The German report reveals that Wiedemann's Battalion 'was severely bombed by our own aircraft ...but repulsed enemy counter-attacks and shock troop operations'.

Captain Hornner's has been ordered to advance astride the road to the wadi west of the road fork at Perivolia. Despite covering fire from a 3-inch mortar and a German 81mm equivalent that was well supplied with bombs, the attack came to a halt a thousand yards from the objective, with a fire-swept, 'horribly open', slope down to the wadi in front of them.

Late in the afternoon word arrived that Captain Jackson's company was moving forward to support him; Captain Honner elected:

Fallschirmjäger medics unloading a stores container.

>*...to make a leap-frogging attack in the darkness with both companies between the road and the coast, where three parallel ditches spaced at intervals of a few hundred yards and about two feet deep offered some cover.*

As the light faded, Jackson's Company advanced to the second ditch 'without difficulty'. Honner was following with his own company but, with the Germans now alert the growing volume of German fire made it 'appear doubtful whether a frontal attack would succeed across the open ground ahead'. When Major Sandover arrived with information that the Greeks were about to attack the Church of St. George and anxious to avoid a 'Blue on Blue' clash with the Greeks, he ordered his two companies to remain where they were and dig in. From the noise and shooting around Perivolia, it was apparent that the Greeks did attack; 'advancing, capturing some prisoners, and withdrawing'.

On 23 May, the unsupported Greeks were again unable to make much headway against the enemy positions in Perivolia from the west but a company of 1 Rangers was on its way from Force Reserve. Equally, progress from the east was limited but 2/11 Battalion, under cover of a machine gun barrage, managed to get across the open ground to the third drainage ditch, 200 yards from Wadi Perivolia and the enemy positions. Casualties were heavy and a major attack was not made. The Germans, however, were driven from vantage points in the church when the 2/11 Battalion engaged the tower with high explosive from Hill B and solid shot from a captured anti-tank gun. But the German position in the village was still strongly held.

By dawn on 24 May, the company of 1 Rangers had arrived from the west and prepared their attack on Perivolia. Thinking that the enemy were only seventy strong, the hundred plus Rangers were in fact heavily outnumbered by the 300 *Fallschirmjäger* and the attack predictably failed. The company was then called back to the Hania front where pressure was mounting.

Meanwhile, Lieutenant Mason, an RAOC equipment specialist, was directed the recovery of the Matilda stuck in the drainage ditch. Due to the lack of any recovery equipment and the absence of the tank crews, this proved to be more difficult than anticipated. Once out of the ditch, the tank was moved to the rear of Hill A. Here a crew from the Carrier Platoon of 2/1st Battalion, commanded by Lieutenant Lawry, worked out how to drive the Matilda and to use its weapons. Meanwhile, B Company had the more difficult task of digging and dragging the second Matilda out of Wadi K. On 24 May, the first Matilda was deployed east to assist the 2/11 Battalion's dawn attack on Perivolia, scheduled for the following morning (25 May). However, the tank, with its amateur crew, became stuck again in one of the ditches, while moving up to the start line and the attack was postponed.

Things did not work out any better for the Matilda crew the following morning (26 May). The post operational report recorded:

At dawn 2/11 Battalion began its attack on the Germans. The Besa [machine gun] *of the tank, however, jammed almost as soon as it got into action, and the improvised crew being unable to remedy the defect, the tank withdrew and 2/11 Battalion, meeting MG fire from well-dug positions to the east of the village as well as from the houses, was forced to halt its attack.*

Another twenty-four hours would pass before further attack could be launched and Colonel Campbell's command suffered yet another setback when a rare RAF supply drop scheduled for the night of 26/27 May could not locate the drop zone due to a lack of flares.

By dawn on 27 May, both tanks had been repaired or recovered and were ready for battle in support of 2/11 Battalion's next attack on Perivolia. Once again, the tanks were both put out of action, one by a lucky mortar round that broke a track and the other by an anti-tank gun that set the other on fire. The two companies (Gook's and Honner's) that had fought their

145

way forward to the German Forward Defence Line spent an unpleasant day, pinned down under fire from ground and air. They were only able to withdraw under cover of darkness during the night of 27/28 May.

Meanwhile, unbeknown to Colonel Campbell, with the withdrawal of the main force in the Hania/Souda area, to the south coast, getting under way, yet another attack was ordered to be launched on Perivolia during the night of 27/28 May. The Australians were to attack, with the two companies that had not been engaged the previous night, astride the road from the high ground to the south-east, while the Greeks were to assault from the direction of Rethymno. The post operational report of July 1941 records that leading the attack, Captains Jackson and Wood set off with their companies into Perivolia 'at 0320 hours on the 28th but the Greeks opened up during the approach and surprise was lost'. The head of the Australian column came under fire at short range. According to the Australian Official History:

> However, the company pressed on, gained the crossroads and penetrated along the wadi towards the sea. Wood's company advanced and bombed the houses on the main road, but ran into heavy grenade and mortar fire which wounded Wood, and two platoon commanders …The responsibility had been placed on Wood of deciding whether the attack could continue or not. At 4.33 Lieutenant Scott, the only unwounded officer, on orders of Wood, who lay mortally wounded fired two green Very lights – the signal that the company was withdrawing, and repeated the signal a few minutes later.

Some eighty casualties were inflicted upon the Germans. However, the official after action report, with many of the Australians still at large on the island or in PW camps, recorded the view that: 'The village was virtually taken and should have been held … D Company then fought its way out of the village, leaving B Company in an impossible position.' The withdrawing troops 'were caught in a dreadful fire' and D Company came back with only forty-three survivors. The majority of B Company remained stranded in Perivolia in strongly built houses, which was just as well, as the enemy exerted every effort to destroy them.

On the evening of 28 May, Captain Jackson initially tried to break out to the east but the enemy were expecting this and blocked him. Consequently, he took his men on a long route to the west and then south of the enemy position. Meanwhile, with the failure to overpower the Germans, Campbell, with his force now so badly reduced and with Captain Jackson's Company missing, decided to abandon further offensive action at Perivolia and concentrate on his main task; the defence of the airfield.

Stavromenos

With the *Fallschirmjäger* cleared from Hill A on the morning of 21 May, and driven east to where they were confined to the Olive Oil Factory, astride the Iraklio Road, at Stavromenos. By dawn on 22 May, Colonel Campbell was ready to launch 2/1 Battalion against them. The attack started with a fifteen minute bombardment but the few small field guns that the Australians had and limited stocks of ammunition, it proved to be largely ineffective against the stout brick building. Another factor was that whenever the artillerymen in their exposed gun pits on Hill A opened fire on the Germans, the *Fallschirmjäger*'s mortars replied with 'deadly accuracy', discouraging prolonged on accurate bombardment.

The main attack was to be delivered by two companies of Australians, each minus a platoon left to guard their positions on Hill A. They were to be joined from the south by Greek troops. The initial attack at 1000 hours should have been mounted by Captain Moriarty's company but he was killed by rifle fire on a recce of the approaches to the objective and the only other officer was also killed. 'The attack did not start' but half of 2/1 Battalion had deployed from the crest of Hill A to positions near Stavromenos.

The Greeks and Colonel Campbell were keen to attack and another attempt to destroy the enemy in the factory was prepared for 1800 hours. The plan was:

> ... *after artillery and mortar bombardment: 200 Greeks would move secretly down one wadi and forty Australians would crawl down another, and then charge, while the remaining troops of Captain Traver's company fired down into the factory from the heights overlooking it 100 to 200 yards away.*

In the event the Greeks failed to attack to around a spur just east of the factory on time but A Company, commanded by Captain Dick Mann, assaulted from a narrow wadi to the south of the factory, 'with a yell'.

Many Australians fell, and survivors took shelter behind a bank about 40 yards from the factory. Campbell was nearby, and called to Mann not to move until the Greeks attacked. Captain Mann had, however, been seriously wounded and Corporal Thompson was now in command of the remnants. Colonel Campbell decided to withdraw the remnant of A Company after dark, with the Greeks giving covering fire. The Australians were sent back to their positions on Hill A, leaving the Greeks to contain the *Fallschirmjäger* in the Olive Oil Factory.

On 23 May, Colonel Campbell received a message from General Freyberg that 'You have done magnificently' but the main event of the day was a truce between 1000 and 1300 hours to enable the clearance of casualties both German and Australian, from the area around the Olive Oil Factory and evacuate them to the joint field Ambulance at Adhel. There were now so many casualties, approximately 200 *Fallschirmjäger* and 100 Australian, that even the generous supply of German medical equipment was stretched and all those prisoners who could be categorised as 'walking wounded' were transferred to a section in the PW cage.

At the conclusion of the truce a *Fallschirmjäger* officer appeared from the Olive Oil Factory, with a white flag; not, however, to offer the German surrender as had been hoped but to invite Colonel Campbell's force to surrender. 'He alleged that the attacks on the other sectors had succeeded.' The offer was declined and to make the point the German positions were shelled. Also recovered during the truce and buried were 300 German dead from Hill A and a further 200 from Hill B.

During the morning of 25 May, a captured 81mm mortar, now with plenty of ammunition thanks to efficient but erroneous German re-supply, was used to very good effect against an isolated building (Mortar House) on the extreme right of the *Fallschirmjäger* position. About forty Germans withdrew west to Refuge Point. This withdrawal was covered by German mortar fire from the enemy in the Olive Oil Factory against Hill A, which continued to be a dangerous place to be seen above ground level. Lacking proper or in some cases any sights and having to rely on direct laying of their guns, the gunners suffered badly from this fire. The party from Mortar House were joined at Refuge Point by Major Kroh who, at 0300 hours the following night, also withdrew with about thirty men from the Olive Oil Factory, leaving approximately forty Germans guarding their few prisoners, which included the RTR tank crew.

One of the Australian-crewed Matildas was back in action east of Hill A on the morning of 26 May, when what started out as a recce by the tank, ended in capture of the Olive Oil Factory. Captain Embrey (B Company) and one of his platoons were approaching the Stavromenos area 'covered by the tank and fire from the 75mm guns on Hill A' but received little fire from the Germans. With the exhausted Germans taking cover Captain Embrey seized the opportunity to attack. Charging forward with his small band of men, he jumped the factory wall and burst into the factory where he took the surrender of the forty *Fallschirmjäger* and a similar number of wounded Germans. The number of PWs and wounded were now becoming a serious problem as they needed treatment and guarding, as well as feeding.

The capture of the factory ended the immediate threat to Colonel Campbell's eastern flank. Captain Embrey wrote: 'the capture of Stavromenos practically ended offensive action by us, as the CO refused to be drawn away from his objective to deny the use of the aerodrome by the enemy.'

Surrender

On the night of 28 May, while the night battle was going on in Perevolia, two days' worth of rations had been delivered by a lighter from Souda Bay captained by Lieutenant Haig RN. They left before dawn, telling Colonel

148

Campbell that they had been ordered to abandon their craft and make their way across country to Hora Safakion on the south coast. This was the first that the isolated Rethymno Garrison had heard of the evacuation. The always intermittent and tenuous communications had been finally thwarted because of Campbell's lack of CREFORCE ciphers. Consequently, orders for the evacuation were not passed and only able to guess what was going on outside Rethymno, Campbell elected in the absence of orders to continue to hold the airfield. Attempts over the next few days to drop messages by aircraft failed for a variety of reasons. The Australians finally accepted that things elsewhere were going badly when they heard on the BBC that 'the situation in Crete is extremely precarious'.

Following the failure of the latest attack on Perivolia, most of the 29th was spent quietly between air raids, which were apparently, and unsuccessfully, designed to draw Australian fire.

With little official information from the outside world and indications from the BBC that the situation was bad, there was little surprise when it was reported by the Greeks, on the evening of 29 May, that a large enemy force was approaching from the west. '300 motorcyclists had entered Rethymno.' This was *Kampfgruppe* Whittman which was leading the advance of *5th Gebergs Division* from the Souda area. The Australian official history recorded:

> Next morning at 6 o'clock Honner's company [2/11 Battalion], *again on the left flank watching Perivolia, reported that they could hear what sounded like many motorcycles, warming up beyond Perivolia, and that the ridge they held was under artillery and mortar fire. About 9.30 three tanks appeared on the left of the 2/11th followed by a procession of about thirty German motorcyclists, accompanied by some light field guns. A little later Campbell was informed that German tanks were behind the 2/11th and in the valley behind Hill 'D'.*

These were Panzer IIs and IIIs from Panzer Regiment 31 who had eventually been landed in the west near Kastelli once the Royal Navy had been driven from the sea of Crete with heavy losses.

As Germans streamed through Perivolia and heavy fire was being directed at Captain Honner's company blocking the road from the east, it was clear to Colonel Campbell that he could not hope to defend the airstrip against such a powerful and numerous force but for the men, 'defeat seemed inconceivable' after maintaining the initiative over the previous days. Lew Lind summed it up when he said 'Oh Jesus. I don't bloody well believe it'.

Royal Navy officer, Lieutenant Haig, had told of his orders that suggested Sfakia was the evacuation point but it was three days' journey away and Colonel Campbell's force 'had been on half rations for three days and now had food only for that day'. He later wrote of his controversial

General Student talks to the Crew of a *Panzer II* on the road to Rethymono.

decision to surrender:

> *The only hope, would be every sub-unit for itself, which would, I knew, result in many being shot down, because, though olive trees are excellent cover from aerial observation, their widely dispersed bare trunks offer little protection against ground observation. I considered that the loss of many brave men was to be expected from any attempt to escape now, and the dangers and penalties to which we must expose the Cretan civilians, were not warranted by the remote chance we now had of being evacuated from the south coast.*

Campbell then telephoned 2/11 Battalion and told Major Sandover 'that further resistance would result in useless waste of lives' and asked his opinion. Sandover said that he would not surrender and that 'he proposed to tell his men to destroy their arms and make for the hills'.

Consequently, forward elements of 1/11 Battalion fought their way back with the Germans shouting 'The game's up Aussies' amidst clouds of dust thrown up by the increasingly heavy air and artillery bombardment. Lieutenant Cunnington fought his way back to the remainder of his company by 'leap-frogging in perfect tactical style, one group blazing at the Germans (who were held on the hill south of the road) while another streaked past to the next patch of shrubbery'. Thirteen officers and thirty-nine other ranks of 1/11 Battalion eventually escaped to Egypt.

Meanwhile, Colonel Campbell on Hill D ordered a white flag to be made and to be flown visibly:

> *At the same time he sent messages by telephone or by runner to all units*

151

A single *Fallschirmjäger* NCO guards the prisoners.

and sub-units informing them of the surrender and telling them to display white flags and assemble at the north-west corner of the airfield. A quarter of an hour later, as the German fire continued, he himself tied a towel to a stick and walked down the track towards the airfield.

Captain Embrey wrote that Colonel Campbell 'instructed the QM and myself to accompany him with a white flag, as further fighting was useless'.

At the time of the surrender about 500 German prisoners, including *Oberst* Sturm, were held by the Australians, of whom the non-injured were immediately released. 'The Australians had lost about 120 killed but some 550 Germans had been buried and it was believed that their total loss considerably exceeded that number.'

Chapter Seven

THE DEFENCE OF IRAKLIO

The battle for Iraklio in many respects reflects those fought elsewhere, including the fact that the Germans again grossly underestimated the Commonwealth Force that was garrisoning Crete's main airfield, its largest town and its most significant commercial port. It was not just an underestimate of their enemy's numerical strength but also of the quality of troops available in Brigadier Chappel's reinforced 14th Infantry Brigade. The British battalions, typically 750 strong, had not suffered losses of men and equipment that the Australians and New Zealanders had in escaping from Greece.

The fertile coastal plain at Iraklio was generally wider than any other area and cultivated more intensely with a greater variety of produce. The success of agriculture in this area and hence trade made this the most prosperous part of Crete since the time of the Minoan civilisation. Brigadier Chappel forced a similar problem to that of Colonel Campbell at Retymno. He had to hold the airfield, three miles east of his other principal location, Iraklio and its port. In between was a beach where the threatened amphibious landing could take place. Consequently, Chappel's defenders were spread along four miles of coast and extended almost two miles inland. Important pieces of terrain included AMES (Air Ministry Experimental Site (radar)) Ridge to the east of the airfield and, at its foot, the East Wadi. In the southern part of 2 Black Watch's position East Hill was important, while in 2/4 Australian Battalion's area there were two

Light tanks in rough terrain.

distinctive conical hills known as the 'Charlies', which the Australian official history confides to us is 'the vernacular for breasts'. The Minoan palace of Knossos is three miles south of Iraklio.

14 Brigade Group consisted of three Regular Army British battalions most of whom had been on Crete since January 1941, and the war-raised unit 2/4 Australian Infantry Battalion, which had been evacuated from Greece. The infantry was supplemented by the gunners of 7 Medium Regiment in the infantry role and three Greek regiments, of which two were little more than recruits. This force was supported by two of 7 RTR Matildas and six Light Tanks belonging to 3rd Hussars, along with twelve Bofors anti-aircraft guns and a mixture of thirteen 75mm and 100mm artillery pieces in a similar state of dilapidation as elsewhere.

14 Brigade had far more time than the New Zealanders and Australians elsewhere to prepare their positions, which formed a relatively tight perimeter. Brigadier Chappel's HQ was sited in the area held by 7 Medium Regiment, with 2 Leicesters, the brigade reserve, holding only a very small part of the defensive perimeter, nearby. With a Complete Equipment Schedule of three battalions to share around, there were sufficient tools to dig proper defences and to build sangars from the copious quantities of loose rock but, as elsewhere, defence stores including mines and wire, were in short supply.

German Plans

Gruppe Ost was the responsibility of *Generalleutnant* Ringel; however, as a non parachute trained officer and so as not to dilute the airborne nature of the invasion, he was not to fly to Crete until X-Day plus 1. Consequently, *Oberst* Brauer would lead the assault, with *Fallschirmjägerregiment 1 (FJR 1)* reinforced by a fourth battalion, *II/FJR 2*. This force, dropping in the second or P.M. wave, was considered to be more than sufficient to seize the Iraklio airfield and port from 400 British troops plus 'various Greeks' assessed as garrisoning the area. They would be followed by one of the first amphibious convoys, who would land elements of *7th Flieger* and *5th Gerbirgsdivisions* in the port at Iraklio late on 20 May. They in turn would be followed by the majority of Ringel's mountain troops by air and sea, who would deploy from the Iraklio lodgement to secure the central and eastern parts of the island.

In detail, two battalions of *Gruppe Ost* were to secure the airfield and the town/port, with the remaining two battalions being dropped to the east and west flanks. Responsible for seizing the airfield were *II/FJR 1*, by dropping at the eastern and western ends of the runway. *III/FJR 1* would land around the town and secure the port. Of the two flanking battalions, *I/FJR 1* was to jump two miles to the east where they were to take out the wireless station at Gurnes, in order to help isolate the Iraklio area, and to

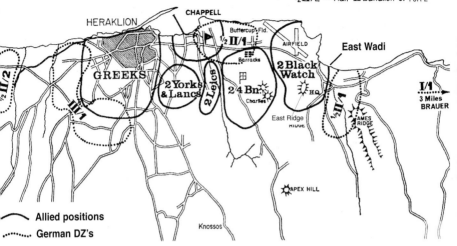

14 Brigade's Positions at Iraklio and Locations of *FJR 1's* Drop.

Scale
0   1   2
Miles

½ II/2 = Half II Battalion of FJR 2

CHAPPELL

HERAKLION

Buttercup Fld.

½ II/1

AIRFIELD

East Wadi

Barracks

2 Black Watch

GREEKS

2 Yorks & Lancs

2 Leics

2/4 Bn

Charlies

HQ

½ II/1

East Wadi

I/1
3 MILES
BRAUER

½ II/2

II/1

East Ridge
RIDGE

AMES
RIDGE

APEX HILL

Knossos

⌒ **Allied positions**

······· **German DZ's**

form an easterly flank. *II/FJR 2*, weakened by the Corinth Operation, were to be dropped four miles to the west as flank protection, but in the event only two companies, 7 and 8, jumped on X-Day due to aircraft losses in the first wave.

The Initial Drop

As at Rethymno the plan for the pre-drop bombardment by von Richthofen's aircraft was dislocated by delays caused by clouds of dust and refuelling of the transports. Australian infantryman Dick Parry, however, recalled:

> At 1600, one of the worst imaginable blitzes started. From a careful distance, no less than 300 aircraft fell upon us at the same time. They were flying at between 50 and 200 feet.

Fallschirmjäger emplaning on their Ju-52.

Our sector was as big as a handkerchief and they could not miss us. They appeared to have thrown in every type of German and Italian aircraft: Me-110s, Dorniers, Junkers, Heinkels, etc.; in fact any plane capable of carrying bombs or firing a machine gun. Many of these planes had shark's teeth painted on their noses, which made them more terrifying.

They flew so low that the engines threw up clouds of dust into our trenches. Meanwhile, they dropped hundreds of bombs and fired hundreds of bursts. The sound was deafening and we could not see further than ten yards because of the big clouds of dust and smoke.

If the defenders could not see nor could the pilots and again the bombardment was largely ineffective. The German fighter aircraft remained above the target for as long as possible to support the drop but, eventually, they were running low on fuel and had to head back to their airfields in Greece. Dick Parry continued:

The planes slipped away and the smoke dispersed. Suddenly, somebody shouted:

'Look at the sea!'

And what froze us was the sight of transport planes, dozens of them, enormous lumbering Ju-52s, each as big as a ballroom approached slowly at 50 mph at an altitude of 100-150 feet above the sea. They approached in waves of eight, ten and fifteen machines. We counted sixty or seventy and they continued to come. They were above the aerodrome and seemed to hang there when the first paratroopers jumped.

The anti-aircraft gun crews that had been driven to ground by the bombing had now recovered from its effects and opened fire, without fear of attack by enemy dive bombers. The guns were well sited and the aircraft dropping in the area of the airfield bore the brunt of the fire from the well sited guns. Another Australian infantryman, Private Harry Wheeler, had a grandstand view of half of *II/FJR 1* jumping directly in front of him. 'It was at that moment that hell gave all that it had. The AA guns opened up and many planes were hit whereas we let loose with our rifles and machine guns.'

Corporal Johnson wrote:

I was spellbound by the futuristic nature and the magnificence of the scene before me ... They were about 100 feet above the water and rose to about 250 feet as they came over the coastline ... I saw many Huns dropping like stones when their parachutes failed to open. I saw one carried out to sea trailing behind the plane with his parachute caught on the tail. One plane caught fire as the paratroopers were jumping, and each dropping parachute vanished in a little puff of smoke, its passenger hurtling to the ground.

More than one Scot from the Black Watch has confessed that he '... lived with the horror of that scene etched on my mind', while others scoffed at

Ju-52s under repair between sorties.

the PWs' notion that it was 'unsporting to shoot at paratroops who had not yet reached their weapons'.

It is estimated that approximately two hundred *Fallschirmjäger* were hit during the drop, which left the enemy reasonably concentrated around their drop zones. Reports are all adamant that no enemy actually dropped onto the airfield.

About fifteen of the 240 Ju-52s were brought down over Iraklio and there were further losses to damaged aircraft on the return journey and on landing. The delay in launching the squadrons accounts for the relatively high aircraft casualties, as the anti-aircraft gunners were able to concentrate their fire on the waves of aircraft that came in between 1700 hours and 1920 hours when the last of the outer or flank battalions were dropped.

Gruppe Ost had dribbled in to Iraklio, not at all like the anticipated 'clap of airborne thunder', minus six hundred men for whom there were no serviceable aircraft. If the *Fallschirmjäger*'s chances of overcoming a numerically superior force were slim, now they were virtually non-existent and they themselves were vulnerable to destruction. However, one *Fallschirmjäger* landing near 14 Brigade lobbed a grenade into the HQ building and temporarily prevented the staff from conducting the battle.

The Hunt

Immediately the first sticks of *Fallschirmjäger* were down the British and Australian battalions, who had suffered negligible casualties, were deployed to destroy the dispersed enemy before they could organise themselves. The first action, as elsewhere, was to clear the defended areas. The soldiers, well briefed on the drills for dealing with parachutists, needed few orders.

Private Logan of B Company 2 Black Watch was at the far end of the

Ju-52, well alight, comes down over one of the Charlies.

airfield on the lower slopes of East Hill:

> They came down in front of us mostly in the dead ground but we had a darn good shoot at the closest ones. I don't know how many we hit but we were out of our trenches to get the bastards before the rest could get their weapons, which came down in containers on white parachutes. There were groups of Huns scattered all over the place, some shot at us with pistols and others threw grenades but they were soon out of ammunition and easy to finish off. We killed a few of the nasty little bastards and the others soon started to surrender. The young ones were frightened and thought that we would kill them. The older ones, when they realised that we weren't, got cocky and told us that they wouldn't be PWs for long.

Adolf Muller, of *8 Kompanie II/FJR 1*, was one of the lucky ones. He explained:

> The signal came to jump ...the container had not been placed correctly to get it out quickly. Time was wasted and we found ourselves beyond our planned zone. It was all shit down below! The delay saved our lives. Few of the 2nd survived: they landed on barbed wire and were mown down by enemy fire.

The Black Watch and Australians cleared most of the perimeter of the airfield, with the exception of some *Fallschirmjäger* who had dropped into the Greek

158

barracks near the airfield, and with elements of B and A Companies, advanced down into East Wadi or the 'Gorge'. The remnants of *5* and *8 Kompanies* were driven east to cover by this move, to where just 60-70 shocked survivors waited for the *I Battalion*.

In the centre where *6* and *7 Kompanies* dropped the destruction was even greater, as the *Fallschirmjäger* had the misfortune to drop in the centre of 14 Brigade's position around Buttercup Field. C Company of the Black Watch 2/4th Battalion and 7 Medium Regiment were all immediately in action. Australian Dick Parry was with 2/4th:

> As they landed, the earth seemed to disgorge men – they appeared from everywhere, firing running and falling on the parachutists, who had been dropped right into the middle of a hail of fire.
>
> There was another surprise for them, two tanks which had started when the paratroopers had been dropped and were now firing in all directions. One of them was just under the drop zone and was turning in all directions, crushing a good number of those who had landed.
>
> About twenty landed in a crop field on the edge of the aerodrome. It was set on fire; the tanks ...picked them off as they escaped from the fire. No quarter was asked neither for nor given; we didn't have time to keep prisoners nor what was more we did not have anywhere to put them.

According to 7 RTR's after action report, the fleeting targets proved to be too much for the tanks' various machine guns' limited arcs of fire and slow traverse. Consequently, tracks were used as weapons by default.

For Brigadier Chappel it was an easier decision to deploy his Matildas at the initial stages of the drop on Iraklio, as he had six Light Tanks in reserve. As described above, and confirmed by the *Fallschirmjäger*, the tanks had a decisive effect. *Oberjäger* Franz Mitz, a veteran of the May 1940 invasion of Holland recalled:

> Most of my section were replacements in their first battle. None of us were expecting panzers waiting for us on our landing zone. Those that were not hit landing were killed reaching the containers. With nothing but pistols, soldiers who tried to surrender were killed. I hid by a bank until the first killing fest was over.

The gunners of 7th Medium Regiment took to their unaccustomed infantry role well. Sweeping through their area towards the Buttercup Field, the unarmed men of 234 Battery gathered enemy weapons and used them 'to collect a bag of 175 dead Germans'. Presumably some of these were jump casualties.

At the end of the 'killing *fest*' little remained of *6* and *7 Kompanies* and the *AA Machine gun Kompanie*. As many as 300 *Fallschirmjäger* were killed and most of the remaining 100 were wounded, with only a few going to ground and making a nuisance of themselves by shooting at the careless. The price of a reckless determination to get into battle based on wholly

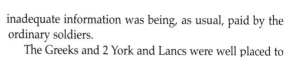

inadequate information was being, as usual, paid by the ordinary soldiers.

The Greeks and 2 York and Lancs were well placed to take the sting out of the attack by *III/FJR 1*, whose drop was 'late and well extended'. The Greeks mopped up most of those who landed in the open fairly quickly and effectively. The medical officer of *III Battalion*, Doctor Eiben, had landed on his own south of Iraklio and managed to evade the initial sweep but:

Suddenly, I heard the sound of engines and tracks. A group of 39 or 40 Greeks were approaching. An officer gave orders and I had to go back. After 40 metres, I was in front of barbed wire. In spite of the concentrated fire, I overcame that obstacle...

Some *Fallschirmjäger* who had dropped near the walls of Iraklio forced their way through the north and west gates and into the town.

Throughout the night there was bitter fighting in the streets, the Greek soldiers and civilians alike, attacking the invaders with any weapons that came to hand. The Greeks were reinforced by a detachment of the York and Lancs. By 2230, however, a party of Germans had reached the quay, and by morning others had dug in at the southern edge of the town.

The remainder of *III Battalion*, under Major Schultz, were unable to break through the Greeks and into the city, so withdrew to the west and dug in. Meanwhile, *II/FJR 2* landed further to the west of Iraklio, with only two companies and made no contact with 14 Brigade.

Attack and Counter-Attack

The initial battle resolved itself within an hour of the landing. During this time, the respective commanders, Chappel and Brauer, were both out of the action; the former thanks to the enemy grenade in his HQ and the latter because of delays in taking off due to refuelling and dust on the airfields.

As a measure of the Commonwealth control of the situation, at 1815 hours, Brigadier Chappel had only to order a small counter-attack by elements of his reserve, the Leicesters, to clear groups of enemy from the Buttercup Field area, immediately west of the aerodrome. The Leicester's Carrier Platoon supported a platoon of the York and Lancs and by 2130 hours the area was clear.

Oberst Brauer and his HQ did not drop until 1940 hours and then they were mis-dropped well to the east. Reaching the battle, Brauer found the situation in his command was 'unsatisfactory' but he believed that the airfield at least had been taken by *II/FJR 1*. He took *Oberstleutnant* Count Blucher and a detachment from the three companies of *I Battalion* that had been dropped very late, several miles to the east of the airfield in the growing darkness. According to the German report:

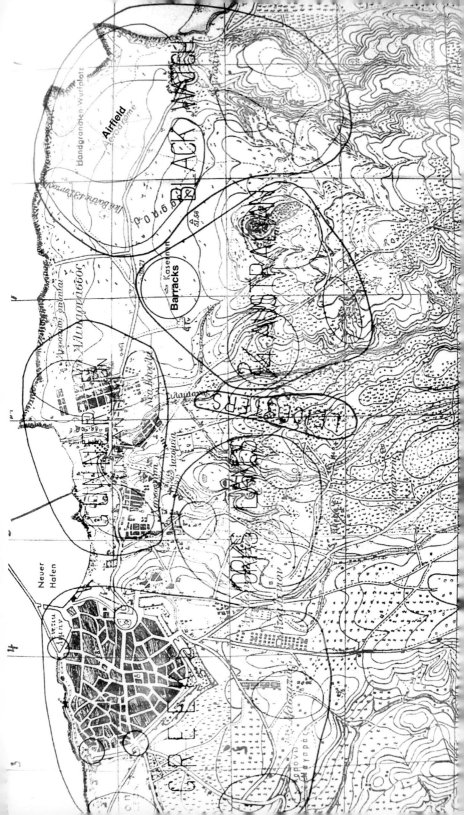

Airfield
Aerodrome

Handgranchen Wurfplatz

Kaserner
Barracks

Neuer
Hafen

BLACK VAULT

RODGROD

SURF

GREE

About 12.40 a.m. he reached the eastern slope of the airfield plateau and to his surprise, encountered strong enemy fire from the Black Watch. During the night Blucher and one platoon reached the high ground east of the airfield.

With the airfield and most of Iraklio in Commonwealth hands, the Australian official history reported: 'All night there was intermittent rifle and machine gun fire throughout the eastern area and much firing of flares by groups of Germans trying to assemble their scattered men.' Summing up the situation at Iraklio, the British July 1941 report recorded that the 2,000 *Fallschirmjäger* that dropped on X-Day had failed badly. Significant groups of Germans were, however, to the east and west of the town/airfield, while small groups were holding out at the port, in the Leicesters' QM's store and in the Greek Barracks. The Black Watch's historian recorded that the Battalion was 'tired but delighted with themselves and with the feeling that months of heartbreaking preparation, the digging, the incessant improvement of position had been utterly worthwhile'.

Subsequent Days

The first night was relatively quiet but in a 'letter from the front', reproduced in a British Army training publication, an officer complained,

During the night they filtered down into Bn HQ Officers' Mess, which was outside the perimeter [east of East Hill]. *They had the neck to sleep on my bed, pinch my shaving kit ...and put a bullet through the heart of two of my jackets which were hanging up under a nearby olive tree. Next morning we blew them to bits with our mortars.*

For the most part 21 May was devoid of major activity. The number of enemy air sorties increased and started to make life difficult for 14 Brigade. Numerous air re-supply drops were mounted by the *Luftwaffe*, with the Commonwealth troops, as usual, securing a proportion of the stores. The Greeks, who were running out of ammunition, particularly benefited from unwitting German largess and fought the remainder of the battle with enemy arms and equipment, including a light artillery piece, which was regularly re-supplied with ammunition!

Around dawn, the Black Watch platoon guarding the radar unit on AMES on the ridge, to the south-east, helped the technicians complete the destruction of their equipment and withdrew to the battalion perimeter. The ridge was subsequently occupied by the *Fallschirmjäger*.

Oberst Brauer, with *I/FJR 1* and the remains of *III Battalion*, who had been halted the previous night coming up out of the East Wadi Gorge, renewed the attack. Brauer's tactics were based on platoon infiltration under the cover of mortar fire. The small groups of Germans failed to make any progress against the Black Watch, and the lone enemy platoon on East

Hill remained isolated.

While this was going on, a supply drop, including light guns and anti-tank guns (some of which were immediately taken into use against their providers) was in progress and a Ju-52 made an attempt to land on the airfield under cover of fighters strafing the surrounding area. This entirely speculative landing, ordered by Student's HQ in Athens to take place at the same time as that at Maleme, resulted in the loss of another Ju-52.

Between 0900 and 1100 hours Brauer attempted a better coordinated attack. The operation was to start with bombing of the airfield by *VIII Fliegerkorps* which was followed by attacks from east and west. As the German account explains, *III/FJR 1*'s attack on the town from the west did not receive all the support it might have.

Schultz (*III Battalion*) did not receive Braver's orders, but intercepted a signal from *VIII Fliegerkorps* that Iraklio was to be attacked from the air … and decided to follow up this bombardment by attacking Iraklio at 1030 hours. He asked *Hauptmann* Schirmer of the *II/FJR 2* for assistance and Schirmer sent him a platoon and a section, but said that he could not spare more men for the task of protecting the force against attack from the west even though he was engaged there only with weak guerrilla forces. Schultz formed his force into two groups, one (*Leutnant* Becker) was to enter the town through the North Gate and occupy the harbour, the other (*Leutnant* Egger) would enter by the West Gate. Egger's group forced its way into the town but Commonwealth counter-attacks thrust it north on to Becker's force which succeeded in capturing an old Venetian fort in the harbour.

About 1700 hours, a major of the Greek Army offered the surrender of

Major Shultz, wearing his Knight's Cross.

the town, but the British in the town forced the Greek officers to fight on and 'advanced with strong forces from the east.'

The wavering Greeks had been stiffened by elements of 1 Leicesters and the York and Lancs and according to German sources, 'Because of lack of ammunition the *III Battalion* was forced, under cover of darkness, to fall back to its starting place west of the town'.

To the east, Brauer's force made up of the remnants of *II/FJR 1* and most of *I Battalion,* for the third time attacked East Ridge with support of light guns and mortars, whose observers were now occupying useful positions on AMES Ridge. These attacks were again piecemeal in character, with small groups being thrown into battle against the entirely unshaken Black Watch. However, having performed well the previous day the Matildas were now engaged by enemy artillery and with an attack assembling at Rattling Bridge (in East Wadi), both vehicles were out of action by mid-day; one with broken traversing gear and the second's engine seized when its cooling system was damaged by anti-tank fire.

To the south, 2/4th Battalion had smaller parties of enemy to deal with. The battalion history records that:

> ... a patrol of the 2/4th moved out to Babali and drove off a small German force; a German party moving towards Iraklio along the Knossos road was repulsed with severe casualties.

The Australians also cleared the last enemy from the lower slopes of the Charlies and surrounded and destroyed the *Fallschirmjäger* in the Greek Barracks.

Some of the missing companies, principally from *I/FJR 1*, were dropped at 1705 hours in positions well to the east and west, representing a small but to *Oberst* Brauer a welcome reinforcement. However, he still lacked the combat power to achieve anything at Iraklio.

The following day, 22 May, it is reported that 950 German corpses were removed from the Commonwealth area and that a further 300 were piled in the Greek area. It is likely, however, that these figures are exaggerated but German casualties were without a doubt crippling and ground activity tailed off. Air raids however remained frequent.

On 23 May it became apparent that the enemy were concentrating in the east with the intention of securing the airfield, and a report was received

A broken down Matilda being inspected by a German soldier after the battle.

that troop-carrying aircraft were landing east of East Ridge.

Two companies of the Leicesters who were sent east to make a raid in this direction returned in the evening with the news that the Germans there were not strong in numbers but had a large proportion of machine guns.

Elsewhere the Brigade extended its area of control. An Australian platoon occupied Apex Hill, 'a high knoll overlooking Babali' and more than a mile outside the perimeter, and from there watched 'the movement of German troops in the hill country through which they might be switched from one flank to another'.

See map page 155

About mid-day two Matilda tanks arrived from the south coast on the way to Souda, having fought their way through *Fallschirmjäger* blocking positions at Kaireti Farm. They brought with them the news that the 1 Argyll and Sutherland Highlanders (1 A&SH) were on the way from Tymbaki on the south coast and the South coast to Iraklio. The two tanks and the only Matilda of the 14 Brigade that could be repaired to running order, along with two 75mm field guns, were loaded on a naval lighter and dispatched onwards to Souda Bay. This was, however followed by an unfortunate event.

Early in the afternoon six Hurricanes arrived overhead from Egypt, but the naval anti-aircraft guns [Royal Marines], *mistaking them for Germans, fired and shot two down. Three then returned to their base, but the sixth landed. Later, during a particularly heavy raid by about fifty German aircraft, chiefly on the town itself, six more Hurricanes arrived, fought the attacking aircraft and finally landed on the field, four of them with damaged tail wheels. Thus few remained serviceable out of these two flights sent from Egypt to attack transports arriving at Maleme.*

After a heavy air raid on Iraklio, the enemy to the west sent a message that the town would be destroyed unless the Greeks surrendered, which was rejected. Because of the mounting civilian casualties and the threat of further bombing, Brigadier Chappel ordered all civilians to leave town, with the York and Lancs taking over its defence, with two companies in the town itself and a road-block to the west. The Greeks, reorganised into two battalions, were concentrated around Arkhania.

The Break in of 1st Argyll and Sutherland Highlanders

In early May, the Argylls were in the Western Desert on guard duty when they were warned for Crete. Their initial tasks on the South coast were:

(a) The defence of Messara Plain and its preparation as an emergency landing-ground for the RAF.

(b) To watch for possible parachute landings on Nida Plateau, in the hills north-west of Ay Deka.

(c) The defence of the beach we landed at, as it was expected to land further reinforcements at the same place.

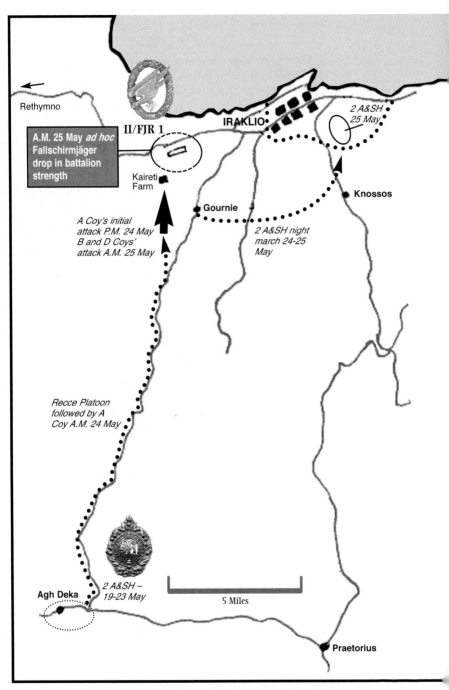

Rethymno

II/FJR 1

IRAKLIO

A.M. 25 May *ad hoc* Fallschirmjäger drop in battalion strength

Kaireti Farm

2 A&SH 25 May

A Coy's initial attack P.M. 24 May B and D Coys' attack A.M. 25 May

Gournie

Knossos

2 A&SH night march 24-25 May

Recce Platoon followed by A Coy A.M. 24 May

2 A&SH – 19-23 May

5 Miles

Agh Deka

Praetorius

Operations of 2 Argyle and Sutherland Highlanders 19-25 May.

166

Arriving with only a part of its stores, plus some RAF stores, the battalion was ashore on the south coast of Crete at Kokkinos Pyrgos, near Tymbaki on the morning of 19 May. By 21 May the majority of the battalion and the two additional Matildas already referred to, were at Agh Deka, with the news that the direct route to Iraklio was cut at Kaireti Farm by *II/FJR 1*. The battalion set about the task of preparing an emergency landing ground.

The regimental historian commented that 'No attack had been made on us at Agh Deka, and it is doubtful if our presence on the south coast was known'. In these circumstances and with little information to go on, as the battalion had not made radio contact with 14 Brigade at Iraklio, Lieutenant Colonel Anderson took action on his own initiative:

> *After all the information had been sifted and considered the CO decided on a change of plan. It looked to us as if the whole weight of the German attack was to be concentrated on the northern ports, and that not until Iraklio was taken was an extension southwards probable. It looked as if we were wasting our time sitting guarding a plain which was not likely to be required by British aircraft. The CO decided, therefore, that on the following day, 23rd May, we should make an attempt to clear up the German positions near Kaireti Farm and so open up the main road into Heraklion. He was influenced in making this decision by the fact that HQ 16 Brigade and the Queen's were expected to land at Tymbaki during the early hours of the 23rd May, and he thought that if he could open the road it would give 16 Brigade Commander more freedom for any action he thought necessary.*

Suffice it to say, 16 Brigade could not get to Crete due to the rapidly deteriorating naval situation. On the morning of 23 May the Argylls' Carrier Platoon carried out their recce of the enemy at Kaireti Farm. At 1000 hours, they reported that they believed a single company, supported by the carriers, could deal with the enemy. A Company were selected and moved off at 1100 hours but with battle procedure (recce, orders and briefings) to complete on arrival it was anticipated that H-Hour would not be until late afternoon. The first objective was Kaireti Farm and the second, a *II/FJR 1* blocking position, a little to the north of the farm near the coastal road. According to the Regiment:

> *The attack went in at 1700 hours and made good initial progress by capturing the first objective. When about half-way between the two objectives an untoward event occurred. The Germans called up more*

paratroop reinforcements, about 200 of whom were dropped in the nick of time just behind the second objective. With this extra padding they staged a counter attack, which forced A Company back through its first objective to its starting point, where it was finally held. At dusk A Company had established itself on high ground west of the road and overlooking Kaireti Farm, and the Germans were holding their initial positions. Casualties had not been heavy. But for the last minute intervention of the German parachute reinforcement, A Company would, in all probability, have succeeded in its task.

The dropping of *Fallschirmjäger* on top of the Argylls' attack was entirely coincidental but the result was a confusing battle and a boost to the Germans' flagging morale.

Meanwhile, with the refusal to surrender Iraklio, waves of Germans bombers began their attempt to destroy the town. A Company's attack was under way, when Colonel Anderson was ordered to attack with not less than three companies. Consequently, with the CO's recce group leading, two companies and Battalion HQ moved off but with little transport, by marching and running a transport shuttle, they were in the Forming up Place at 0445 hours.

After the experience of A Company during their recent attack, a frontal assault was ruled out, so it was decided that B Company on the right would attack east of and parallel to the main road, and that D Company would make a detour round the left, both companies to be guided by personnel of A Company who had already been over the ground. A Company was to remain in situ, but to be ready to exploit success on either flank. Such was the plan for what was going to be an unrecced night attack against opposition whose strength was unknown, and without the knowledge as to whether artillery support would be available or not. We were landed in this difficult position by the complete breakdown in communications.

Not only was there to be no artillery support but also no coordinated attack elsewhere on the Brigade perimeter to draw the enemy away from 1 A and SH. Brigadier Chappel's command was having the same communication problems as his opponent.

At 0500 hours on the 24th the attack commenced. It was important that we should succeed before 0730 hours, the normal hour the German Air Force started play for the day. At 0530 hours, very heavy German machine-gun fire opened on D Company's front, but there was no sound from B Company axis of advance. At 0730 hours, when the air offensive opened up, D Company were still well short of their objectives, having encountered heavy fire from machine guns firing on fixed lines and located in the entrance to caves. A Company were also pinned down by heavy small-arms and mortar fire, and B Company had vanished into the blue, no message having been received from them since the attack had started. It

Fallschirmjäger search an Argyle prisoner taken during their 'break-in' battle.

soon became obvious that an all-day slogging match was in front of us, so a message was sent back to Agy Deka for the immediate dispatch of C Company and the mortar platoon.

By 0830 hours some of B Company had been located, held up in line with A Company near Kaireti Farm, but:

At this hour complete disaster nearly overtook the Battalion. The Germans, as they had on the previous evening, again called up parachute reinforcements, and approximately a Battalion were dropped in front of, and to the left of D Company Those that fell in the rear of the Company were actually between the Company and Battalion HQ. The position of D Company was now hopeless. Heavily attacked on three sides by these new reinforcements and under heavy fire from the air, there was no way out, and

169

it became a case of every man for himself. There was nothing for it now but to sit tight and try and hold on where we were. The intense air attacks over the whole battlefield made an attempt at movement impossible.

Again fortune was on the Germans' side. *II/FJR 1* had seen little action so far and the good fortune of an *ad hoc* battalion of *Fallschirmjäger* rear details dropping exactly when and where needed confirmed the situation. The lack of artillery or mortar support for the Argylls was also telling.

During the afternoon, a York and Lancs officer arrived from Brigade HQ, who had heard the sounds of battle. 'He brought orders to the effect that we were to break off the battle forthwith and go to Iraklio by the cross country route he had used, guided by local Cretans whom he had brought.'

The first problem was to break off the action and withdraw to Gournies. The withdrawal was covered by C Company who had arrived from Agy Deka at 1800 hours. 'The withdrawal went according to plan'.

Leaving a platoon, stretcher-bearers and the regimental Medical Officer at Gournies to collect the wounded and evacuate them to Agy Deka, the remainder of the Battalion prepared for what was expected to be a seven hour night march. To avoid moving in daylight, they planned to set out at 2200 hours, which would allow sufficient time before dawn and the return of the dive bombers. Unfortunately, exhaustion and guides who were unfamiliar with the route by night meant that the Argylls did not arrive in the 14 Brigade perimeter until P.M. 25 May, whereupon the Highlanders took over the small sector held by the Leicesters, which released that battalion into a true, uncommitted, reserve for 14 Brigade.

The End of the Battle
With both sides reinforced, there was little change in the balance of combat power. The Germans decided to concentrate on the south-east flank. On 26 May, *Hauptmann* Schrimer of *II/FJR 2* recalled that:

I sat down with Major Schultz, commander of I Battalion, to decide what had to be done. We had to carry on. We advanced east with the two battalions in line, one man behind the other, leaving the old front line only thinly occupied.

We marched off, headed south, right up to the edge of the mountains, and then bore left, heading east. We passed Knossos to reach the Lion Mountain [Apex Hill] with heavy losses.

Hauptmann Schrimer continued his account of his advance on Apex Hill: 'We wanted to take the mountain. The English (sic) still held it, though somewhat feebly now. We took this mountain on I think 28th or 29th.'

On the 27th, Brigadier Chappel received word via Cairo that Crete was to be abandoned. For 14 Brigade this was not entirely surprising, despite

Oberst Brauer gives orders to a runner at Iraklio.

their lack of detailed information and not unwelcome as they were running low on stores of all kind. Orders for the withdrawal were given to the battalions the following morning, coinciding with further drops of *Fallschirmjäger* and renewed bombing of the town and defended area. That night, a force of cruisers; HMS *Orion, Dido* and *Ajax* (the latter turned back damaged) and six destroyers braved the *Luftwaffe* and arrived at Iraklio to evacuate the waiting Commonwealth Troops. The last troops slipped away from the perimeter at 0100 hours, undetected by the enemy. They had to hurry, however, as the loading timetable was brought forward by an hour, to 0300 hours, due to the ships' need to be well south of Crete by dawn. The Greeks, who were now operating as a guerrilla force, were neither informed of the evacuation or allowed precious spaces on board the overcrowded ships.

The Germans reported that they took five hundred prisoners and released two hundred of their own men. Of the Greeks, 1,000 capitulated, while approximately 1,000 took to the hills or 'prudently became civilians overnight'.

Chapter Eight

REINFORCEMENTS AND COUNTER-ATTACK

When on the 21st May all reserves had jumped and conquered the aerodrome of Maleme, from that time the battle of Crete was won for Germany.

General Student

While the two smaller and independent actions were being fought at Rethymno and Iraklio the decisive battle between *Gruppe West* and the New Zealand Division was being fought around Maleme and Galatas. We left Lieutenant Colonel Andrews' and most of 22 New Zealand Battalion having, unilaterally, withdrawn eastwards, from their position on Hill 107 and the Maleme Airfield, to join 21 and 23 NZ Battalions across the valley on Vineyard Ridge. Andrews had been left to fight his battle unsupported, either physically by significant reinforcement or emotionally by a remote and passive commander 5 NZ Brigade; Brigadier Hargest.

Ceding Hill 107 and positions surrounding the airfield offered an unwitting General Student his only success. It would seem that neither Andrews nor Hargest appreciated the fact that Hill 107 was now the vital ground for the airborne invasion. However, with the lack of information, compounded by poor passage of messages, they were not to know that elsewhere the Germans had failed, nor could they have anticipated that cession of Hill 107 could be quite as vital for the enemy as it was. There have been persistent accusations that some of the older New Zealand commanders held to a Great War 'line holding' concept rather than a focus on ground, manoeuvre and destruction of the enemy.

On the morning of 21 May 1941, the *Fallschirmjäger* of the *Luftlandesturmregiment (LLSR)* believed they had failed. Failed to take more than what amounted to a toe hold on the Maleme airfield and failed to secure the dominating Hill 107 and were, consequently, surprised to find only isolated detachments of 22 NZ Battalion left on the feature and its surrounding area.

Student's Plans

Overnight in Athens, General Student, unaware of Andrews' withdrawal, pored over his maps seeking a way of recovering the situation. Communications with Rethymno and Iraklio were virtually non-existent and Prison Valley offered little opportunity for flying in troops, even if the surrounding heights were not occupied by New Zealanders. If, contrary to the principles of war, he was going to 'reinforce a failure', Maleme was the place for Student to concentrate his effort. He described this as:

A very grave decision. I decided the whole mass of the reserve [this was not in reality a formal reserve] *of the* Fallschirmjäger *would be put into action at the aerodrome of Maleme. It was a critical night for me. If the enemy had made a united all-out effort to counter-attack during the night 20th-21st or on the morning of the 21st then very tired remnants of the* Sturm Regiment, *lacking ammunition would have been wiped out.*

Student ordered, further proving Ju-52 flights to both Iraklio and Maleme airfields to take off at dawn. The fate of the earlier flights to Maleme and Iraklio have already been recorded but the aircraft, flown by *Hauptmann* Kyle to Maleme on 21 May, landed successfully on the western end of the airfield, despite machine gun and rifle fire on his approach. In landing, he had proved that the Tavronitis end of the airfield was not swept by small-arms fire, even if aircraft had to brave fire on the final approach and 27 NZ Battery's shells (3.7-inch mountain and Italian 75mm) were bursting at the eastern end of the area.

At the same time, another Ju-52 flown by *Leutnant* Koenitz managed to land on the pebble beach to the west of the mouth of the Tavronitis River. This flight was apparently unauthorised. His radio operator records that Koenitz had spent all evening listening to the situation briefs and the radio traffic from Maleme and realising that *LLSR* were in trouble decided on his own initiative, to fly a load of ammunition to the beleaguered *Fallschirmjäger*. Not long after Kyle landed on the airfield Koenitz put his amazingly tough Ju 52 down on the beach – a tremendous feat of flying but

Maleme airfield with wrecked Ju-52s scattered about.

N

Beach

Coast Road

RAF
Cam

The shingle beach at Maleme, present day. *Leutnant* Koenitz managed to land a Ju-52 transport on this surface.

landing here was clearly not practical for the scale of fly-in that *XI Fliegerkorps* planned. However, light aircraft with vital stocks of ammunition were able to use a strip of cleared and levelled beach throughout the day.

With the ammunition being offloaded and the beach being cleared for the indestructible Ju-52 to take off again, Koenitz went to find the *LLSR*'s HQ. Here he found the wounded *Generalmajor* Meindl delirious; apparently believing that he was still in Norway. The General and seven other seriously wounded men were flown back to Athens by Koenitz.

The result of the information gained and the presumed loss of the aircraft sent to Iraklio, led to a glimmer of hope developing into a course of action for Studert. Maleme was to be reinforced at the expense of the other areas, which would have to hold out until relieved. Orders were issued; Maleme was the *schwerpunkt*. The *LLSR* was to drive the Commonwealth troops back beyond artillery range of the airfield, the amphibious force would all head for Maleme and *5th Gerbirgsdivision* would also fly to Maleme rather than to Iraklio. The first of the *ad hoc Fallschirmjäger* battalions would be formed from the 850 men left out of battle or left behind the previous day due to insufficient aircraft. They were placed under *Oberst* Bernhard Hermann Ramcke, an officer who was 'too old for airborne operations' and as already mentioned had only come to Greece to train the *Gerbirgsjäger* in air portability techniques. The *Fallschirmjäger* had to first re-rig the Ju 52s back into the parachute role, which meant that their drop could not be until late afternoon.

The operational aim was to drive west to link up with *Gruppe Mitte* and advance on Hania and seize Souda Bay. The aircraft of *VIII Fliegerkorps* were, of course, to support this advance in strength.

Meanwhile, the *LLSR* could not believe their luck. They pushed forward on to Hill 107, overwhelming small parties of New Zealanders, of D and A

Companies who had blocked all earlier attempts to capture it. But they were now isolated detachments and were easily surrounded. Swastika air recognition panels were soon laid out on the olive trees and vines of Hill 107. However, the remnants of 22 NZ Battalion slowed the cautious Germans by putting up fierce resistance. Stukas were called on to support the advance, dive bombing targets, particularly the New Zealanders' artillery, indicated to them with air panels and flares. By 1100 hours, the eastern end of the airfield was clear and the Germans had occupied the hamlet of Maleme and closed up to Pyrgos where they were in contact with the remainder of 5 NZ Brigade.

Reorganising his defences, Brigadier Hargest did little to oppose the advance of the *LLSR*, let alone deliver an immediate counter-attack from his own resources that the situation required. This passive stance, however, highlights the difficulty of any daylight move, which invariably attracted the attention of the circling *Luftwaffe* dive bombers. At 1115 hours, Hargest did propose to Brigadier Puttick that a counter-attack should be made under cover of darkness. In the meantime, a relative period of quiet settled over the battlefield, punctuated by bursts of fire from the New Zealanders' Vickers guns, as the Germans prepared their next move.

Reinforcement

The enemy plan was for *HQ 100 Gerbirgsjägerregiment* and its *II Battalion (II/GJR 100)* to fly in from 1700 hours onwards, while *Oberst* Ramcke's reinforcement was made up of elements 5 and 6 *Kompanies* of *II/FJR 2* that could not be dropped at Iraklio the previous day and other left out of battle *Fallschirmjäger*, totalling about 250 reinforcements. They were to drop at 1800 hours, onto a DZ on the coastal strip between Pyrgos and Platanias, a mile behind the front line. The drop was to coincide with an attack from the airfield that would link up with the *LLSR* from the west.

Oberst Ramcke was to jump east of the Tavronitis and take command of the *LLSR* and leading elements of the *Gerbirgsjäger*, as they arrived.

At 1700 hours, the familiar roar of fighter and dive bomber engines over Maleme was supplemented by the deeper throb of massed Ju 52s. 'Here they come again' was the resigned comment of many New Zealanders.

Oberst Ramcke.

Oberleutnant Rossenhauer of GBR 100 was aboard the leading group of Ju 52s:

> We were flying towards Crete! Quiet, without any turbulence and at low altitude ... Wearing our lifejackets, our weapons and our bags by our side, we looked into the deep blue sea...
>
> Passing in front of the island of Theodori, the Cretan coast was now in

front of us. Here we are! The AA guns opened up and welcomed us. We could see little spots of light around our Ju-52s. The planes lost altitude and got ready for landing. The machine-gunner aboard was emptying his magazines one after the other.

The airfield was on the edge of the sea, there seemed to be no obstacles. Three Jus from the first wave landed and threw up a huge cloud of dust which marked the landing strip. This was too short and because of the dust nothing could be seen. We were on edge. 'Hold tight,' shouted the pilot.

The landing was perfect! A few seconds later, he pulled the aircraft abruptly to the right to a standstill. Immediate disembarkation!

The noise of engines and exploding shells was all mixed up. Our aircraft were submitted to terrible punishment from artillery and machine-gun fire. Petrol flowed from the tanks. Would they catch fire?

Crates and [motorcycle] sidecars were unloaded. All very quickly, but unfortunately it was too late. Our Ju was so severely damaged that it could not take off again. Near the plane, the battalion commander was wounded; he was evacuated from the firing zone aboard a sidecar. It was unbelievable, but nobody was wounded inside the plane.

Our planes were landing non-stop, one after the other, some of them on their bellies. The pilots were blinded by the dust. Destroyed Jus very quickly blocked the strip making it unusable. Half the planes could not land and circled over the strip, shooting with the weapons on board. Many of them landed on the beach, under enemy fire, but the beach was not made for our heavy Jus. We the Jägers were on the battlefield and that was the main thing.

Captain Baker watched the landings on the beach east of the Tavronitis' mouth, '…apparently having filled the aerodrome they commenced to land along the beach until finally they had landed right down past where we were taking cover'. C Troop, 27 NZ Battery 'at once switched fire onto those planes on the beach'. Captain Baker witnessed the result.

They gave a first class exhibition of gunnery and accounted for the six planes nearest to us in a matter of moments. Certainly in practically all cases they were set on fire before the occupants had the chance of alighting and out of these six planes I saw only twenty men who ever left that beach.

German war reporter, Kurt Neher was aboard one of the Ju-52s that crash landed.

Germans capture Hill 107.

Left: *Gerbirgsjäger*
emplaning Greece.
Above: The Edelweiss,
motif of the German
mountain troops.
Below: On their way to
Crete and arriving safely at
Maleme airfield.

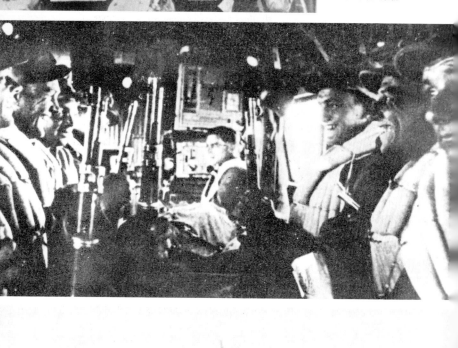

Men, packs, life jackets, ammunition were thrown forward ... for some
seconds we lost every bit of control over our bodies. Then the Ju came to a
halt half standing on its head ... Only two hours before we were lying in
the shade of our planes on the mainland and now we were being fired on
from everywhere.

Even though the landing on the airfield and beach had produced a
graveyard of twisted metal airframes, to make a difference, sufficient of the
52 aircraft delivered their passengers and cargo. Some 650 fresh troops of
Oberst Utz's HQ *GJR 100* and his *II Battalion* were available for tasking by
nightfall.

While the desperate fly-in to Maleme was under way, the attack of the
LLSR and drop of two rifle companies and part of the anti-tank battalion
was taking place. The *LLSR's* attack against the well dug-in 23 NZ
Battalion, despite close air support, lacked sufficient punch to make much
impression. This is what the defenders had to say about the attack:

About 4 p.m. a more definitely organised attack from the north came in
on the platoons commanded by Lieutenants Thomson and Ensor. These HQ
Company men stood their ground and repelled or killed the enemy with
their steady fire. We estimated, perhaps a little optimistically, that nearly
200 German dead were left in front of the 23rd positions. But, in the main,
the day was one of attacks, recurring attacks, from the air rather than of
serious attacks from the troops on the ground.

With regard to the parachute reinforcement, despite recommendations
passed back to Student in Athens, again the enemy paid a high price for
dropping on top of Commonwealth forces. Franz Rzeha of *5 Kompanie,*
II/FJR 2 was amongst them:

We could see our escorts, Me-110s on both sides. Just before our arrival
we flew over the island of Theodori to the west. It was there that the AA
started shooting. We could hear and see the host of AA shells which
perforated the skin of our Junkers. Looking through the window we could
see two Junkers which had been damaged, and which were returning to the
continent. One had an engine on fire, the other had fuselage damage.

'Get ready.' A light anti-aircraft battery fired at the Ju 52s with all its
might. The signal 'Go' delivered us!

The drop from 70 metres up was a jump into hell. We dropped in front
of and behind the English and the New Zealanders, into a vineyard near
Pirgos. I could hear the sound of bullets. We had the impression of being
expected and were getting shot at from the enemy positions. But we had to
get through. A lot of comrades were killed or seriously wounded, still
attached to their parachutes. When we got down, we could hear their shouts
for help, asking for a medic. There weren't any. The shouts were very loud
to begin with, then went calm and then ceased altogether.

The surviving comrades identified the centre of resistance and advanced

179

Ju-52s crashland into old stone walls and 22nd NZ Battalion's abandoned sangers.

[i.e. withdrew!] *in the direction of the hill from where the best part of the shooting was coming.*

The engineers and 19 Army Troops Company were on the ground near the DZ, along with 28 Maori Battalion. Twelve Ju 52s dropped their *Fallschirmjäger* on top of 19 Company and another twelve sticks dropped over the westerly elements of the Maoris. There was fierce fighting in the Maori battalion's area. Across the DZ running fights developed similar in nature to those of the previous day and prevented the Germans from forming up into a cohesive force. Captain Anderson, an NZ Army Service Corps officer, wrote:

> At one stage I stopped for a minute or two to see how things were going and a Hun dropped not ten feet away. I had my pistol in my hand – what for I can't imagine – and without really knowing what I was doing I let him have it while he was still on the ground. I had hardly got over the shock when another came down almost on top of me and I plugged him too while he was untangling himself. Not cricket, I know, but there it is.

The logistic troops of 19 Company were in the infantry role. Captain Anderson continued:

> Our fellows behaved well and did some good destruction. Every man who could handle a rifle did his bit. Officers – cooks – bottle-washers – all were at it. Unfortunately we only had one Bren on the strength but the two chaps using it did a magnificent job.

The drop was a disaster and did little to assist the *LLSR*'s progress being almost entirely dealt with by the troops on the spot and the Maori's D Company. About eighty *Fallschirmjäger* escaped westward towards the airfield but small groups, however, remained in cover near the drop zone and proved to be a considerable nuisance and were to have a significant impact on the coming night's operations.

Oberst Ramcke made his first operational jump just to the west of the Tavronitis, amongst the last men to drop on a DZ near the bridge. He was lucky, as up to forty others were caught in a sharp offshore breeze and blown out to sea to drown. Ramcke immediately took command and confirmed orders already given to deploy the *Gerbirgsjäger* in defence of the newly captured airfield, mostly occupying captured New Zealand

180

positions. With the fly-in of the *Gerbirgsdivision*, the newly arrived Ramcke could also expect further reinforcement during the night from the amphibious force.

With the situation looking more positive but the overall outcome still unclear, the *Gerbirgsjäger*'s war diarist wrote:

> On the evening of the second day of the invasion the situation seemed to be on a knife-edge. If II/GJR 100 had landed with light casualties, the defences of Maleme Airfield would be considerably strengthened, but a heavy concentrated British [sic] counter-attack would force the defenders to fight for their lives.

And it was a counter-attack that General Freyberg had in mind.

Counter-Attack Plans

While the German reinforcement of Maleme was under way, General Freyberg held a conference with his chief of Staff, Brigadier Puttick (Commander NZ Division) and two of the brigade commanders, Inglis and Vasey. Hargest and Kippenberger, however, were committed to fighting the current battles on their front and sadly did not attend. The conference resolved to mount a counter-attack, with two battalions, to retake Hill 107 and the airfield, supported by 3nd Hussar's Light Tanks and an RAF bombing raid. The operation was, perforce, to begin after dark and was to be complete by dawn, in order to avoid the depredations of the morning bombing.

Two battalions, 28 Maori and 20 NZ Battalions, was a relatively small force considering the amount of uncommitted infantry in the area. However, 'economy of effort' is a principle of war and, at the time he made his decision, Freyberg had no knowledge of the enemy's efforts to reinforce the *LLSR*.

The concept of the plan was simple but ULTRA's warnings of the presence of the German Amphibious Force over the horizon, 'heading for the Hania area', was a factor that weighed heavily on Freyberg's mind. The General believed that leaving 20 NZ Battalion's positions on the ideal landing beaches just west of Hania unoccupied would be a risk too far, as his interpretation of the ULTRA intelligence was still that he faced an assault landing force rather than a reinforcement. Consequently, he ordered Brigadier Vasey to dispatch one of his two Australian battalions from Georgioupoli to take over 20 NZ Battalion's positions. Eighteen miles away, 2/7th Battalion had no transport of its own, consequently, it was appreciated that moving 580 men would take time and Zero-Hour was set for 0100 hours, leaving five hours until dawn or six and a half until the dive bombers arrived for the morning attacks.

CREFORCE's basic time appreciation was, however, subject to the 'resistant medium of war', that renders 'the simplest action difficult'. To start with, the Australians were neither connected to Souda by radio or telephone, which meant that there could be no concurrent activity while the trucks drove from Souda to Georgioupoli. Their arrival with the Australians coincided with a *Luftwaffe* raid on an ammunition dump and the drivers scattered into cover, from which it took some time to round them up. It wasn't until well after 1700 hours that the main body set out for Hania, under Major Marshall, following Lieutenant Colonel Walker who had gone ahead with his Recce Group.

Major Marshall wrote:

> *Just as we had completed embussing of the battalion … some enemy planes discovered us… I started off with the planes still around. It followed our idea from Greece that the best way is just to go on in the face of attack … We whizzed down the road … Then we turned a corner and found half a dozen planes above with the obvious intention of attacking us. It was rather exhilarating. The planes had now obviously got on to us, but the road was winding along a valley and there were few straight stretches. The planes cruised about waiting for us … Twice I watched a plane single us out, bank and turn to machine-gun us along the straight and I told the driver to crank it up. It then became a race to the curve … We streaked along and I hoped the battalion was following.*

Meanwhile, the remainder of the force was assembling including Lieutenant Farran and his troop of Light Tanks.

> *We stopped at Platanias village, where the New Zealanders had their Brigade Headquarters. When the Squadron Leader told me that my troop had been selected for the counter-attack, I slightly resented it, since we had been in action almost non-stop for forty-eight hours and I felt that this was almost certain suicide.*
>
> *Together we mounted the steps of an old farmhouse to receive the orders from the Brigadier [Hargest]. He was a red, open-faced man, who looked like a country farmer and it was obvious that he was suffering from acute fatigue. He asked us to wait for half an hour while he had some sleep. Disgusted, intolerant, we sat on the steps until he was ready. Then he began to explain his plan, which had the merits of simplicity if nothing else. There was no artillery apart from a few captured Italian guns, which had to be aimed by squinting down the barrel, so we were to advance without a barrage. There were no mortars … There were no spades, so weapon-pits would have to be dug with steel helmets. My orders were to advance at a slow pace down the main road, since the ground was too rough to get off into the open country. Parallel with my middle tank, the 20th New Zealand Battalion would advance on the right and the Maori Battalion on the left. In particular, I was to be aware of two Bofors guns, recently captured by the enemy, which were said to be mounted near the village [Maleme] and would blow large holes in my tanks. I protested that my tanks were only*

thinly armoured perambulators and that this was a job for Matildas, but I was sharply brought back to reality by the reminder that beggars cannot be choosers. All the Matildas had been knocked out the day before. He acceded to one request, which was that a section of Maoris should advance behind each tank, so that I could better judge the pace and to prevent Molotov Cocktails from being thrown from the ditches.

The delays imposed by air attacks on the road to Hania meant the last company of 2/7th Battalion did not leave Georgioupoli until 2000 hours and that the relief in place of 20 NZ Battalion was not complete until about 2330 hours, which left the New Zealanders just an hour and a half to reach Palatanias in trucks, receive orders and to join the Maoris on the start line. This proved to be far too little time and it was not until 0245 hours that they were approaching the Maoris who had been waiting for four hours. Zero-Hour was eventually set as 0330 hours. With the amphibious threat, it would have been a brave commander to have released 20 Battalion before relief but failure to do so had a profound effect on the attack.

Major General Freyberg went to bed at his HQ at Venizlo's Grave, on the evening of 21 May, optimistic that, with the Royal Navy having located the enemy shipping, they were set to intercept the German amphibious flotilla. With this counter-attack, as he believed, under-way, he felt he had matters under control.

Naval Action

The German Naval Commander Southeast, Admiral Schuster, having no major *Kriegsmarine* vessels under his command had to rely on some sixty-three commandeered, Greek crewed, motor sailers (principally fishing boats or *caiques*), seven cargo ships, each capable of carrying 300 tons and an Italian destroyer (*Lupa*) and several motor torpedo boats as escorts. They were formed into two convoys at the Piraeus near Athens; one originally bound for Iraklio, the other to Souda Bay. The convoys were to each carry a battalion of the *5th Gerbirgsdivision*, some heavier support and administrative units of *7th Fliegerdivision* that were not air portable or could not be lifted with the number of aircraft available. Mules and similar heavy equipment belonging to *5th Gerbirgsdivision* were also to be in the *caiques*. The tanks (Marks II and III) of *5 Kompanie Panzer Regiment 31 (5th Panzerdivision)*, the heavier anti-aircraft and anti-tank guns, bulky equipment, as well as further stores and ammunition were also to be carried by sea in the cargo vessels and converted barges in a thind, Heavy Flotilla that on the night of 21-22 May, had not yet left Piraeus.

Armed with ULTRA intelligence, at 2300 hours on the night of 20-21 May, a Royal Navy cruiser task force sailed around Cape Spatha, into the Sea of Crete to intercept the German amphibious convoys. Force C seeking to intercept the Iraklio-bound convoy (Flotilla 2), which as the convoy was still at Milos, had a fruitless night. Captain Rowley's Force B, however, had more luck with the western enemy flotilla now redirected to Maleme.

> *Suddenly at about 2300 hours, searchlights from the north were trained on the bright sails [of the caiques] and rolling salvos of medium naval guns, a burning ship, then quiet ... no signal, no light, not a trace of the flotilla remained.*

The German naval officer landed in advance of the *caique* force could only wonder 'What had happened?' The cruiser HMS *Dido* had picked up the flotilla on her radar and fired illuminating rounds. The German report on the operation concluded:

> *Strong enemy surface forces had encountered the advance command vessels of the small Flotilla 1, which was enroute for Cape Spatha. Flotilla 1 had become stretched out considerably due to the varying speeds of the vessels. The flotilla itself was shot up, rammed and dispersed without the possibility of defending itself.*

Feldwebel Gunter Kerstens of *III Battalion, Gerbirgsjägerregiment 100 (III/GJR 100)* was aboard one of the caiques:

> *By our second day in the boat, I was no longer sick and we were nearing our destination, Crete, when ahead searchlights came on and heavy guns started to fire. We could see the English ships getting closer, silhouetted by the flash of their guns. Ships and boats ahead of us were on fire and then it was our turn. The boat alongside us exploded then through the smoke came the bow of an English ship. I could not move. Some jumped but I was stuck to the spot as it came down on us. The boat splintered and was pushed under the big ship, me with it. With my last living breath, I came to the surface to see the ship continuing the Gotterdammerung.*

> *I spent all next day in the water, clinging to wreckage before being picked up. The English Navy made no attempt to rescue us – curse them!*

About fifteen out of thirty-two *caiques* were sunk and between 350 and 400 Germans drowned, most of them from *III/GJR 100* but the *Fallschirmjäger* also lost support elements principally through the destruction of equipment. The dispersal of the force and the attack's concentration on the leading part of the convoy had saved it from total destruction. Also, according to the German report, 'Valiantly the Italian destroyer entered the uneven battle and one of them succeeded in laying a smokescreen'. The destruction would have been greater but for Commander Mimbelli's desperate engagements with the Royal Navy at very short range that allowed the flotilla to scatter.

The second flotilla with *II/GJR 85* aboard, was recalled to Piraeus and amphibious operations were suspended until the Royal Navy had been driven from the Sea of Crete. To that end, on the morning of 22 May, *VIII Fliegerkorps* began an all-out attack on the British fleet, which was forced to withdraw from the Aegean after suffering heavy losses. The battle between

Greek caiques commandeered for the invasion of Crete.

the *Luftwaffe* and the Royal Navy ended in victory for the Germans, who, with air supremacy, controlled the skies and seas north of Crete for the remainder of the campaign.

Counter-Attack

While awaiting the arrival of 20 NZ Battalion at the Palatanias Bridge, the Maoris' B Company conducted a preliminary operation to drive away enemy parties and re-established 19 Army Troops Company in its forward pits.

> This was accomplished by sending Private Timihou with a section to draw fire while the others, with the enemy located, worked in behind them. The result was a dozen dead paratroops and one live glider pilot. Because he appeared to be very young and could speak a little English, he was taken along as a mascot, was lost sight of later, and probably rejoined his own people.

The counter-attack proper was finally under way, two and a half vital hours late, at 0330 hours, when the first two companies of 20 NZ Battalion were ready on the start line beyond the Platanias Bridge. The attack went ahead without the RAF bombing of the objective. 28 Maori Battalion under Colonel Dittmer planned to 'advance on a two-company front, with D supported by Headquarters Company on the right and A leading C Company on the left'. It was anticipated that the 'first part of the advance to just short of Pyrgos village was to be regarded as an approach march'. The Maoris had, however, to be prepared to clear pockets of *Fallschirmjäger* left from the afternoon's drop. 'To this end the forward companies were

See map page 187

HMS *Dido* had picked up the German invasion flotilla on her radar.

instructed to put out a screen of scouts across the front.'

Lieutenant Roy Farran's troop, protected by Lieutenant Reedy's platoon of Maoris, was leading the attack along the Coast Road and was almost immediately in action.

> At half-past three we moved forward from the start-line, a stream outside Platanias. The fighting began almost immediately. I sprayed the front with my tracers and was lucky enough to hit an ammunition dump, which exploded like 'golden rain' at the Crystal Palace. The line of figures marched steadily forward. I saw several parachutes lying in the trees and there were two dead Germans hanging on the telephone wires, blown up like green bladders. A white Very light was fired from a cottage on the left and we gave it a whole belt of Vickers. I was astonished to notice that my section of Maoris had suffered heavy casualties in the dark. I had not even realised that we had been fired at, but the sadly depleted numbers and the bandage round the head of the sergeant were evidence enough.

Away from the road, the approach march had barely gone half a mile before both battalions were in contact with the enemy. D Company, 20 NZ Battalion encountered a large group of *Fallschirmjäger* in a house and after some sharp fighting captured it. The Battalion history describes the situation:

> From in front, on either side, and sometimes from behind came streaks of fire, but the tracer gave the enemy's positions away, enabling men to pick their way between the lines of fire and get close enough to throw grenades. It was a strange sensation for the attackers: the machine-gun fire seemed terrific, and Tommy guns, pistols, grenades, and the shouts and screams of men combined in an unearthly din like nothing they had ever heard before. Through the darkness the troops pressed resolutely on, meeting resistance in depth — in ditches, behind hedges, in the top and bottom storeys of houses, in fields and gardens along the road.

Meanwhile, the Maoris, 'threading their way through trees and around houses, met scattered Germans firing from windows and from behind stone walls'. The tanks provided support by engaging flashes from the houses and covered the infantry's approach; 'grenade and bayonet did the rest'. In the darkness, that perennial problem of fratricide caused delay; 7 Field Company had been instructed to fire on any movement and inquire afterwards. It took time to 'clear up the misunderstanding' that resulted in a sharp exchange of fire between the engineers and the Maoris of A Company. A Company also suffered casualties from the engineers' anti-personnel mines scattered in front of their position, but the battalion continued the advance.

Private Hill-Rennie described C Company's fighting, including the first of a series of actions that led to the award of the VC to Lieutenant Upham:

> Suddenly we ran into our first opposition. A Jerry machine-gun nest

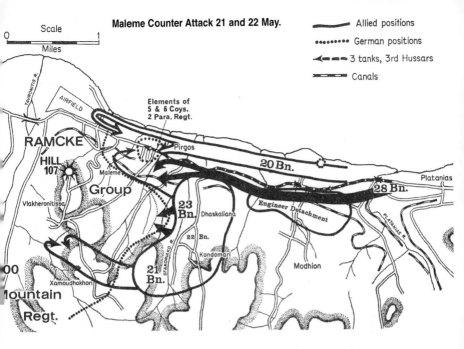

opened fire on us at a range of 50 yards and they got four of our boys before
we could drop to the ground. The man just on my right gave a sharp yelp
and I crawled over to see what was the matter. Two fingers of his right hand
had been blown off by an explosive bullet. Jerry was using tracer and it was
strange to lie there under the olive trees and see the bullets coming. ... We
waited on the ground and finally the order came for my section to advance
and wipe out the nest.

    We edged forward on our stomachs until we were within 20 yards of the
Nazis, who were tucked away behind a large tree, and then opened fire with
our one Tommy gun, one Bren gun and eight rifles. As we kept up the fire
the platoon officer [Lieutenant Upham] cautiously crawled round to the
side and slightly to the rear of the tree. Although it was still dark, we could
tell by the way the Jerries were shouting to each other that they didn't like
the look of the situation. When he got round behind the tree the platoon
officer jumped to his feet and hurled three Mills bombs, one right after
another, into the nest and then jumped forward with his revolver blazing.
Single-handed he wiped out seven Jerries with their Tommy guns and
another with a machine gun.... Two machine-gunners managed to hobble
away in the darkness, but we got them later.

The necessity of platoon actions to destroy every one of the scattered
enemy positions, while technically still in the 'approach march' phase,
consumed hours of vital time. At dawn, when the operation should have
been concluding, forward elements of the two Battalions were half way to
Pyrgos and only a third of the way to the airfield but they had an hour or

Lieutenant Charles Upham VC.

so of grace before the Stukas would arrive. In the meantime, however, both sides' infantry would have to bear a greater quantity of more accurate artillery and mortar fire.

The advance, however, continued against the isolated remnants of 5 *Kompanie FJR 2* who were waiting for dawn before exfiltrating to Maleme:

On 22 May 1941, at dawn, units of the 28th Battalion (Maoris) attacked us. Coming from the east, from three different directions, the enemy twice got very close, a few metres away. We defended desperately, but were running out of ammunition. The enemy retired to its positions to reform and launch a third attack. Heavy mortar fire fell on our trenches and enabled the enemy to get closer and closer. We fired to the last cartridge. Our machine gunner was mortally wounded by grenade splinters. He was the last casualty during the battle of Pirgos.

The final attack began. A drunken Maori, bayonet fixed, advanced on me. I saw him and could smell the alcohol. I had my P08 in my hand, but the magazine was empty. I could already feel the bayonet on my stomach, but at the last moment, a young officer put himself between us and pushed the Maori's rifle away. He took me by the shoulder and said: 'Come on, boy.' I was saved! Our adversaries passed their water bottles around, after having got our comrades out of their holes.

Shortly afterwards, the senior officer approached us. He looked at us and asked us in German … 'Where are the others?' We shrugged our shoulders and one of us answered: 'There's only us.' The officer stood in front of us, looking each of us in the eyes. Tears in his eyes, he saluted us and said 'All right boys'.

Lieutenant Farran's tanks had been keeping pace with the advance through Pyrgos and into Maleme village, providing fire support with his machine guns.

My leading tank had got a little too far ahead, in contravention of my orders and had run into trouble in the village. Coming round the corner of the street, it had run slap into two anti-tank guns in the churchyard. The first shot holed them, mortally wounding the gunner, but he bravely continued to fire until he had despatched one of the enemy guns. The tank tried to turn to get out of its impossible position, but another shell hit them in the middle. The gunner was killed, the commander, Sergeant Skedgewell, was mashed up with the seat, and Cook, the driver, received a serious wound in the foot. What was worse, the tank was set on fire.

It wasn't long before Farran was himself in trouble. An hour after dawn '… now there was all hell let loose in the sky'.

A swarm of Me 109s like angry buzzing bees beset our remaining two tanks. Hot flakes of burning metal flew off the inside of the turrets into our

188

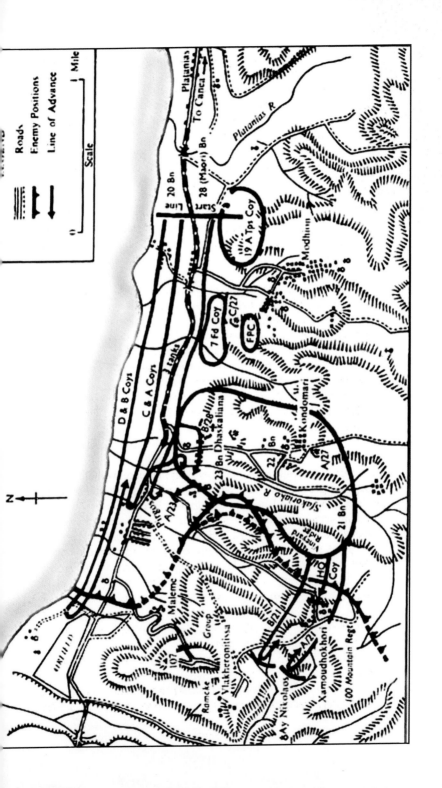

faces. We tried to minimise their dives by halting under a tall tree, but it was of no avail. Finally, like a wounded bull trying to shake off a cloud of flies, I crashed into a bamboo field. In the long green plants we lost them, but a final disaster overtook my tank. The rough treatment had been the last straw for the bogey wheel I had damaged in the barbed wire two days before. It collapsed as though it had been made of cardboard, having also been damaged by a grenade, and there we were as immobile as the Rock of Gibraltar.

The loss of the tanks was keenly felt by the New Zealanders, especially as they were now vulnerable to attack from the air but the battle continued. 20 Battalion had become strung out, D Company fighting along the beach on the right flank, with fewer buildings to contend with, forced their way through the small fields and bamboo windbreaks and reached the eastern end of the airfield but according to Private Hill-Rennie, C Company 'in the middle sector came up against Maleme village, where Jerry had taken up vantage points in the houses. We slowly blasted our way from house to house, wiping out one nest after another …'. Casualties were high as the *Fallschirmjäger* sniped at the New Zealanders keeping 'up a constant, deadly fire'. The Germans did not have things entirely their own way. Lieutenant Maxwell of D Company recalled:

> *We reached the clear part of the 'drome all right—there were stacks of aircraft, some crashed, some not — I remember P. Amos saying 'I've carried this anti tank rifle all this way and I am going to have one shot'. He fired two shots into one aircraft and made a mess of it.*

The Battalion history recorded that 'Casualties were heavy: some sections had only one man left. Lieutenant Maxwell then pulled the survivors back about 100 yards to the cover of some bamboos where sections of B Company were found'.

B Company and the scattered remains of D were in an un-enviably exposed position and sought permission from Colonel Burrows to withdraw, which, with mounting casualties, was reluctantly given around

Germans pose around a captured Light Tank.

0800 hours. Colonel Burrows set about revising his plan to capture the airfield by coming in behind the Maoris and attacking from Hill 107 once it had been taken. But in the meantime, his battalion had to withdraw from contact around the airfield, which was easier said than done. Some groups of New Zealanders did not receive the order and others failed to read beyond the withdrawal order and missed Colonel Burrows's revised intent.

Lieutenant Charles Upham continued to perform beyond the call of duty. An extract from his VC citation reads:

> When his Company withdrew from Maleme he helped to carry a wounded man out under fire, and together with another officer rallied more men together to carry other wounded men out. He was then sent to bring in a company which had become isolated. With a corporal he went through enemy territory over 600 yards, killing two Germans on the way, found the company, and brought it back to the Battalion's new position. But for this action it would have been completely cut off.

Even though a member of 20 NZ Battalion reported that 'Over on my left I could hear wild shouts coming from the Maori lines as they forged ahead', 28 Battalion was unable to make much progress through or around Maleme. 'Ace' Wood described an incident in the attempt to bypass the village:

> All I remember was ordering a number of the boys up the track and jumping off into a bayonet charge in the direction of the stone house. I remember feeling an utter ass because, realising the seriousness of the position with our lads packed like sardines, I shot off yelling to the boys to follow and after going about thirty yards and hearing no yelling, I stopped and looked back – I was on my own. But they followed and we cleaned up what turned out to be a patrol of about Platoon strength. Half the bods we speared and shot in the middle of the ridge, the other half, including the commander, in the vineyard.

Lieutenant Colonel Dittmer's intention was to outflank the enemy at Maleme and the Maoris fought their way forward on their left flank, until they reached the top of the ridge that ran south towards 21 NZ Battalion's position. Here they were halted by fire from Hill 107. The Official History commented, 'All the élan and gallantry of the Maoris and their commander could not get them to the final objective', in spite of a series of local but spirited charges that were described in the following terms:

> The Maoris were going forward crying 'Ah! Ah!' and firing from the hip, the Huns with their fat behinds to us running for their lives down the gully and then our job to hold the Maoris in – the ancestral fighting urge was a truly magnificent thing.

Meanwhile, 21 NZ Battalion, who were to join the attack on the left flank could hear the noise of battle drawing closer and they 'made ready to do

191

its share'. Their task, at a time when it was assumed that the 20 and 28 Battalions would have completed their attacks, was to establish a line from Hill 107 to AMES Ridge, where the now abandoned ruins of the Wireless (radar) Station was located. The enemy in this sector was *II/GJR 100* who held the southern flank of the enemy position.

Headquarters Company, acting as riflemen, cleared a few snipers and secured these ruins and A Company then advanced along the road to Xamoudhokhori. 'The village was entered without much opposition and B Company went forward.' It was not, however, until they tried to advance beyond the village that enemy resistance hardened. The Battalion's history continued:

> *Heavy fire from the direction of Vlakheronitissa killed Captain McClymont and wounded several men before the others were forced to take cover. Lieutenant Yeoman posted Corporal McCabe and his Lewis machine-gun section in the tower of the village church and, though targets were difficult to pick up among the trees and grape vines, the enemy fire slackened considerably. Eventually a machine gun got onto McCabe's section and, when bursts of fire started coming through the open window and ricocheting off the stone walls of the empty room, they had to move.*

By 1030 hours, B Company's advance had come to a halt and A Company was ordered to outflank the opposition but the enemy had blocked all progress by about mid-day. Eventually, a runner arrived from Major Harding at Rear Headquarters in Kondomari, with a message from 23 Battalion, stating that the counter-attack had not gone well. This merely confirmed the existing situation of stalemate. However, this state of affairs did not last long, as the enemy's 'flanking patrols, snipers, and mortar fire had forced them [A and B Companies] into the village'. The *Gerbirgsjäger*, realising that the New Zealanders had withdrawn, followed at a discreet distance and sensing an advantage 'his fire increased'.

During a lull in the fighting, a *Gerbirgsjäger* approached carrying a white flag. He delivered a note to Colonel Allen who, after reading its contents, which demanded immediate surrender, 'screwed it up and threw it in the emissary's face. The gesture was sufficiently obvious, for the man retired quickly along the way he had come'.

The New Zealand counter-attack had failed. Thanks to a combination of the amphibious threat and delays in moving battalions, the attack had been late in starting, leaving only a few hours of darkness and cover from air attack. The presence of the remainder of 5 and 6 *Kompanies II/FJR 2* had not been a planning consideration and inflicted serious delay in the approach phase, which was ultimately fatal for the attack. A preliminary recce and clearance operation by 5 NZ Brigade would have paid a healthy dividend. On the other hand, 20 NZ Battalion reached the airfield and one is left with futher 'what if' questions.

Chapter Nine

THE BATTLE OF GALATAS

In the daylight hours of 22 May 1941, while the 5 NZ Brigade's soldiers were struggling to maintain their counter attack on the airfield, Ju 52s were landing at the rate of twenty per hour, delivering the remainder of *Oberst* Utz's *Gerbirgsjägerregiment 100 (GJR 100)* and *I Battalion GJR 85*. With a growing strength, the enemy's lodgement in Maleme was beginning to slip beyond the New Zealanders' capability to destroy. The tide of the battle for Crete had turned.

While the New Zealanders were falling back from Pyrgos to their original position, *Hauptmann* Gericke and his much reduced *Fallschirmjäger* followed and occupied the ground. On the inland flank, reinforced by the newly arrived *Gerbirgsjäger*, *Oberst* Utz was able to exert mounting pressure on 21 NZ Battalion. Later in the day the *Gerbirgsjäger's* Pioneer Battalion 95 took responsibility for defence of the airfield, on arrival, releasing the *Luftlandeslurmregiment (LLSR)* to be reconstituted into *Kampfgruppe Ramcke*. This was the situation at the time *Generalmajor* Julius Ringel and his headquarters *5th Gerbirgsjägerdivision* took command of the battle.

Back in Athens, with Hitler and Göring furious at the delay in the redeployment of von Richthofen's *VIII Fliegerkorps* to its BARBAROSSA positions, rivalry came into play. With Student suddenly out of favour, he was to be excluded from further operational control, although for reasons of morale, he was to remain 'in command' of his *Fliegerkorps*. Consequently, Ringel was ordered to fly to Crete to take command and Student was instructed to remain in Greece. *General der Flieger* Lohr *(HQ Luftflotte IV)* and his staff were to take a more active role in supervising the campaign's conduct.

The German Advance and the Withdrawal of 5 NZ Brigade
With the airbridge from the Greek mainland to Maleme now well established and, with a growing strength, Ringel set about implementing his orders from Lohr; linking with the other airborne lodgements and clearing the island from west to east. The advance would be on two fronts. *Kampfgruppe Ramcke* would advance towards Hania using the Coastal Road, while Utz's mountain troops would strike towards Galatas and link up with *Fallschirmjägerregiment 3 (FJR 3)*, via the foothills of the mountains to the south. Meanwhile, *FJR 3* was to attack north from Prison Valley, between 5 and 10 NZ Brigades and cut the Coast Road near Agh Marina.

General Julius Ringel.

These moves were aimed at of outflanking 5 NZ Brigade and of course, mitigated against another attempted counter-attack, would have sucked additional Commonwealth troops into the encirclement.

On 23 May, as the Germans resumed their advance, Brigadier Hargest's command was already withdrawing in small groups to reduce the effect of enemy air supremacy. The commanding officers 'All were of the opinion that we could hold the position' but the progress of *Oberst* Utz's flanking move confirmed that holding was not actually a viable option. The Brigade would fall back to positions adjacent to 10 NZ Brigade in the area of Agh Marina and be in position by late morning.

Lieutenant Farran was again mobile in his Light Tank, the REME fitters having carried out front line repairs. He wrote:

I received orders to proceed back up the road towards Maleme to cover the withdrawal of the New Zealanders ... I took up my position in a garden half-way between Platanias and Maleme. I had been told to fall back on the Platanias position ... but when the time came to go back, there was still one company of Maoris to return. I could see long lines of grey figures advancing towards me across the fields and I knew them to be Germans. An anti-tank rifle began to snipe at my turret, but he was not much of a shot. There were bullets whistling about everywhere. And then the last Maoris came along with the Germans hard on their heels, but not a shadow of fear showed on their smiling, copper faces. As they passed my tank, they winked and put up their thumbs. Some fifty yards behind the rest came two Maoris carrying a pot of stew across a rifle. There is something so engaging about this cheerful race that it is no wonder that there is no colour bar in New Zealand.

28 Maori Battalion withdrew to their old positions around Platanias. D Company was, however, ordered to counter-attack their former trenches around the bridge, a mile in front of the village. Captain Baker led his men forward to see off the *Fallschirmjäger* who could be seen bringing up mortars in captured RAF trucks. Even though they tried to move discreetly they were seen at about 800 yards from the bridge and were deluged with mortar and machine gun fire. Captain Garriock wrote 'We were not there long before Jerry turned all his fury loose at us. MG and Mortar fire was terrific, I think it was the hottest hour I had during the war'. However, small groups of determined Maoris avoided the enemy's fire:

Lieutenant Markham with one party, by taking advantage of the bamboo clumps skirting the road, got to within 100 yards of the bridge and Lieutenant Maxwell, with another, reached the river bed. They captured a Bofors gun and put another out of action, but casualties, shortage of ammunition, and the sight of more enemy approaching with more guns necessitated a speedy withdrawal.

Also taking part in the withdrawal was the sixty strong Divisional Field Punishment Centre, made up of staff and soldiers serving 'a few days' detention'. They had fought very well during the first day of the battle under command of 22 Battalion. Now they too were withdrawing westward in small groups. Private Follas's group were reluctant to abandon their large collection of enemy weapons and 'found' a donkey, 'loaded it with four *spandaus*, carried the ammunition themselves and, after taking part in a brisk skirmish yielding twenty prisoners, met 22 NZ Battalion in their new position'. Follas recalls seeing Colonel Andrews, looking approvingly at the donkey, the *spandaus*, and the ammunition and asking 'What have you been pinching this time?'

Sergeant Alfred Hulme VC.

During this period Sergeant Alfred Hulme, Provo Sergeant of 23 NZ Battalion and staff member of the Field Punishment Centre was also active against the enemy, in actions that contributed to him being awarded the VC.

Hulme returned to the 23rd the day before the unit left its area near Maleme. By this time he had acquired two items from parachutists he had shot which gave him some protection on his stalking patrols and may possibly have misled the Germans. These were a camouflage suit or blouse which he wore over his battle-dress tunic and a camouflage hat, which could be worn either rolled up like a balaclava or down in a hood, with eye-slits, over the face. He killed two other Germans before the order to withdraw came. On a visit to Brigade Headquarters, he ran into a small party of New Zealand engineers held prisoner by one German sentry. Afraid to shoot for fear of hitting a New Zealander, Hulme crept up behind the sentry, jumped on him and killed him with a short German bayonet. Directed to find out how many Germans were in Pirgos, Hulme ran into two unguarded aircraft which he set on fire with German fusee *matches.*

Stalos

After 'quiet' days in Prison Valley on 21-22 May, the part to be played by *Oberst* Heidrich in the German plan to envelope 5 NZ Brigade was the dispatch north of a force from *FJR 3*, who would advance into the void between the two New Zealand Brigades. In the event Brigadier Hargest's Brigade had already started to move back and Colonel Kippenberger, active as ever, did his best to strike into the flank of the *Fallschirmjäger* with his temporary infantrymen. The result was a sharp encounter in the village of Stalos.

One hundred and fifty men of *Kampfgruppe Heilmann*, the remains of *III Battalion*, were on the move north from Prison Valley and occupied Stalos shortly after dawn. Meanwhile, Kippenberger ordered the 'Infantillery' of the Composite Battalion to advance westward by a thousand yards to narrow the gap between the two brigades. This move was preceded by patrols that were told by civilians that Stalos was occupied by the enemy, which proved to be *Fallschirmjäger* pioneers who had taken over from Heilmann's men, as the Kampfgruppe continued north. The historian of the New Zealand artillery wrote:

> *Two strong patrols, one from the RMT [NZ Army Service Corps] and one from the 4th Field [artillery], went forward to snipe and observe. One of these sent a detachment forward towards Stalos and it engaged in a skirmish which lasted for an hour, caused the enemy the loss of 14 men and two machine guns (at a cost of one RMT man wounded), and ended only when a company of 18 Battalion arrived to take over. A platoon of this company attacked and brilliantly captured the village, driving out or killing the strong enemy force. While this action was going on the Composite Battalion formed a forward line of standing patrols to guard against further infiltration in this area.*

Major Evans, of B Company 18 NZ Battalion decided to attack Stalos with a single well supported platoon. 'He set up the 3-inch mortar, which the company brought and selected 11 Platoon to make the attack.' By about 1100 hours, the platoon was forming up and, after a short mortar

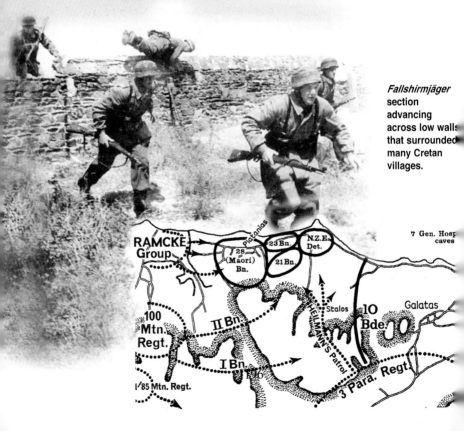

Fallshirmjäger section advancing across low walls that surrounded many Cretan villages.

A tripod mounted MG 34 covers the advance of *GJR 100*.

bombardment, it attacked, one section going south of the village, one north of it, and the other into the village itself. The divisional history records:

> The attack went very well and the enemy was driven out of the village, leaving behind at least five dead and two machine guns. One house, however, kept on holding out with a machine-gun post. As the platoon was about to deal with this one also, an order came forward from Major Evans for the platoon to withdraw; for Evans had by now come to the conclusion that the enemy in the area was about 200 strong and so too much for his force. The platoon therefore reluctantly let go its grip and fell back to its original positions.

Major Evans may well have overestimated the enemy in the Stalos area but the *Fallschirmjäger* pioneers 'make much of the fighting it had that day, so 11 Platoon must have given the enemy a sharp shock with its spirited assault'. The effect of this lesson and the closing of the gap between the two brigades meant that the German encircling operation failed.

However, the threat remained and, at 1700 hours, detailed orders arrived at Brigadier Hargest's HQ for a further withdrawal of 5 NZ Brigade, this time through both 10 and 4 Brigades into reserve in the east of the Divisional area. The withdrawal of the 800 men still on their feet began with evacuation of as many of the wounded as possible at 2100 hours; with the fighting units leapfrogging back an hour later.

> We withdrew under orders soon after midnight, carrying our wounded on improvised stretchers down the steep cliff face and then along a difficult clay creek bed to the road. Then we marched until nearly dawn. I was very impressed by the continued discipline of the men. Mile after mile we trudged. Everyone was tired. All were vaguely resentful, although none of us could have put a finger on the reason. Those who could bear the strain better carried the rifles and Bren guns of those who were fatigued. Len

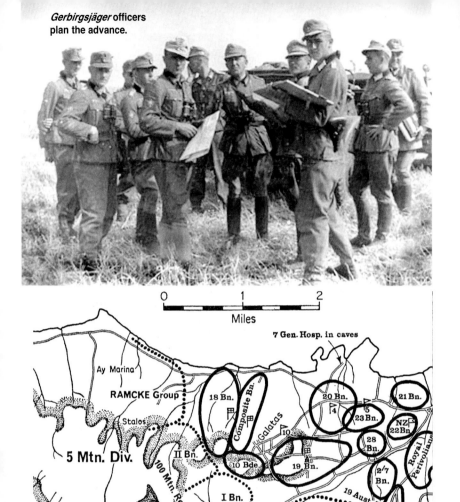

Gerbirgsjäger officers plan the advance.

Diamond, a rough and lovable West Coast miner with a difficult stammer, raised a smile whenever things seemed a bit much.

It is interesting to note that the Field Punishment Centre, whose staff and inmates had performed so well in battle, 'dissolved itself' during the withdrawal, as:

> *The sight of their own units in the withdrawal had been too tempting for the men. They had one by one slipped away and, back with their own*

battalions, they could be sure of a welcome and not too many questions.

In recognition of their stout service in Crete, the bad lads were formerly pardoned after the campaign.

Advance through the Hills

Oberst Utz's ten mile advance through the inland hills had begun on the evening of 22 May and by the following morning his men were beginning to make their presence felt. While two battalions of *Gerbirgsjäger Regiment 100* were advancing across the hills, *I/GJR 85* were heading further inland.

With only their motorcycles, mules and half-track motorcycles to transport heavy weapons, equipment and ammunition reserves, the rugged *Gerbirgsjäger* were in their element, although the heat of a Mediterranean spring was testing. *Gefreiter* Karl Meyer wrote:

> *The first night in Crete we dug [trenches] on Hill 107, fought all day and now on the second night we march. In the morning, I was more tired than I had ever been and hot – so hot - in full battle equipment and load. The hills were dry, there was no water and the advance march became slow. A few comrades left the column as we climbed the hills in the unaccustomed heat. The mortar* Kompanie, *whose vehicles we normally envied, were worse than we were.*

With the eventual arrival of *II/GJR 100* south of Stalos, in the afternoon of day four of the operation, the reinforced *Gruppe West* had finally linked up with *Gruppe Mitte* in Prison Valley. However, before Ringel could mount a proper attack on the Galatas Heights he had to build up his combat power, particularly in respect of artillery and other support weapons.

With Maleme now securely in German hands and now out of range of Commonwealth artillery, General Ringel could count on more speedy reinforcement and plan the capture of Souda Bay, his next objective. Encouraged by the New Zealanders' sensitivity to moves on their southern flank and 5 NZ Brigade's withdrawal, *GJR 85* were tasked to take a wide sweep through the foothills aimed at Souda Bay. *Kampfgruppe Ramcke* would continue to exert pressure on the coastal plain, *GJR 100* would assault the Galatas Heights from the west and the much reduced *FJR 3* would push east up Prison Valley towards Hania to the south of the Hania–Aghya Road.

Brigadier Puttick also made a few changes of disposition on the Galatas Heights. 18 NZ Battalion took over responsibility from the 'Infantillery', who in a static role under constant fire from ground and air had become 'dispirited' and were moved to supporting positions near the Divisional Petrol Company. The Divisional Cavalry remained west of Pink Hill. Even though 10 Brigade was now subsumed into 4 NZ Brigade, Colonel Kippenberger remained in command of the Galatas sector under Brigadier Inglis.

A *Gerbirgsjäger* photographed on the Galastas Heights looking north to the coastal plain, illustrating the key nature of this ground.

The final move of the 23rd to consider was the reinforcement of 19 Australian Brigade which was deployed by Major General Weston, under MNBDO command to block Prison Valley. Brigadier Vasey received his fellow countrymen of 2/7th Battalion who with 2 Greek Regiment formed a line through the hills south-east from the Hania–Aghya Road.

The Attack on Galatas

The renewed German attack on Galatas began on 24 May, as enemy artillery and reinforcements poured into Maleme and moved up to face the new Commonwealth defensive positions. The *Luftwaffe*, some of whose fighters were now operating from Maleme, had focused its attention over the previous day on Souda Bay, were now softening up the New Zealand positions on the Galatas Heights. Throughout the morning, across the hills and into the valleys the number of German troops steadily increased, filling the vacuum left by the withdrawal of 5 NZ Brigade during the night.

18 NZ Battalion, on whom the brunt of the defensive battle would fall, were in an unenviable position. They held a long frontage (2,500 yards) and Ruin Hill, which had steadfastly been held by the Composite Battalion, was no longer occupied and, consequently, Red Hill could be completely and Wheat Hill partly overlooked. As already recorded, the trenches and

See map
page 202

weapon pits were in a poor state and there was little effective protection in the form of mines or wire. 18 NZ Battalions historian wrote: 'The position had to be accepted for what it was, although there was some resiting of section posts during the morning. 'The Petrol Company was still on the slopes of Pink Hill, as already recorded, supported by a platoon of 'infantillery'.' The official history records that 'Morning on the Brigade front was one of great tension and feverish preparation for what was expected to be a formidable onslaught and one that would come soon'.

However, to the surprise of the New Zealanders and the annoyance of General Student, nothing in the way of a 'formidable onslaught' materialised on 24 May. *5th Gerbirgsdivision* described its actions of the morning and early afternoon as 'a reconnaissance in force' but these operations saw *I/GJR 100* occupying Ruin Hill, bringing fire down on 18 NZ Battalion and mounting probing attacks, which led to minor withdrawals and counter-attacks. Meanwhile, 19 NZ Battalion was unsuccessfully attacked by *FJR 3* whose advance towards Hania failed.

The battle for Galatas proper began the following day and the course of the day's fighting, despite Student's criticism, supports Ringel's assessment that he lacked sufficient combat power on the 24th to take the Galatas Heights. The attack was to be delivered by the two battalions of *GJR 100*, now enjoying the full range of fire support normally to be expected from a division. The remains of *FJR 3* were to fix 19 Australian Brigade in its position by maintaining pressure on Brigadier Vasey's units deployed in blocking positions across Prison Valley. *GJR 85* was at last beginning to make progress through the hills to the south. A *kampfgruppe* of two motorised units, *Recce 95 and 95 Anti-Tank Battalions*, were to form a reserve for exploitation of success. General Student was finally released

Oberst Ramcke greets *General* Student on arrival in his HQ.

from Athens and arrived at Ringel's HQ that morning (25th May). One commentator wrote, 'The attack was not likely to lack élan with him to spur it on'.

Ringel's subsequent objective remained Souda Bay and the road to Rethymno, avoiding becoming embroiled in Hania.

The assault was to be preceded by air attacks at 0800, 1230 and 1315 hours, 'with all the aircraft the sky could find room for'. Zero-Hour for the attack on Galatas was at the relatively late hour of 1320 in order to ensure that all the artillery resources would be concentrated. An indication of the level of artillery support that the Germans could now call upon is given by Captain Sinclair, who reckoned that 'shells and mortar bombs were bursting at a rate of perhaps twenty a minute'. Added to this, fire from captured Bofors and from *Spandaus* 'the storm of sound' made it difficult for officers to exercise any control.

Pressure mounted as the *Gerbirgsjäger* advanced and a growing stream of New Zealand casualties were making their way to the rear. 18 NZ Battalion, with its extended front was being pushed back by Ramcke and *II GJR 100* but Russell Force made up of the 'Infantillery', the Petrol Company and the Divisional Cavalry in the Pink Hill area were holding firm, despite 'the usual stiff thrust against them'. Local counter-attacks resulted in hand to hand fighting. One such attack was mounted by the CO of 18Nz Battalion on the right flank, against *Kampfgruppe Ramcke,* which Corporal Bishop describes, as viewed from his position behind D Company on the battalion's right flank:

> Some D Company posts at the seaward end of the line had just been overrun and had surrendered when Colonel Gray hove in sight armed with rifle and bayonet and leading perhaps 20 men and yelling to Don Company 'No surrender. No surrender.' Sergeant Scott asked if we were to join in but was told to wait for the second wave. However, he took half a dozen men with him and left almost immediately, the rest of us following. We had just got to the top of the ridge when we met the CO coming back, Sgt Scott and others having been killed.

The official history commented that 'The gallant and hopeless counter-attack had failed. Its members were few and motley, the enemy numerous and better armed. All it may have done was to hold the enemy back a little longer'. Only eleven men of D Company, under the quartermaster-sergeant, got away. Meanwhile, Captain Bassett had come forward from Colonel Kippenberger's HQ:

> …flights of dive-bombers made the ground a continuous earthquake and Dorniers swarmed over with guns blazing incessantly. It was like a nightmare race dodging falling branches, and …and got on their ridge, only to find myself in a hive of grey-green figures so beat a hasty retreat until I reached Gray's HQ just as he was pulling out. I had to admire the precise

way he was handling the withdrawal — he greeted me with 'Thank God Bassett, my right flank's gone, can you give us a vigorous counter attack at once', and I promised to put in the two 20th Companies and he insisted on my taking a signaller with me in case I got hit ... My way led through the town, and I found all our sectors undergoing the same massed attack.

Colonel Kippenberger, still acting as forward commander of 4 NZ Brigade, supplied the promised two companies of 20 NZ Battalion. Meanwhile, Colonel Gray 'charged madly round gathering up odd groups of stragglers, and in a little while the line was intact again'. It was, however, a patchwork line, but for the time being 'fairly solid' between Galatas and the sea.

Wheat Hill was now a key to the defence of the Galatas Heights. Its loss would threaten the flank of Russell Force on 18 Battalion's left and 'would leave a hole for Jerry to push through to Galatas and smash the whole New Zealand line'. The battalion's history goes on to comment that 'So for A Company it was – hang on, cling to the hill at all costs'.

A Company was, however, being steadily reduced in strength by constant enemy bombardment, and the *Gerbirgsjäger* were closing in and would soon 'beyond a doubt overrun the position'. Rather than be destroyed, the company fell back through Galatas, with the enemy following close behind. The Galatas Line was broken!

The *Gerbirgsjäger* swarmed forward from Wheat Hill through the gap in the line, pursuing A Company right to the outskirts of Galatas. Battalion HQ, C and B Companies on Murray Hill hit a great number before they too were forced back to avoid envelopment. Other *Gerbirgsjäger* set up machine guns to the right of the gap and poured fire into the flank of Russell Force.

Helped by enfilade fire from Divisional Cavalry, the Petrol Company held up *I/GJR 100's* attack on Pink Hill. The Divisional Cavalry also came under heavy machine gun fire, and as the battle developed Major Russell had considerable difficulty in maintaining communication with his force, as telephone lines were cut, and he had to resort to runners. Soon the elements of Russell Force were fighting independently in an information vacuum.

The Last Stand of the Petrol Company

Russell Force was by mid-afternoon 'in a most perilous position', not helped by the lack of information on what was happening on their right. Captain Rowe wrote:

I had no indication that there was going to be a withdrawal, but as the afternoon progressed, more and heavier fire came from our right flank and on several occasions I tried to contact 18th Battalion and at one stage sent a Sgt and runner to definitely find out what had happened. Late in the afternoon I received a call from Major Russell to say that he was hard

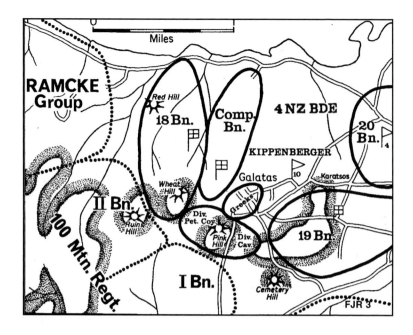

pressed and must withdraw but would try and hold out until we came through. He said that the 18th Battalion had been withdrawn some hours before. This was my first definite advice of a withdrawal on this flank.

A little later the Divisional Cavalry retired towards Daratsos. This left the Petrol Company and the 'infantillery' platoon, undefeated by direct attack in an extremely dangerous position. Captain Rowe ordered the Company to retire in extended line, using the left flank on Pink Hill as a pivot in order to form a fresh line in front of Galatas facing Wheat Hill. 'Rowe hoped in this way to contact troops who had been between Galatas and Ruin Hill in the morning. Those troops [of 18 NZ Battalion], however, had also been withdrawn...'

Private Sparks, when a lean and spry eighty-seven-year-old, described to the author how he had been on the outer edge of the wheel:

I was running hard from tree to tree, weighed down by the platoon's only Bren gun, stopping to fire a short burst to keep the enemy back. Going back through the trees on the reverse slope, I was struggling to keep up as I had furthest to run but eventually we came to this road.

The Petrol Company wheeled their right flank back in good order, in a manoeuvre that in the face of the enemy, would have tested the most skilled infantry. The NZ Army Service Corps' soldiers deserve the highest of praise. Pointing out the place where he had taken up a fire position, Ray Sparks continued:

I had five mags [magazines – usually filled with twenty eight rather than thirty rounds each to prevent stoppages] left and coming up the hill on the road were more Germans than I had ever seen before or since. I let them have it with long bursts. They scattered, running for cover in the scrub on either side, leaving the road covered with crumpled green heaps, some of whom screamed for help and their mothers. No one tried to help them. I fired away steadily at any of sign of movement up the hill towards me, until I was on my last mag. It was at that point we were ordered back. If we had more ammunition we could have held the bastards. At close range their bombers couldn't get us.

To this day Sparks knows that he and the Petrol Company were not defeated and proudly, and justly, tells how the Service Corps took on everything the Germans could throw at them.

The Fall of Galatas

The Petrol Company was ordered to fall back through Galatas with the aim of linking up with 19 Battalion behind the village. This was extremely hazardous, as the remnants were exposed to enemy fire as they stood up. CSM James says:

Passing through the southern outskirts we discovered the Div Cav was being fiercely attacked and we carried out some of their wounded. Pet Coy had very heavy casualties. These seemed to come from box barrages laid by mortars sited on Ruin Hill, which overlooked the whole area.

Galatas was a hell of exploding shells, burning buildings and falling masonry.

While the Galatas front was failing, to the north of the village, Colonel Gray was struggling to stabilise a line with the remnants of his battalion, the Composite Battalion and the 20th's reserve companies. The situation was, however, becoming desperate and Brigadier Hargest's very last and unlikely reserves were sent forward, including:

... such reinforcing parties as could be scraped together from his own Brigade HQ. He at once set to work having these latter organised, and as a result an officer and 14 men from J Section Signals were hastily sent forward, the Brigade Band, the pioneer platoon of 20 Battalion, and the Kiwi Concert Party. All these were promptly put into an improvised line along the stone walls north of Galatas...

Around the village, where the situation was at its worst, Colonel Kippenberger was trying to stem the dangerous tide of withdrawal. He recorded:

Suddenly the trickle of stragglers turned to a stream, many of them on the verge of panic. I walked in among them shouting 'Stand for New Zealand!' and everything else I could think of. The RSM of the Eighteenth, Andrews, came up and asked how he could help. With him and Johnny Sullivan, the intelligence sergeant of the Twentieth, we quickly got them organised under the nearest officers or NCOs, in most cases the men responding with alacrity. I ordered them back across the next valley to line the ridge west of Daratsos where a white church gleamed in the evening sun. There they would cover the right of the Nineteenth and have time and space to get their second wind. Andrews came to me and said quietly that he was afraid he could not do any more. I asked why, and he pulled up his shirt and showed a neat bullet hole in his stomach. I gave him a cigarette and expected never to see him again, but did, three years later, in Italy. A completely empty stomach had saved him.

Amongst others, the Australian gunners of C Troop 2/3 Field Regiment RAA, with their four 75mm guns, on the outskirts of Galatas did a great deal to stabilise the situation. Each gun fired at point-blank range, under its own commander's orders. Major Bull wrote:

When I got to C Troop, stragglers were starting to come through them and from the ridge you could see Germans on the outskirts of Galatas. The only thing to do was to protect ourselves so we hauled the guns up to the ridge. It wasn't very difficult to persuade the stragglers to lie down along the ridge to form a sort of firing line on each side of the guns. It was all very primitive but it seemed the only thing to do. There was a little potting but no one in the position got hit. Our gun fire was gloriously accurate using the open sights and [individual] gun control, and very soon all Jerries hastened out of sight.

The Galatas Counter-Attack

Still struggling to establish a line east of Galatas, Colonel Kippenberger in his roadside HQ received word that 23 NZ Battalion were on their way to help but as the 23rd advanced towards Galatas, Colonel Leckie was wounded by machine gun fire and Major Thomason took over command. Already arrived with Kippenberger were Lieutenant Farran and his two remaining Light Tanks. He volunteered or was sent (the Farran and Kippenberger accounts differ on this detail) into Galatas on a recce and it was soon apparent that the village was filled with Germans. Farran wrote:

They were in all the cottage windows, in the orchard, behind chimney stacks and in the schoolyard. I, the leading tank, sprayed one side of the street, while my corporal sprayed the other. When we reached the far side of the village, we turned round and came back in the same fashion. An anti-tank rifle pierced the turret of my corporal's tank, wounding both the commander and the gunner, but it did not put the tank out of action.

On his return, Farran reported to Colonel Kippenberger that 'The place is stiff with Jerries' and requested for two men, who understood Vickers guns, to replace the two wounded turret crew. He recalled that 'About three hundred volunteered'.

Lieutenant Roy Farran.

The Colonel described the troops of 23 NZ Bn assembling who were to deliver the attack:

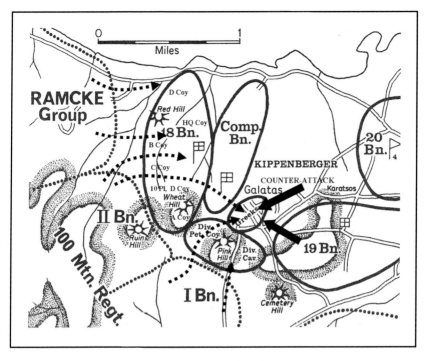

The men looked tired, but fit to fight and resolute. It was no use trying to patch the line any more; obviously we must hit or everything would crumble away. I told the two company commanders they would have to retake Galatas with the help of the two tanks. No, there was no time for reconnaissance; they must move straight in up the road, one company either side in single file behind the tanks, and take everything with them. Stragglers and walking wounded were still streaming past. Some stopped to join in as did Carson and the last four of his party. The men fixed bayonets and waited grimly.

In almost full darkness, with 23 NZ Battalion ready, the scene was now set for one of the extraordinary feats of arms in the history of the Commonwealth.

On the right, C Company was to attack along the road; on the left, D Company was to follow a route parallel to the road, and another platoon was to come in from the left flank.

The 150 men of the 23rd were joined by detachments from 18 and 20 NZ Battalions, in additions to stragglers from various other units. All were hastily briefed, 'bayonets were fixed and all were ready'. But what was it like waiting for that order? Platoon commander Lieutenant Sandy Thomas provides an insight:

Everyone looked tense and grim and I wondered if they were feeling as afraid as I, whether their throats were as dry, their stomachs feeling now frozen, now fluid. I hoped ... that I appeared as cool as they. It occurred to me suddenly that this was going to be the biggest moment of my life.

The Battalion's history records:

> About 8.10 p.m. Colonel Kippenberger gave the word to the tanks to lead the way and the attack was on. This time the 23rd was not withdrawing, as had been too often the case, but was going forward to attack the enemy. The onset of darkness meant an end to Stuka raids ... Their spirits rose! As the tanks moved off, the infantry gave a cheer and the cheer changed quickly to a deep shout of defiance and determination.

Lieutenant Thomas recalled:

> ... suddenly ... I found myself shouting to my men and we were away ... And then it happened. I don't know who started it, but, as the tanks disappeared as a cloud of dust and smoke into the first buildings of the village, the whole line seemed to break spontaneously into the most blood curdling of shouts and battle cries...the effect was terrific – one felt one's blood rising swiftly above fear and uncertainty until only an inexplicable exhilaration quite beyond description surpassed all else, and we moved as one man into the outskirts... By the time we entered the narrow streets, every man was firing his weapon to the front or in the air and every man, you could feel it, was flushed with confidence. Nothing could stop us.

Those who heard the counter-attack have left graphic accounts of its chilling sound. Colonel Gray, 18th NZ Battalion's CO, is quoted in the official history: 'I shall never forget the deep throated wild beast noise of the yelling charging men as the 23rd swept up the road. There was a hell of a battle in the village.' Private Adams of the 18th's 'I' section recorded

Lieutenant Farran's tank, finally knocked out in Galatas.

how he was too late to join in the attack but how, *'It was quite dark now and suddenly from Galatas 400 yards away we heard the most ungodly row I have ever heard – our chaps charging and yelling and screaming to put the wind up them, cat calls and battle cries, machine guns, rifles, hand grenades all going at once'.*

Private Ferry, a volunteer gunner in one of Lieutenant Farran's tanks, said: 'The howling and shouting of the infantry sounded like the baying of dogs … as it rose and fell, it made my flesh creep.'

Lieutenant Farran's tanks led the way and blazed away at 'the slightest sign of the enemy, who shot up flares, called for mortar fire'. Fortunately most of this fell behind the advancing Kiwis. The *Gerbirgsjäger* threw stick grenades and fired from the buildings. On the right, C Company cleared the first few houses one by one but, finding more Cretan civilians than enemy, they pressed into the centre of the village, not bothering to clear the houses.

A matter of a few hundred yards across the valley, 18 NZ Battalion could hear and understand what was happening. Captain Dawson, witnessed the reaction to Colonel Kippenberger's message and told them 'to join in'. 'I … found that amazingly virile warrior, John Gray, who no sooner grasped Kip's message than he fixed his own bayonet, and jumping out of the ditch cried "Come on 18th boys, into the village." And blow me if most of the line didn't surge out after him.' Gray led the few dozen survivors of his battalion into battle. Private James was amongst those who followed Colonel Gray across those few hundred yards:

Suddenly we were going forward; I followed at the run, joining in the mindless war cries. We were going forward across the valley and at last were going to give it rather than take it. I wasn't frightened, I was elated! And the climb up the slope to the village, where we could see the towers of the church silhouetted against flame and explosion, didn't cool our determination.

Falling on the enemy, who we hit in the flank in the main square, we gave vent to all the frustrations of the last days. On guard! Thrust with the

37 mm anti-tank gun was more than a match for the thin armour of the Light Tanks.

bayonet. Take the Jerry down. Stamp on the body, twist the rifle, pull the bayonet out and on guard again. Parry a German Krupp steel blade and up with the butt below his chin. The enemy run and we follow them through the streets crazed and still elated, still killing.

Meanwhile, Lieutenant Farran was in front of the charge up the 'High Street':

> *... there was a blinding flash inside the tank and my gunner sank groaning to the bottom of the turret ... I felt a sort of burn in my thigh and thought it probable that I also had been wounded. I told the driver to turn round, but as we swung broadside to the enemy we were hit again. My driver was wounded in the shoulder and in consequence pulled the tiller too hard, putting us into the ditch. We sat there, crouched in the bottom of the turret, while an anti-tank gun carved big chunks out of the top. ... Stannard, my gunner, was in a bad way, having stopped one in the stomach. I pushed them both out through the driver's hatch and crawled out myself. I pulled myself along on my elbows until I was under cover of a low stone wall. There I lay in the infernal din ... praying for the New Zealanders to arrive.*
>
> *They came up the main street in a rush, but were met by a hail of machine-gun bullets on the corner. Several went down in a heap, including the platoon commander [Thomas]. I shouted, 'Come on, New Zealand! Clean 'em out, New Zealand!'*

The other tank withdrew but was turned back by Lieutenant Thomas and returned to the village as the New Zealanders surged forward. 'Streams of tracer bullets came from the windows and from behind low stone walls. They were ill-aimed but caused casualties nonetheless.' Against the surging tide of New Zealanders, many yelling school or club hakas to add

Galatas is a traditional village little changed from the time it became a bloody battlefield.

Galatas the following morning. The remains of Farran's knocked out tank can be seen at the end of the road.

to the bedlam, the Germans fell back. Lieutenant Thomas described the scene in the Square where his platoon joined Colonel Gray's men.

The boys rose as one man, we jostled each other for the lead, and firing from the hip we advanced across the square. The consternation at the far side was immediately apparent. Screams and shouts showed desperate panic in front of us and I suddenly knew, with that peculiarly clear insight which sometimes comes in battle, that we had caught them ill prepared and in the act of forming up...By now we were stepping over groaning forms, and those which rose against us fell to our bayonets, and bayonets with their eighteen inches of steel entered throats and chests with the same horrible sound, the same hesitant ease as when we had used them on the straw-packed dummies in Burnham. The Hun seemed in full flight. From doors, windows and roofs they swarmed wildly, falling over one another to clear our relentless line. There was little aimed fire against us now.

The hunt went on through the streets, leaving behind the wounded. Amongst them were Lieutenant Farran, his tank crew and Lieutenant Sandy Thomas who had been hit while in the area of the square. Farran continued:

The platoon commander [Thomas] was also shouting to rally them from his position in the middle of the street. I shouted across to him to ask where he had been hit and he said that he was wounded in both legs. And then someone shouted that the enemy were on the roof. I saw the Platoon Commander lift himself up on his elbows and take careful aim with his pistol. The German machine-gunner came tumbling down the slates on to the street below. It was an astonishing shot in such light and at such a range.

The New Zealanders were going in again now at the point of the bayonet and I heard a German scream like a small child in pain. Another New Zealander came up and put one foot on me as he took aim from behind the wall. I protested and he apologised: 'Sorry, joker, thought you was a corpse!'

Both officers were subsequently evacuated but Lieutenant Farran was taken prisoner while in the field hospital.

With few surviving officers and NCOs to control the charge the soldiers lost direction in the houses and streets and the Germans were able to halt the advance and without the tanks the New Zealanders were unable to overcome the stiffening resistance. Now was the time to reorganise to hold the village against the inevitable counter-attack but such had been the ferocity of the New Zealand assault that the *Gerbirgsjäger* did not counter-attack. Colonel Kippenberger, the architect of the sudden attack on the Germans in Galatas, at the moment when it seemed that the destruction of the New Zealand Division was already assured, sent off a report to Brigadier Inglis.

Despite the success in checking the Germans at Galatas, Brigadier

211

An Italian 75mm gun.

Puttick had already decided that the situation required a shortening of the line by a further withdrawal to the east, in order to bring the remains of his division into line with 19 Australian Brigade. While orders were being promulgated for the withdrawal, Brigadier Inglis with a senior representative from Puttick's HQ had to decide whether or not to counter-attack in the coastal area. The situation boiled down to the fact that if a battalion counter-attack was not launched, Crete would be lost but in committing the Maori Battalion to an uncertain operation, the last reasonably complete battalion would not be available to help form a line to prevent imminent defeat. This Catch 22 decision resulted in the mooted counter-attack being shelved in favour of a withdrawal that would give a better chance of survival for the New Zealand Division. The die was cast.

Chapter Ten

SOUDA BAY AND 42ND STREET

Over the night of 25/26 May 1941 the New Zealand Division fell back from the Galatas Line to one that ran from the sea in the area of the 7 General Hospital to the northern flank of 19 Australian Brigade in Prison Valley. It was another exhausting night for the Kiwis.

Overnight, Brigadier Puttick sent General Freyberg a message 'Am exceedingly doubtful on present reports, whether I can hold the enemy tomorrow' and a liaison officer with the Greeks 'made it clear that the Greeks were about to break'. The situation, despite the success at Galatas, was still near crisis point and during the 26th fundamental decisions would have to be made. Having delayed sending a signal to Wavell regarding the implication of the latest turn of events, finally at 0930 hours Freyberg signed the message pad and handed it to a clerk:

> *I regret to have to report that in my opinion the limit of endurance has been reached by the troops under my command here at Souda Bay. No matter what decision is taken by the Commanders-in-Chief from a military point of view our position here is hopeless. A small ill-equipped and immobile force such as ours cannot stand up against the concentrated bombing that we have been faced with during the last seven days. I feel that I should tell you that from an administrative point of view the difficulties of extricating this force in full are now insuperable. Provided a decision is reached at once a certain proportion of the force*

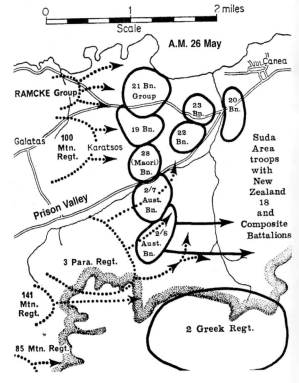

213

← North

4 NZ BRIGADE   2/7TH BATTALION   2/8

Perevolia   Hania   Akrotiri Peninsular

View looking east towards 19 Australian Brigade's positions south of the Hania – Aghia road.

might be embarked…The troops we have with the exception of the Welch Regiment and the Commando are past any offensive action. If you decide in view of whole Middle East position that hours help we will carry on. I would have to consider how this would be best achieved. Souda Bay may be under fire within twenty-four hours…

There was to be no 'immediate decision' and Freyberg would have to wait a full twenty-four hours before he received an answer.

Meanwhile, as Brigadier Puttick's men were enduring another night of marching and digging, *Generalmajor* Ringel was ordering a resumption of the attack of the previous day. *Kampfgruppe Ramcke* was to continue along the Coast Road and *Gerbirgsjägerregiment 100 (GJR 100)* to resume its advance eastwards through Galatas and Daratos. Starting from below Galatas, Heidrich's *FJR 3* would continue up Prison Valley, while in the foothills to the south, *GJR 85*, now with all three of its battalions and *I/GJR 141* (from *6th Gerbirgsdivision*) were to push east to cut off the Commonwealth troops. The advance of *GJR 85* was cautious following an early morning *Luftwaffe* fratricide bombing incident in the hills south of Galatas.

With command of the air the Germans could rove at will over the Allied positions.

By dawn the Commonwealth troops were more or less where they should have been and defensive schemes were being tied up. The fact that the Germans were feeling their way forward, assisted by recce aircraft, to locate the New Zealanders amongst the hills, gullies and trees, gave the defenders precious time. GJR

BATTALION

2 GREEKS

White
Mountains

100 did not report Daratos clear until 1030 hours. However, behind the Commonwealth front line, communications that had always been poor were breaking down, as the various headquarters relocated to positions further back and the enemy aircraft continued to attack any movement they could identify, including dispatch riders. The effect of this was that by the time information had been gathered, decisions made and orders reached those who were supposed to implement them, the situations had changed to the point that the new orders were often irrelevant. The resulting confusion, amongst staff officers and their commanders did much to erode the in resilience of mind and confidence that had been so remarkable amongst the front line troops.

Against this background and awaiting instructions from Wavell, General Freyberg insisted that the line be held despite the entreaties of his subordinate commanders that his men were reaching the end of their tether and that they would not hold the enemy for long. Men from the Composite Battalion, which had finally disintegrated after a highly creditable performance over the past days, were beginning, along with infantrymen who had lost their units during the withdrawal, to make their way to the rear. Men no longer required to operate the port had already been instructed to head across the mountains to Hora Safakion and in the atmosphere of rumour and uncertainty, word of this instruction spread like wildfire and the withdrawal to the south coast began way of its own volition.

Operations on 26 May 1941 – Overview
Closing up to the New Zealanders' line, the Germans directed dive bombers and increasing quantities of mortar fire against the defensive positions, particularly those on forward slopes, where due to the lack of tools and the rocky ground soldiers had little in the way of adequate

protective cover. Some, as indicated in the following typical 'sitrep' of the day, were forced to withdraw. Colonel Allen of 20 NZ Battalion wrote:

> Right flank has caused me considerable anxiety all day. Have had to counter-attack once and regained lost ground. Since then have reinforced once; and am standing by to reinforce again. If I have to do so I shall have used all my reserves, but at present line is holding. Left flank position alright but a good deal of mortar fire coming over. 19th Battalion have withdrawn Coy from ridge in front of me.

However, the battle was not entirely one-sided, as this entry in *5th Gerbirgsdivision's* War Diary indicated:

> The enemy is offering fierce resistance everywhere. He makes very skilful use of the country and every method of warfare. Mainly snipers, MG nests and positions partly wired and mined. Shellfire has so far only come from the western outskirts of Hania for the most part. Armed bands are fighting fiercely in the mountains, using great cunning and are cruelly mutilating dead and wounded. This inhumane method of making war is making our advance infinitely more difficult.

The continuous pressure by the Germans was held but in most places at a considerable cost to both sides.

The Attack on 19 Australian Brigade

Hitherto, Brigadier Vasey's two battalions had not seen much action, despite being brought forward by 1,000 yards the day before, but had endured the *Luftwaffe's* bombing and strafing by day and *Fallschirmjäger* patrols by night. Vasey was, however, confident that his line centred on the village of Galaria would hold that day and the next; but at 1700 hours, 'he was convinced that the situation on his left was critical'. During the day the far south of the line, held by 2 Greek Regiment, finally started to crumble. While organised defence may have ended, groups of Greeks fought on as guerrillas to the discomfort of the *Gerbirgsjäger* as indicated in their War Diary. The Australian official historian wrote:

> 2/7th and 2/8th Battalions, in reality just a battalion and a half strong in terms of manpower, had been brought over land from their original positions at Georgioupoli and with few tools and virtually no defence store they dug hasty defensive positions. These shell scrape defences only afforded the minimum protection from enemy fire and short of ammunition the Australians could not realistically be expected to hold for long.

From 1030 hours, the *Fallschirmjäger*, well supported by air and mortar bombardment, attacked. The threat to two Australian platoons on the left was such that they were withdrawn some distance towards Perivolia, and there held on.

Hauptmann von der Hydte's *I/FJR 3* was not in action until late afternoon:

I had ordered that two strong detachments of Fallschirmjäger *should be formed, the first, from No. 1 Company, to take Perivolia, and the second, from No. 2 Company, to attack Pyrgos. Both detachments fell in at 5 p.m., the first advancing down a densely overgrown trough-shaped valley, the second along the Cladiso. [in Prison Valley] I followed in the wake of the latter.*

The two detachments met initially with trifling resistance, and it appeared that the British [sic] had left only a weak rearguard. At the first contact with the enemy, however, an M.O. accompanying the second detachment was seriously wounded in the stomach. I came across him during the advance...He was fully conscious, and his voice, though weak, was quite clear. 'Go on, Herr Hauptmann,' he said. 'I am a doctor...My wound is fatal...I know...Let me die...I don't need anyone any more... .'

On the fringes of Pyrgos the shock-troops encountered barbed wire entanglements. Assuming that British positions could not be far away, they took cover and scanned the ground before them. But they could see nothing, and an absolute calm prevailed. Where could the British be? The leader of the detachment raised his steel helmet on a stick in the hope of drawing enemy fire. But still nothing happened.

Eventually our men crawled cautiously forward, expecting at any moment to come under fire. Wary of mines, they cut a path through the entanglements. Beyond the wire they found a deep trench, but it was empty, abandoned. Where could the British have gone?

Even in the village of Pyrgos itself they encountered no more than token resistance from a weak rearguard which retreated after a brief exchange of shots.

Hauptmann von der Hydte's battalion had pushed into a gap between 2/7 Battalion and the Greeks who were by now no longer in place and following pressure from the attacks earlier in the day, at almost exactly the time *I/FJR 3* were advancing, 2/8th Battalion was ordered to withdraw to its original positions outside Mournies. The 2/7th received similar orders. The Australian official history records that 'They withdrew about 5 p.m. and fitted in among the Marines [of the Souda Brigade] around Mournies'. That night they and most of the rest of the force were to join in another withdrawal.

Despite Freyberg's insistence that no mention be made of a withdrawal from Crete, by the end of the day, the retreat was becoming general. The official report commented:

... the units which had withdrawn from the front line had done so in some order, maintaining military formations which enabled them to fight further actions. But the rear units began to move without orders and without organisation. Units got inexorably mixed up, and it was never possible to sort them out again.

Destruction of Force Reserve

During the day with the New Zealand Division having been forced to withdraw again, this time onto the Mobile Naval Base Defence Organization (MNBDO), Major General Weston took command of what was to become the rearguard for the withdrawal. However, in an attempt to hold General Weston's new line, General Freyberg instructed Brigadier Inglis to take command of the Force Reserve, consisting of 1 Welch, The Rangers and the Northumberland Hussars. He was to take them forward to relieve the 5 NZ Brigade during the night 26/27 May. Colonel Kippenberger would replace him in command of 4 NZ Brigade.

Brigadier Hargest described the withdrawal of 5 NZ Brigade to between Hania and Souda:

> *All arrangements had been made and at about 10:30 we moved each* [battalion] *on its route with the Australians on our flanks to the south. The going was terribly hard, the roads had been torn up, vehicles burned across them, huge holes everywhere — walking was a nightmare. Our guide lost us with* [the] *result that we went through Hania itself, transformed from a pleasant little town to a smouldering dust heap with fires burning but otherwise dead.*

While the remainder of the force were withdrawing to what was reffered to as the 42nd Street position, through one of the increasing number of communication failures, at General Weston's insistence, Force Reserve were carrying out orders that were no longer relevant. They were moving forward, in the opposite direction to Weston's/Puttick's troops, and preparing positions covering the western outskirts of Hania. The Rangers and the Northumberland Hussars were under command of Lieutenant Colonel Duncan of 1 Welch.

The 1,300 strong Force Reserve had spent most of the previous week after clearance of the two *LLSR* companies from around Hania, awaiting

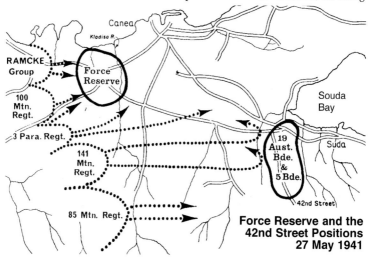

**Force Reserve and the
42nd Street Positions
27 May 1941**

the amphibious landing but even after that threat was disposed of they were given only low-level tasking. General Freyberg appears to have maintained them as a reserve for a reserve's sake, in the manner of the Great War. Their deployment on 21, 22 or even 25 May would have, arguably, had a significant impact on the situation.

The positions that the Force Reserve were to occupy were those the Welch had prepared four weeks earlier. Therefore, battle procedure was considerably shortened and they were, consequently, more effective in the very limited time available than if they had had to start from scratch. Even so, on a moonless night, it was a difficult procedure, with troops having to pick their way through bomb craters, wreckage and bodies of the dead, before reaching their position at 0230 hours.

Well before dawn on 27 May, patrols of *Gerbirgsjägerregiment 100 (GJR 100)* started to filter into the southern outskirts of Hania through the void left by the withdrawing Souda Brigade. A small detachment of Welch guarding the battalion's transport was amongst those who had sharp encounters among the trees at dawn. Sergeant Creighton wrote:

> One of the drivers asked me if he could go for a short walk to stretch his legs. He went, but did not return. Presently two little Greek boys came out of the wood, one of whom had been shot in the back by a German. We grabbed our rifles and moved stealthily into the wood. I hadn't got far when I saw a German officer about fifty yards from me. He was immaculately dressed, with beautifully polished helmet and boots. He wore no equipment but was holding an automatic pistol in his left hand. He waved the pistol and shouted in English, 'Come on boys'. I saw no other movement and I think he was bluffing. I shot him in the chest and he fell dead.

By dawn Colonel Duncan had heard nothing from General Weston since his deployment the evening before and 'Right from the start we had been trying to make contact with Weston's HQ by wireless but our operators never got them and consequently, no message of any sort reached us. Runners could not find their way through the infiltrating *Gerbirgsjäger* and the Battalion's Bren-carriers that could have got through had been redeployed days earlier'. With a lack of information, at dawn, Colonel Duncan sent patrols to probe up the Kladiso stream and who almost immediately encountered the enemy but they found no sign of friendly forces that they assumed to be on their left flank. Worse was to follow, sounds of battle could clearly be heard behind their position; 'soon proclaiming beyond all doubt that the enemy had penetrated far to the

A member of *Kampfgruppe Ramcke* observes the withdrawal of Force Reserve.

rear'. Meanwhile, General Weston's HQ MNBDO had already departed for Neo Horio, eighteen miles down the road to Sphakia, having left no instructions for Force Reserve. Accusations are consistently traded that 'he had long since written off Colonel Duncan and his men' and that two dispatch riders were sent to recall Force Reserve but these could not get through. Weston himself remained in the Souda area trying to restore some order but with a breakdown of the command and control system he had a limited effect on this stage of the battle.

The Germans, however, did not immediately realise that there had been another Commonwealth withdrawal and probing attacks only began after the end of the *Luftwaffe*'s morning attacks. To the south of Force Reserve, the enemy advance went well facing only sporadic resistance from

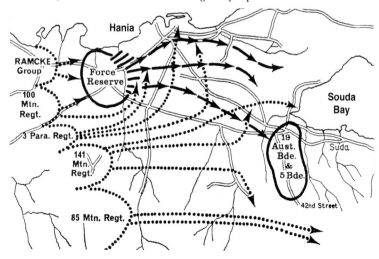

Commonwealth troops who had become separated from their units. The *Fallschirmjäger* of *Kampfgruppe Ramcke* found that there had been no reduction of the opposition along the coast at axis. At 1000 hours, *Oberst* Ramcke informed *Generalmajor* Ringel that the enemy had 'reoccupied the positions ... which he had evacuated yesterday' and requested close air support, while urging his men to renew their attacks.

Advancing at the same time up the Cladiso stream, *GJB 100* found that they had struck Force Reserve's scattered companies who were quickly bypassed and the Germans poured heavy fire in on them from all sides. From his command post, under a bank two hundred yards west of the bridge, Colonel Duncan could hear what was happening and decided to bring back B and D Companies from the left flank.

With great difficulty, orders were got through to them. At last, a few men began to come running in groups out of the trees, splashing through the shallow water of the river and dropping for a moment behind the stone walls to fire at their pursuers before stumbling on.

The *Gerbirgsjäger* were hot on their heels making their way through the olive groves to the east of the Kladiso. Colonel Duncan realised that he was all but surrounded and ordered his 2IC, Major Gibson, to take a total of about four hundred men including those men of the Rangers and the Northumberland Hussars that could be found, through Hania in small parties, and to reorganise on the Souda Road. They made their way in cover as best they could across the battlefield littered with enemy dead, while one group used the surviving vehicles to burst through a German cordon. Others using a ditch as cover passed the body of their Quartermaster, a Welch Regiment Great War veteran.

Colonel Duncan remained at his post with a few men but early in the afternoon, with the Germans all around, he was joined at the Kladiso Bridge by survivors of A and B Companies who had been driven off the ridges to the right. With thrusts from *Kampfgruppe Ramcke* and *GJR 100* converging, the battle would not last long. *Oberleutnant* Kurt Meyer was with *II Battalion GJR 100* moving north along the bed of the stream and witnessed the Welch withdrawing from the bridge:

> We bring to bear all the machine-gun fire that we have in order to cover the last seconds of our comrades' advance. A croaky hurrah breaks out from half-dried throats. Hand grenades fly. The defenders tear their machine-guns round . . . and set them in the face of the attackers, but the German machine-pistols are quicker. With hand grenades and bayonets the yellow shadows spring out of their holes and defend themselves. They won't surrender. Nearly fifty . . . cover with their bodies this last bulwark before Hania. Only four men, pale and shattered, are taken as prisoners.

About two hundred Welch, thirty or so Rangers and Northumberland Hussars, escaped into Hania. With Colonel Duncan carrying a Bren gun, they fought their way back through the ruins of the town but their bitter resistance ended late in the afternoon on the rocky slopes of the Akrotiri Peninsula. Brigadier Hargest was a distant witness to their last stand and wrote in his personal diary:

> Up on Souda Hill enemy bombers and fighters were blasting at a village to our surprise until we found that the Welch Regt and Rangers, who had gone out to beyond Hania with the mistaken idea that they could hold the line Vasey and I had left, had been smashed to bits in a few minutes and had been driven up to the hill village where they were annihilated. Whoever sent them should be shot.

A distant view of another example of 1 Welch's heroism was had by wounded New Zealander prisoners, who watched in admiration the remains of a platoon that had been left behind, fighting on in their trenches on a small knoll near the site of 7 General Hospital. An officer saw a Bren gun team:

> ...fire bursts all day ... Then must have run short of ammo. One man got out and in full view of the Germans walked 100 yards round the hillside — walked with no intention of hurrying though bullets were hitting the bare hillside. We could see every strike at his feet and above him on the slope. He got into a gun-pit, emerged with two Bren mag carriers and walked back at the same pace despite bullets and mortars. The gun went into action again ... Patients cheered the inspiring sight.

The Charge at 42nd Street

> 'Big battle at Souda. Gave Huns a good dishing.'
> WO2 Bill Foxwell, 2/7th Battalion - personal diary.

As already recorded, at first the Germans did not understand that the New Zealanders had withdrawn and it was not until 0645 hours on the 27th that *Oberst* Jais (*GJR 141*) received word from *Generalmajor* Ringel that *II/GJR 100* had lost contact with the enemy south of Platanos, on the Prison Valley Road. Jais was ordered to strike across country, around Hania, to the head of Souda Bay and cut off the enemy's retreat. After the departure of the bombers, at 0730 hours, *I Battalion* began its advance, with its *Gerbirgsjäger* companies widely spread among the olives.

Overnight, the Commonwealth troops had withdrawn to positions to the south-west of the head of Souda Bay. Brigadiers Puttick and Vasey, in the absence of General Weston, chose positions along a feature called 42nd Street. Properly known as Chickalarion Street, this was an obvious country lane, with earthen banks on either side, running south from the main Hania–Souda road towards the Malaxa Escarpment. It received its nickname from 42nd Field Company RE, who set up camp here in late 1940, as a part of the British garrison in Crete. The name was inspired by

One of the few remaining olive groves on 42nd Street containing old trees that must have witnessed the charge.

the 1930s' musical, 42nd Street, winner of the 1933 Oscar for best movie. In due course, military maps marked the road as 42nd Street.

The commanding officers tied up arcs of fire, with the battalions making the most of the earthen banks for defence and dug shallow trenches. 'There was a 50-yard field of fire with patches of oats and olive trees beyond' obscuring the view.

According to 21 NZ Battalion, during this routine liaison, word circulated that the Maoris were fed up with being pushed around and were going in with the bayonet when the enemy approached. Left largely to their own devices the commanding officers agreed that 'if the enemy attacked they would let him come right up and then have a go at him ...' attack being the best form of defence, in this circumstance. This offensive spirit reveals that the infantry were not yet defeated and offers a tantalising glimpse at what might have been if the middle ranking officers had been in overall command in Crete. Putting aside the 'what if' questions, the result of this plan was without a doubt, wholly remarkable.

In the pause while the enemy closed up to their positions the soldiers who, as Lieutenant Cockerill recorded, 'were thoroughly tired by now ... were all hungry, thirsty, and desperately in need of sleep'. So having dug themselves trenches behind the banks and 'eaten such hard rations as they had brought with them, they mostly prepared to bed down'. Their rest was not to be long.

I/141 GJR were advancing on the head of Souda Bay and, in doing so were crossing in front of the Commonwealth defensive line at an angle, unaware of the new position. Nor were they aware that their progress was being watched and reported on by patrols and observation posts provided by the Australians and New Zealanders.

Some of the *Gerbirgsjäger* halted in their advance to loot food from a Commonwealth engineer supply dump that was now abandoned in no-man's-land. Australian company commander, Major Miller of 2/7 Battalion, had sent forward a patrol to keep the enemy under observation, while he planned a counter-attack. Receiving agreement of Captain Nelson, commander of the left company to support the venture; 'When the shooting started he signalled his company forward to the patrol and engaged the enemy. It took a few minutes to establish superiority of fire and after this was effected the enemy broke and ran'. Having won the fire fight both companies charged. Private Carter took part in the assault and his account forms a part of the 2/7th Battalion War Diary:

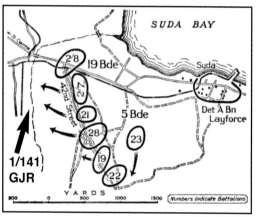

The charge at 42nd Street.

I was platoon runner of No. 13 Platoon under command of Lieutenant McGeoch. About 1000 hours on 27 May, we were told that we were to attack the enemy who were then about 250 yards ahead of us ... Both C and D Companies attacked together. After covering about 200 yards we went to ground and opened fire at the enemy who were then very close. Major Miller called for the mortars who fired about six bombs, and the enemy started to run.

We immediately charged forward at them, on the order of Major Miller who went with us; during the charge some Maoris came up and joined us. We shot a considerable number of Germans.

I/GJR 141 had been advancing with its companies, probably well spread out, bumped the whole Commonwealth position more or less simultaneously and a fierce fire-fight broke out, spreading south down 42nd Street. 21 NZ Battalion reported that they could hear '... yells that could come only from Maori throats. It was a blood-stirring haka. The Australians produced a scream even more spine-chilling than the Maori effort'. The sight of the Maori Battalion charging 'with vocal

224

Soldiers of FJR 3 were facing Greek soldiers and Cretan civilians to the South of Souda Bay.

accompaniment' sent the whole Commonwealth line surging forward.

The Maoris' regimental history records:

> A rumble followed by a series of explosions and a cloud of smoke from the direction of the engineers' dump. A ragged rattle of small-arms fire, surprisingly close, and bullets mowing the leaves off the trees…. The Maori reaction was immediate – there was a glint of steel and a rattle as bayonets were fixed, then another rattle as magazines were filled and safety-catches released.

> A, B, and C Companies jostled for starting positions in the confined area of 42nd Street, now immediately in front of the battalion; B Company, led by Captain Royal brandishing a bamboo walking pole like a taiaha in one hand and a revolver in the other, and C Company following Captain Scott got into 42nd Street first and deployed across the battalion front. By this time the Germans were within 200 yards of the sunken-road start line and advancing in sections dispersed in frontage and depth.

The appearance of two companies of bloodthirsty, howling Maoris, along with a 'few stray Greek soldiers who adding their Hellenic yells to the blood-curdling din',

Maoris practising their blood-chilling haka.

225

sent the enemy to ground and 'they opened heavy defensive fire'.

Captain Baker recalled:

> B Company were subjected to deadly fire as soon as they commenced to move forward and by the time they had moved to 50–55 yards they were forced to the ground where from the cover of trees, roots, and holes in the ground they commenced to exchange fire with the enemy, who had likewise taken up firing positions as soon as the attack commenced. I therefore gave immediate orders for A Company to advance. We moved forward in extended formation through B Company and into the attack. At first the enemy held and could only be overcome by Tommy-gun, bayonet and rifle. His force was well dispersed and approximately 600 yards in depth and by the time we met them their troops were no more than 150 yards from 42nd Street. They continued to put up a fierce resistance until we had penetrated some 250–300 yards. They then commenced to panic and as the troops from units on either side of us had now entered the fray it was not long before considerable numbers of the enemy were beating a hasty retreat. As we penetrated further their disorder became more marked and as men ran they first threw away their arms but shortly afterwards commenced throwing away their equipment as well and disappearing very quickly from the scene of battle…

Commonwealth Commanding officers struggled to retain control of their men who were flushed with success.

Fallschirmjäger from *Kampfgrupe Ramcke* in the outskirts of Hania.

The pursuit of the enemy paused briefly at a wadi some 600-800 yards forward of 42nd Street, while its clearance took place. However, there was practically no German resistance, as 'those still alive threw away much of their equipment and disappeared westwards'. They were chased for another 400–500 yards before fire from houses and a road where a second German battalion was deployed gave the harried *I Battalion* some relief. 21 NZ Battalion describe the hunt during this phase of the battle:

> *The forward elements of the enemy did not wait. They threw away their packs and ran. They were shot from the hip, and those who hid in the scrub were bayoneted. Some mortar teams that tried to get into action were overrun and dealt with. Patches of crop were trampled flat, drains were peered into and buildings ransacked. The chase went on for about half a mile without a prisoner being taken, before it was checked at a group of houses with rifles firing from every window.*

I/GJR 141 had been virtually destroyed, with over 300 bodies being counted in the olive groves in front of 42nd Street. The New Zealanders' and Australians' total of dead and casualties from this remarkable action was around a hundred. The effect can be summed up in the words of the New Zealand history: 'The ground troops gave no more trouble that day.' *Oberst* Jais and his *Gerbirgsjäger* were shocked by the Commonwealth counter-attack. *I/GJR 141* fell back on the *III Battalion* who were dug in, having earlier lost contact with them and it was only later that *Oberst* Jais adopted a prudent course keeping clear of the 42nd Street position and took a literal interpretation of his orders to secure the head of Souda Bay. The result was that 'By the middle of the afternoon the road was cut, but patrols sent towards Souda were soon forced back by fire from 19 Brigade'.

It can be argued that despite Jais's later assertion that 'The counter-thrusts, in so far as they were not the imagination of his forward troops, were no doubt mere feints to cover withdrawal', the later, much criticised, performance of his regiment was shaped by their experience at the hands of the Commonwealth infantry on 42nd Street.

In the aftermath of the campaign, accusations of brutality and violation of the laws of war at 42nd Street were made by the Germans. Controversially, British officer Alexander Clifford wrote 'The Australians, of course, had not the faintest notion of the laws of war ... They were a brutal lot of men, and they made up their rules as they went along'. Reg Saunders of 2/7th Battalion, refutes claims that Germans had been killed 'unfairly' and described the fight as 'a short range very bloody action. Certainly skulls were broken and men stabbed ... it was hand-to-hand combat, and that's what happens'.

Accusations of breaches of the laws of Armed conflict were not only made by the Germans. Lieutenant Bennett reported:

> The German machine-gunners had taken up positions on our flanks and an attacking party of infantry were moving up between them. The enemy had put out a screen of Cretan civilians and these poor people received the full blast of our weapons and several were killed. One of them was a policeman I knew well ...

Despite the accusations, the charge at 42nd Street was a truely remarkable event and did much to enable the Commonwealth rearguard to break clean that night and begin the withdrawal to the south coast and evacuation.

Chapter Eleven

WITHDRAWAL AND EVACUATION

After the action on 42nd Street, the remnants of 5 NZ and 19 Australian Brigades remained in position but according to 21 NZ Battalion '... parties of enemy troops could be seen moving across the ridges in the south. The main road across Crete passed through a defile near Stilos, and the enemy's object undoubtedly was to block the only practical way out'. A further withdrawal was planned for that night to extract as many of the defenders of 42nd Street as possible. They just succeeded in making the point where the road headed south to Hora Safakion before the *Gerbirgsjäger* in the hills cut them off.

A typical comment on the mood of the front line soldiers, as the inevitability of defeat confronted them is that:

> *It was a tough 15-mile night march back but, in spite of eight days' fighting with little sleep or food, the spontaneous bayonet charge at 42nd Street had raised the troops' morale. It was generally felt that if the movement had been allowed to continue the enemy would have been pushed right off Crete into the sea.*

Withdrawal Orders

Wavell's answer to General Freyberg's request for authority to evacuate eventually arrived at 1550 hours on the afternoon of 27 May, long after the withdrawal to the south coast had started and orders had been issued!

To set the scene for the final and torturous withdrawal to the south coast it is worth examining parts of the orders given by Generals Freyberg and Weston to CREFORCE. First Freyberg's directive:

To: *Major General Weston*   SECRET

1. ORGANISATION AND COMD
All the tps formerly in the Souda Bay and Maleme Sectors are placed under your command for operational purposes. Force HQ will make all arrangements for the evacuation of tps.

2. The operations henceforth must be based on the evacuation programme which is:

Night 28/29 May 1000
Night 29/30 May 6000
Night 30/31 May 3000
Night 31 May/1 Jun 3000

3. As far as can be foreseen 5 NZ and 19 Aust Inf Bde and Layforce
[commandos – see below] will withdraw through the line of the [Mountain]
Pass immediately N of the 'SAUCER' [Kares/Askyfou] *which is to be*
occupied this evening by 4 Inf Bde.
The 5 NZ and 19 Australian Bde will almost certainly be very tired and should,
subject to the tactical situation, be withdrawn S of the SAUCER into assembly
areas.
It is suggested that Layforce or at least a part of it, on reaching the line held by 4
NZ Inf Bde should be placed under command of that formation.

4. The C-in-C directs that you should put the R.M. Bn into a defensive posn
immediately S of the SAUCER forthwith.

5. FUTURE OPERATIONS
It is anticipated that the enemy will make contact with 4 NZ Inf Bde in the
afternoon of 29 May. In order to keep the enemy at a distance from the beaches it
would appear that the 4 NZ Inf Bde will have to hold its posn until dark night
29/30 May when it is hoped to withdraw it direct to the beaches for embarkation…

7. POLICY OF EMBARKATION
The C-in-C has laid it down definitely and irrevocably that fighting troops embark
first and that those who have fought the longest have priority. Wounded are
included in the first priority. Only after fighting troops have embarked will non-
combatants be provided for.

The key portion of General Weston's orders are:
1. All troops whether Aust, NZ or British will withdraw to Sphakia (S coast) for
embarkation (name of port not to be mentioned).
2. The withdrawal will be carried out under cover of a rearguard, which will
consist of 'Layforce'.
3. The intention is, in view of the enemy's air superiority, troops will march by
night and lie up under cover by day.
The march will be carried out in stages. At each stage rations, water and POL
[fuel] will be available.
4. OC. L and M Unit (Royal Marines) will provide guides at each staging camp,
the general intention being that Aust, NZ and British troops shall be routed to a
separate camp where some degree of reorganisation of units can be carried out by
day. …
It should be appreciated that in contrast to individuals' reminiscences, unit
War Diaries stressed that, on the whole, these and further detailed orders
issued by General Weston's HQ worked well.

German Orders

In contrast to the Commonwealth commanders, *Generalmajor* Ringel and his HQ were in a state of euphoria. They had on the 27th made significant gains, including *FJR 3* securing Hania and the enemy were finally moving back apace. Either poorly served by his intelligence staff or through a premature loss of attention Ringel failed to realise that the Commonwealth forces were not falling back on their other garrisons in the east but heading south for evacuation. According to the New Zealand official history:

> ... the pursuit was now on and Ringel determined at once to exploit the day's successes and hasten to the relief of Rethymno and Iraklio. He does not yet seem to have realised that these two objects were not identical. For his orders for 28 May were: 'Ringel Gp will pursue the enemy eastwards through Rethymno to Iraklio without a pause. First objective Rethymno and the relief of the paratroops fighting there.'

Enter Layforce

The Middle East Commandos were in mid-1941 working under the codename of LAYFORCE, after its commander Brigadier Bob Laycock. Two of the commandos units, also for security, referred to as 'battalions', were sent to reinforce Crete, under its brigadier. These were A Battalion (formerly No. 7 Commando) and D Battalion (formerly an amalgamation of 50 and 52 Middle East Commandos), each with five companies of two troops. Layforce in Crete totalled around 900 lightly armed men, with few of the heavy weapons commandos had to support them later in the war. They were in short, organised as a light raiding force, not as line infantry but included nationals from various Mediterranean countries, including Spain.

Brigadier Bob Laycock.

The first indication that Layforce would be needed in the battle was received about midnight on the 22/23 May when Brigadier Laycock was told that his command would be 'carrying out raids on German air bases on Crete' in order to help attack the enemy's air superiority. The original plan was to a cross to the south coast of Crete by troop ship but these were too lightly armed and any ship in that area was in great danger. Consequently, Layforce was to be shipped to Souda Bay. On the morning of 24 May 200 men of A Battalion were landed from a mine sweeper. The remainder of the force left Egypt that day but the state of the sea and the destruction of the ships' boats meant that they could not be landed. The commandos were eventually landed:

> ... at approximately midnight the ship crept up to the mole at the western end of the bay. All was quiet and only distant gunfire and

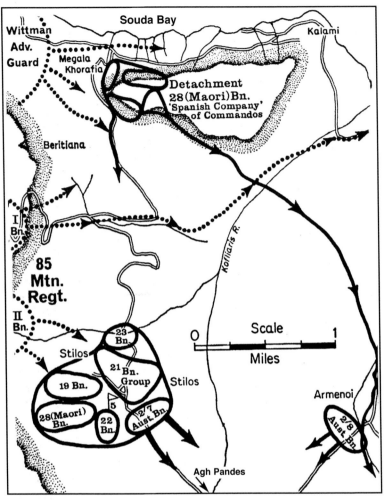

The situation a.m. 28 May 1941.

occasional flashes of light from the direction of Hania marred the peacefulness of the night. Just as the Brigade Commander, myself and other officers were bidding farewell to the Captain of the minelayer, the door of the latter's cabin was flung open and a bedraggled and apparently slightly hysterical Naval officer burst in. In a voice trembling with emotion he said, 'The Army is in full retreat, everything is chaos. I've just had my best friend killed beside me. Crete is being evacuated!' Cheerful to say the least and something of a shock to the little party of Commando officers, armed to the teeth and loaded up like Christmas trees, who stared open-mouthed at this bringer of bad news. 'But we are just going ashore,' I faltered. 'My God,' he cried, 'I didn't know that: perhaps I shouldn't have said anything.' 'Too late

*now old boy,' I said. 'You can at least tell us what the password is.' But he
had forgotten it.*

*We had no time to stay and check upon his story which in any event was
likely to be unreliable in view of his state of mind. Disembarkation started
at once ...*

During unloading via lighters the commandos lost most of their heavier
equipment into the bay through careless handling, as the ships crews were
desperate to get out to sea and south of Crete by dawn.

Once ashore, the confusion was apparent and as Tom Caselli recalled:

*We assembled by companies on the quay, by forcing other military
personnel milling about out of the way... In the darkness we formed up in
column of threes, company orders, and set off out of the dockyard and
Souda. When we got onto the actual road it was clogged up by disorganised
soldiery – only two words to describe them – a rabble!*

Layforce marched east to join the advance party of A Battalion who were
in position south-east of Souda. D Battalion passed through A Battalion to
take up a position six miles in depth at Megala Khoratia, on a ridge, at the
point where the road south to Hora Safakion left the coast road. This was
in effect to be the first of the pre-prepared blocking positions ordered by
General Weston.

Megala Khoratia (formerly Beritiana Junction)

Before dawn D Battalion arrived at Megala Khoratia, where Lieutenant
Colonel Young deployed three companies to construct defences covering
the road and the remaining two up on the heights covering the flanks.
Throughout the day the *Luftwaffe* bombed and strafed them but their rock
built sangars on the steep slopes provided plenty of cover and they
suffered no casualties.

In the afternoon Colonel Young was instructed to recce a another
blocking position to further delay the enemy. Once he had found one, he
was to withdraw all but one company from Megala Khoratia. With a single
company remaining down in the valley, this position was unsatisfactory, as
it was overlooked by surrounding hills and could be easily outflanked by
a larger force. Despite D Battalion's protestations, General Weston's
headquarters ordered 'that it had to be done' and after dark, leaving E
Company, including a troop of Spanish volunteers. Lieutenant Russo
commented to his company commander Maj McGibbon 'Christ Bob, we
will never get out of this mess'. His commander '...silently agreed', as
Colonel Young 'had explained there was only a slim chance of us ever
getting out, but he was very fair about it'.

Lieutenant Russo recalled how the single company of commandos
received a welcome reinforcement.

Shortly afterwards a platoon of New Zealand Maoris came through us

233

N ←—

Souda Bay and
coast road

The block at Megala Khorafia looking across the deep valley to the positions of the Cammandos and Maoris, as seen from the position of *GJR 100*.

— commanded by a 2nd Lieutenant. All were carrying not only their own weapons but also German weapons. They asked if they could join us — for a chance to fight the Germans! They stayed and later I sent them in on a bayonet attack.

Around midnight, two companies, numbering 130 Maoris, occupied rock built sangars on the high ground earlier constructed by the remainder of D Battalion, thus providing some depth, which greatly strengthened the position. The commandos and Maoris were to hold the junction until 0900 hours, in order to allow time for further positions to be established to the south. The four surviving Maori officers, according to the battalion history '… made a quick reconnaissance in the darkness while the troops who had found some rations had a meal'. There was, however, a problem.

While the rest of 5 NZ Brigade was passing through an all-round position was organised and the troops put on the ground, but the dispositions had to be altered somewhat unexpectedly. A Canadian captain in charge of the Commandos who were guarding high ground to the west and … Sixty of his men, Spanish [commandos] volunteers under a Spanish sergeant had marched away with the last of 5 Brigade.

These were foreign troops pitched into the chaos of a retreat, and while the Spanish Troop's unauthorised withdrawal was thoroughly reprehensible, it is perhaps understandable. Lieutenant Russo commented, 'It was hard to explain to Spaniards why British troops didn't stand and fight'.

Maori's B Coy

Megala Khorafia

Commandos covering the Old Road

Maori's A Coy

New road to Stylos

With the withdrawal of 5 NZ and 19 Australian Brigades around midnight on 27 May, the commandos of A Battalion, positioned to the south-east of Souda became the rearguard and fought their way back, passing through B Battalion before dawn. At 0800 hours, the engagement at Megala Khoratia began.

Following the charge at 42nd Street, *Kampfgruppe Whittman* echeloned through *GJR 141* to continue the advance along the sharply narrowing coastal plain. *Kampfgruppe Whittman* consisted of the *Gerbirgsdivision*'s *95 Recce Battalion*, the Motor Cycle Battalion and two troops of self propelled anti-tank guns, plus motorised artillery and engineers. Their task was to be ready to move off before dawn and drive through to Rethymno and then on to Iraklio. From his position on the high ground, Captain Royal of the Maoris could see that the road from Souda Bay was 'lined with enemy transport and troops, light armoured vehicles and field guns'. This was the advance guard of *Kampfgruppe Wittmann*, probably *95 Recce Regiment*, which had been ordered to clear the Megala Khoratia Junction.

The attack opened with the defenders being engaged by a mortar bombardment and then attacked by the *Gerbirgsjäger* from the coastal road to the north and from the high ground to the south-west. The battle took place on the more open high ground and in the close confines of the valley, with fighting taking place at ranges of 100 yards or less, because of the hillside scrub. With only Bren guns, Tommy guns and rifles plus the Maoris' captured weapons the Commonwealth troops were not only outgunned but heavily outnumbered. It was only a matter of time before

**See map
page 232**

235

the Germans identified the extent of the position and attempted to envelope them, threatening to cut them off from the route to the south.

Down in the valley Major McGibbon had been badly wounded and told Lieutenants Russo and Sandbach to leave him and ordered them to withdraw at 0900 hours. Major McGibbon recalled that:

> *After I was finally picked up by the Germans, one of their officers expressed surprise that so few commandos (although he did not know that we were commandos) had held up the German attack for so long. The German said that their losses were very high – especially the number killed.*

Informed of the commandos' withdrawal and with what was almost certainly a company from the Recce Battalion approaching Megala Khorafia to cut the road south to Stilos, Captain Royal led the Maoris into the hills to the south-east, where weak [enemy] patrols did not have the stomach to tackle the determined Maoris.

Having reorganised after their attack and the withdrawal of the Commonwealth troops, half of *Kampfgruppe Whitmann* continued its advance east along the coastal road, while the remainder advanced south down the Megala Khoratia–Stylos Road, which had already been cut by *GJR 85*. *GJR 141* was similarly tasked with objectives in the east and only *GJR 100* had any orders regarding the south and they were only to provide flank protection. As the official history comments, 'The importance of Ringel's failure to appreciate the direction of the withdrawal needs no underlining… he could easily have brought strong forces to bear…'

Stilos

While the commandos and Maoris were fighting at the Megala Khoratia Junction, in the hills to the south of *Kampfgruppe Whittman*, *GJR 85* was advancing with all three battalions forward, due east across country, a task eminently suited to the *Gerbirgsjäger*. Their aim was to cut off the tail of the Commonwealth withdrawal and reach Georgioupoli, thus opening the way to relieve the *Fallschirmjäger* at Rethymno. A company of *I/GJR 85* narrowly missed encountering the withdrawing commandos and Maoris, as it made its way east, while *II Battalion* closed with the Commonwealth position (5 NZ Brigade) that had been identified at Stylos. Further south into the mountain foothills *III/GJR 85* was unknowingly heading south to an encounter with the main body of Layforce at Agh Pandes.

See map page 232

After a gruelling night march, the remnants of five New Zealand battalions and an Australian battalion arrived at Stilos. 23 NZ Battalion's historian commented:

> *All were feeling the lack of sleep and of regular meals, to say nothing of the strain imposed by frequent attacks from the air. The road grew steeper and rougher the farther south it went. At daybreak the battalion reached Stylos. Major Thomason established his headquarters in a cave and ordered*

Most of the withdrawal was on foot, with little water or shelter from the sun.

> *A and D Companies to occupy a ridge to the west of the road, covering the*
> *northern approaches to Stylos.*

23 NZ Battalion were to cover the area of the bridge north of Stilos. The two
company commanders were carrying out a recce of a piece of high ground
just to the south-west before settling down.

> *As they reached a stone wall at the top of the ridge, they saw Germans*
> *coming out of a creek bed about 400 yards away. Machine-gun fire whizzed*
> *over the ridge. In great haste the men of the two companies, many of whom*
> *had already dropped off to sleep, were summoned to the ridge. Major*
> *Thomason ordered those near him to join A and D Companies, shouting,*
> *"Sergeant Hulme! Get men on top of that hill! Whoever gets men there first*
> *wins!"*

Lieutenant Cockerill wrote:

> *There was a terrific scramble up to the ridge and in places the ascent was*
> *almost precipitous. On getting to the top of the ridge we came under fairly*
> *heavy mortar fire and there were, unfortunately, quite a few casualties.*
> *Some of the enemy had advanced to within 20 to 30 yards of the stone wall*
> *which ran right along the ridge like a backbone of a hog's back and these, of*
> *course, were sitters if one cared to take the risk of looking over the wall*
> *which, of course, we had to do.*

The redoubtable Sergeant Hulme was again at the forefront of the action,
according to his battalion's history:

237

Hulme was among the first to arrive and opened fire from behind the stone wall just when the enemy leaders were about 15 yards away. He was joined by Sergeant Bob Young and then by D Company.

These were the leading elements of II/GJR 85 and after they had been sent back down the hill in chaos, Sergeant Hulme was seen 'sitting side-saddle on the hog's back stone wall', shooting at the enemy on the lower slopes. His VC citation stresses that:

His example did much to maintain the morale of men whose reserves of nervous and physical energy were nearly exhausted. At one stage, too, Hulme threw the grenades that were being hurriedly primed by others. Eventually, after shooting several Germans, he himself was wounded in the arm.

With his battalions' way forward blocked, *Oberst* Krakau sent a detachment to the left who, using the cover of the wall, began to throw grenades across. In response, a section of 19 Battalion was sent to deal with the enemy and 'arrived in time to dispatch an enemy officer and about six men who stood up at the wall with a machine gun'. The attack was finally beaten off by about 0930 hours. *GJR 85* later described this engagement in their report: 'The strong enemy force at Stylos: A terrific struggle developed, including bloody hand-to-hand fighting'.

Brigadier Hargest signalled General Weston first thing in the morning: 'We will endeavour to hold small position here today and move back tonight but owing to exhausted state of troops this will be very difficult.' However, while the battle described above was going on, he held a conference at his HQ and asked each of his COs if they could fight and hold all day and then withdraw under cover of night, marching eleven miles to Vryess. The answer was 'No'. 'Well, we'll march at 10,' said the brigadier. In doing so, in full daylight, the force would be risking the attentions of the *Luftwaffe*. However, aircraft were now, fortunately, only available in limited numbers thanks to the requirements of BARBAROSSA. The troops were ordered to make the best use of the cover available; a habit that was now well engrained!

As the most northerly battalions began their withdrawal, at the vital moment, 23 Battalion reported that 'shouts, hakas and yells were heard from the rear of the Germans who suddenly ceased attacking and withdrew in some confusion'. It seems that the new arrivals were a detachment of Maoris that Captain Royal had sent back with the wounded. The official history comments:

Royal, however, says that he had told the escort and the wounded to throw away their weapons. We must assume either that they had acquired fresh weapons on the way or that they had been joined by parties from A Battalion or by men who had had to fall out on the march but who were now ready to make a further bid for freedom.

238

This unplanned intervention significantly assisted the break clear of 5 NZ Brigade which fell back through the rearguard of 2/7 Australian Battalion. It was fortunate that the Brigade was falling back in a southerly direction, for the *Gerbirgsjäger* were under orders to advance east, and this contributed to 2/7 Battalion escaping destruction.

Agh Pandes (formerly Babali Hani)

On the afternoon of 27 May, Colonel Laycock had been ordered to locate a defensive position further back on the road beyond Stylos and occupy it with his force less the company left at Megala Khoratia. He was to hold this last position, which was on a low ridge north of Agh Pandes Crossroads, before the climb into the White Mountains, until dark on 28 May.

D Battalion had four of its own companies to cover a long front. A and D Companies were deployed on the right of the road, with a combined frontage of about 500 yards. This flank against rising ground was reasonably secure. C and E Companies, however, were in better cover, also on a frontage of about 500 yards, to the left of the road but had 'a more or less open left flank' in the valley beyond the ridge. His reserve was a company of A Battalion that arrived during the course of the morning.

Tom Caselli recalls their battle preparations:

> We all deployed roughly in our company areas and as dawn broke, occupied the positions in detail, arranging inter-company junction points, tidying up arcs of fire and getting ourselves fixed up with individual sangars — plenty of stone about and with the steel helmet rim (the back portion only) to scratch out a hollow. If we had used the front of the rim the sun could catch that part where we had scratched off the paint and give our

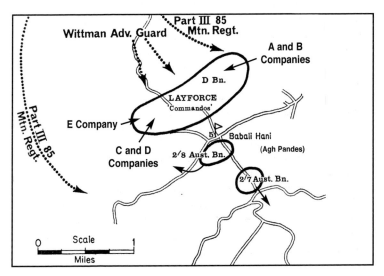

Abandoned Commonwealth transport on the climb up to the mountains.

position away. While this was going on, there was a continual procession of unattended retreating men, straggling through our lines and along the road south, very few carrying any weapons... Our battalion had been joined by the remnants of the 2nd/7th Australian Infantry Battalion, who were giving us invaluable back-up. Gen Weston had given us three of the Matilda Infantry tanks (7 RTR) as a reserve. There was a ravine on the left of our company running roughly east-west, capable of giving the enemy a covered approach and during the morning we had mounted several patrols there, so as not to be surprised, but Jerry was not encountered.

'Jerry' was, however, not far behind the Australians, who withdrew through Layforce from Stilos. George Williams was forward of the main position in an observation post.

We could see quite a long way up the road along which any mechanised vehicles would have to travel. Eventually the first that came into view were Jerry motorbikes and sidecars. Our signallers passed this message with mirrors. There was a church tower some distance over the other side of the road from which a sniper later did some deadly work. But I think someone was there already and had spotted our signals, because just after this they started peppering us with mortars. They soon got the range and were becoming quite deadly. The corporal then gave the order to get back to HQ.

At 1330 hours, the enemy attacked, advancing on the axis of the road where C Company immediately to the left of the road bore the brunt of the

240

attack for thirty minutes. Elements of *Kampfgruppe Whittman*, in the centre, with the flanking support of *III/GJR 85* had attempted a quick attack, with little recce, in the hope of bouncing the commandos out of their position.

> *So there we were in our little stone sangars, watching for Jerry to appear and with our forward scouts posted to spot men or vehicles making an appearance. About mid-day the first German patrol appeared on motorcycle combinations. They were allowed to get well within range before we opened up with concentrated machine gun and rifle fire and some grenades, which sent them hurtling off the road into a quarry. The follow-up troops got the same treatment. Sure enough, up went the blue flares and the mortars began to range in. Star-shells followed and the Stukas turned up and plastered our positions in their own noisy fashion. Curiously enough they caused few casualties and many bombs went wide of the mark. They did manage to set some of the scrub on fire, but their ground troops didn't take advantage of it, but it was hectic whilst it lasted. Then they tried a change of tactics – turning our flanks, but were beaten off.*

An hour and a half later an altogether more serious attack started, this time using the whole of *Kampfgruppe Whittman*, and the *Gerbirgsjäger* battalion. Again it focussed on the left flank but this time threatening to use the valley to envelope the commandos. Tom Caselli was with E Company on the left flank:

> *A Fieseler Storch appeared again, disappeared and the same tactic was repeated. However, the field grey uniforms were soon spotted as they came on and they were easily picked off. They must have had heavy casualties.*

Commando Bren gunner Arthur Noble recalls the second attack:

> *We never had a moment's respite. I had to keep my Bren gun in constant action. The need to estimate distance had by then gone. I dropped my sights down to zero. Boyle [his No.2] was carrying on valiantly, filling and charging magazines as they became empty and changing barrels as they became hot. The Jerries were pressing closer and closer and just as our first box of ammo ran out they appeared to have broken through on our left.*

Tom Caselli wrote about the role that the commandos' senior officer played in the defence:

> *Colonel Laycock must have had a guardian angel because he was here, there and everywhere, wearing his brigadier's cap with its red band and gold peak, which must have been very obvious to the snipers as we were all in steel helmets. . . It wasn't long before the Stukas turned up again and we got plastered, with the infantry following up ... the pressure was increased on our left flank, so much so that the 2/8th Australians were moved up to our left on the edge of the ravine. Colonel Laycock, plus cap, also arrived to assess the situation.*

Colonel Young used every man he could to extend his flank and asked Laycock for reinforcements. As mentioned above 2/8 Battalion were sent

to assist with two companies. This deployment and a counter-attack by E Company, along with the Matildas, which 'kept making sorties up the road', enabled the line to be held but 'It had been touch and go'. Certainly out-gunned and by now outnumbered as well, the commandos only had the troop from A Battalion in reserve. 2/7 Battalion had already been sent to the rear with HQ 5 NZ Brigade.

In his situation report *Oberst* Whittman recorded:

> *The enemy's actions pointed to his intending to hold his positions at all costs at least until the evening and then withdrawing under cover of darkness. He even made small counter-attacks from time to time, and often the fighting came to close-quarters. Observation was too poor for our artillery to be effective, and our tanks had not yet arrived, and so we had to desist from attacking, as it would have been too costly under the circumstances.*

Further reinforced by *GJR 85*, with a company of *GJR 141* approaching the flank and *GJR 100* on their way, the enemy now planned an attack by two battalions of *GJR 85* at dusk but they attacked too late. During the afternoon Brigadier Laycock received confirmatory orders to withdraw at dusk and at about 2115 hours, the commandos began to slip away. Their stubborn stand had made the withdrawal of 2/7 Battalion and 5 NZ Brigade a much less hazardous affair than it would otherwise have been.

Their withdrawal, however, wasn't straightforward. Major Graham recalled that with most of the commandos, including many wounded, still on the road:

> *Imagine my horror, when ... I found a huge crater which was being*

242

admired by the sapper party [42 Field Company] *who had done the deed. In a fury I cross-examined the officer in charge, but all he could say was that a 'senior officer' who said he was commander of the rearguard had ordered him to blow. To this day no one knows who that 'senior officer' was. There was no time for recrimination – desperately we organised working parties to at least partially repair the damage. No vehicle, tracked or wheeled, would ever get through, but we might make it passable for marching troops. After some hours of backbreaking toil, we succeeded in getting the wounded across to the other side, where some ramshackle Cretan lorries were waiting to evacuate them... Two tanks had run out of petrol and been destroyed and the third was slewed across the narrow road on the enemy side of the crater and, after removing oil and water, we abandoned her with her engine running.*

The Mountain Road

Beyond Agh Pandes the road, an earth and gravel track wide enough for a single vehicle, climbs from the hills into the mountains, zigzagging up the steep slopes to the Pass at an altitude of 900 metres. Beyond the Pass, the mountains open up to the small flat fertile Askyfou Plain, a former mountain lake bed, surrounded by bare rocky peaks. The road then makes its way between the deep gorges that run down steeply to the sea. Opportunities to slow the German advance abounded but the mountain troops were trained to operate in exactly this type of terrain. The road petered out into an exposed, steep, switchback track for the final few miles of descent down to the coastal plain. The marching troops, however, were able to take a covered route down via the five mile long Imbros Gorge,

Motorcyclists from the *Gerbirgsdivision* examine the Matilda that blocked the road at the crater.

where they were all but immune from strafing attacks.

Heading up into the mountains at the best of times is demanding but for men who had fought with little sleep, hardly any food and hardly any water for the previous week, the barrier was an extreme challenge 'and not to be able to cross it was to become a prisoner'. No one who took part in the withdrawal could forget the climb up to the Pass:

> For two days and two nights men had been streaming over it, some crammed into the few vehicles that were still functioning, the rest marching, stumbling, and at times reduced to crawling on hands and knees. The natural savage grandeur of the mountain road was overprinted with the chaos of war. Every yard of the road carried its tale of disaster, personal and military. The verges were strewn with abandoned equipment, packs cast aside when the galling weight had proved too much for chafed skin and exhausted shoulders; empty water bottles; suitcases and officers' valises gaping their glimpses of khaki linen and pullovers knitted by laborious love in homes that the owners might not live to see again; steel helmets half

An overloaded carrier pauses under cover of a tree on the mountain road.

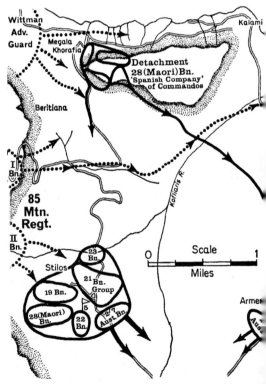

244

buried in the dust; all the grotesque and unpredictable bric-a-brac of withdrawal, the personal property treasured till it became an impediment and then discarded so that its owner could keep up with his desperate urge for life.

On the way up to the Pass, further blocking positions were established to cover CREFORCE's withdrawal. Having been first away from Stilos, it was 23 NZ Battalion who were providing the blocking force on the morning of 29 May. They took up positions as best they could in the dark, 'with D Company on the left of the road, Headquarters Company, A Company, and the detachment of gunners under the indefatigable Captain Snadden on the right'. One man commented that 'We had never slept on such boulders but it might as well be a feather bed; it makes no difference'.

From their naturally strong, rocky but waterless positions astride the road up into the mountains, at 0715 hours, 23 NZ Battalion reported they could see a large number of the enemy below them and to the north. These were *I/GJR 100*, who following the loss of contact with Layforce the night before had been brought up from reserve to follow the enemy withdraw leaving the main force to resume its march east to relieve the *Fallschirmjäger* at Rethymno and Iraklio. Regaining contact would take time and General Ringel was heavily criticised by Student for allowing so many Commonwealth troops to be evacuated but this is to underestimate the effectiveness of the rearguards and to ignore Student's own priority for the relief of his beleaguered regiments to the east.

The upper section of the marching troops route down through the Imbros Gorge or Ravine.

Slowed by the demolitions lower down on the mountain road, the Germans did not make contact with 23 NZ Battalion before they withdrew. They started to thin out after mid-day but not finally abandoning the position until late afternoon, to head south through 18 NZ Battalion who were providing the rearguard on the northern crest of the Askifou Plain.

The Saucer

18 NZ Battalion arrived out of the mountain after a dreadful trek, early on 28 May, onto the lip overlooking the green Askifou Plain:

> It didn't belie its looks. When those weary men stumbled down the mountain to the flat below they found wells — lovely wells, scores of them, scattered all over the fields. Water to drink, water to sluice over your face and head, water to bathe your feet. The men practically wallowed in it. German planes were miraculously absent, and for a while the anti-paratroop role had to wait on the good pleasure of the water.

According to the Battalion's historian 'There was no work to do yet, and a day of inaction was doubly welcome after the fearful march of the night before'. 18 and 20 NZ Battalions were to hold the plain, with the help of four Light Tanks and three old Italian 75mm guns crewed by Australians.

Early on the 29th, 18 Battalion was ordered to send its main body several miles south, to the south end of the Saucer, where it joined 20 Battalion. A Company, however, with fifty men under command of Major Lynch, went back up to the north edge of the Plain to block the entrance. With the company was one of the tanks, a few Vickers gunners who had happened to be tagging along, and 'a 3-inch mortar manned by the 19 Battalion RSM (who had lost his own unit) and a crew of volunteers'.

> A Company, jaded as it was, hauled its weary feet up to the top of the first peak north of the plain, and there spread out over a wide front, covering as much of the approach from the north as possible.

With the withdrawal of 23 NZ Battalion, it wasn't long before A Company was in action, 'putting up a skilful defence against the Germans at close range'. For three hours the enemy probed the company, trying 'to smash this stubborn ring of men who disputed their passage'. Major Lynch, despite the exhaustion of his men fought a mobile battle, and used the rock ridges as cover to 'move a section hastily to counter one of Jerry's thrusts'.

Thwarted on the direct route into the Saucer, the Gerbirgsjäger were forced to feel their way around the flanks in a wide loop, taking a Spandau with them. Eventually they reached a position overlooking A Company's rear and the road down to the plain, and opened fire.

This could have been the end of A Company, but it wasn't. When the situation began to get 'sticky up on the hilltop', Brigadier Inglis sent the three 'Aussie guns' up in support. They were, without much ammunition, but nicely sited to tackle the 'troublesome Jerry machine gun'. The German

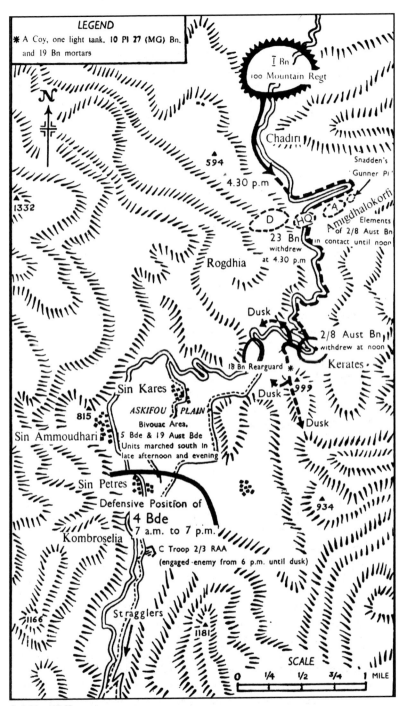

LEGEND
✳ A Coy, one light tank, 10 Pl 27 (MG) Bn, and 19 Bn mortars

I Bn
100 Mountain Regt

Chadırı

594

4.30 p.m

Snadden's 'Gunner Pl'

1332

A

D   HQ   Amıgdhalokorfı   Elements
of 2/8 Aust Bn
in contact until noon

23 Bn
withdrew
at 4.30 p.m

Rogdhia

Dusk

2/8 Aust Bn
withdrew at noon

Kerates

18 Bn Rearguard   ✳

Sin Kares

Dusk   999

ASKIFOU PLAIN
Bivouac Area.
5 Bde & 19 Aust Bde
Units marched south in
late afternoon and evening

815

Dusk

Sin Ammoudhari

Sin Petres

934

Defensive Position of
4 Bde
7 a.m. to 7 p.m.

Kombroselia

C Troop 2/3 RAA
(engaged enemy from 6 p.m. until dusk)

1166

Stragglers

1181

SCALE
0   1/4   1/2   3/4   1 MILE

Safakion 29 May.

247

fondness for firing tracer gave away their exact location, and the Aussie gunners 'gave it the works'. Under cover of their fire A Company began to retire downhill.

Lieutenant Colonel Gray 'had been largely responsible for turning the Aussie guns on to their target', and helped direct their fire. He wrote:

> It was the first time I had ever spotted for artillery and Geoff Kirk and I sat on the rocks above the road directing the fire and calling out corrections to the guns. The range, by trial and error, was 3200 yards and they literally rocked it in, firing, I believe, all the 40 rounds which was all they possessed.

Colonel Gray also secured three trucks from somewhere, and had them waiting, with nervous drivers, at the foot of the hill, where a breathless A Company tumbled into them. Covered by the remaining Light Tanks, the trucks took the exhausted Kiwis to the south end of the plain, where the rest of the battalion was preparing to move on again.

The actions fought between Stilos and the Saucer enabled 6,500 men to be evacuated from Hora Safakion on the night of 29/30 May.

The Final Leg

With *GJR 100* now up in the mountains, preventing the *Gerbirgsjäger* from advancing along the road from Imbros to Hora Safakion or the five miles through the mountains and gorges to the south coast was vital for the slowly proceeding evacuation. Brigadier Vasey was allocated the grim task of commanding the last rearguard. He had under command, his two Australian battalions and the Royal Marine battalion, the three 75mm guns, a platoon of 2/1 MG Battalion with two Vickers, the four tanks of 3 Hussars, and three Bren carriers. His plan was simple; the tanks and

The pass through the mountains south of Imbros was easily blocked by a few determined men.

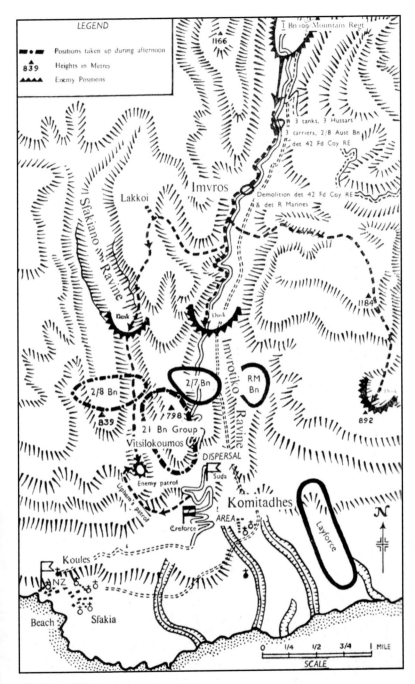

Safakion 30 May.

Brigadier Vasey was allocated the grim task of commanding the last rearguard.

carriers, under Major Keith, were to delay the enemy in front of the defence line until 1700 hours and then fall back, the Sappers of 42 Field Company RE blowing the road behind them. Two miles further down the road, the defence line, prepared overnight 29/30 May, covered the road and the routes through the flanking mountains.

The Covering Force, Sergeant Trethowan's platoon of 2/8 Infantry, mounted in carriers and supported by tanks, were deployed about a mile north of Imbros. At dawn, they spotted the enemy moving into the vacated Saucer, aboard trucks and motorcycles. *GJR 100's* War Diary for the 30th includes a claim that they 'captured' the Plain!

Two companies of *I Battalion GJR 100* with three light tanks, probably Panzer IIs, which had finally been landed on Crete on 26 May, advanced on the Covering Force at 0645 hours. The Australian carrier crews were dismounted and deployed in the rocks astride the road but it was the Light Tank commanded by Corporal Summers that opened the battle with his Vickers machine guns, engaging the infantry advancing on the road. He only managed to get off a couple of bursts before his guns jammed but 'he had disposed of perhaps a dozen enemy'. Sergeant-Major Childs' tank came into action, covering his corporal's withdrawal. However, one of the panzers soon hit Childs' tank, which though still a runner was damaged. Somewhat later, with enemy mortar fire growing in volume, the remaining tanks and carriers withdrew behind the Sappers' first demolition, which they blew at 0855 hours. A delay of over two hours had been inflicted on the enemy, who were now also slow in following up.

The second block was established a mile back, just north of Imbros. Two carrier crews again deployed astride the road. Major Keith's tanks, now up against opposition from their own type, took up positions on the southern outskirts of the village, from where they provided covering fire. After an hour's hasty preparation:

> About ten o'clock the new position was attacked and the enemy moved in cautiously to within a hundred yards of the Bren crews, who held their fire, waiting to be sure of not firing on stragglers.

Once sure that they could see 'field grey and coal scuttle helmets' the infantry opened fire, 'doing a good deal of damage before they withdrew under cover of the tanks'. The infantry and tanks fought from Imbros for a further 30 minutes, before enemy fire mounted and they came under pressure from enemy using the beginnings of the gorge to the left, to outflank them. The Covering Force again withdrew, blowing the second and third demolitions (north and south of the village) as they went. This time they fought their way back to a position a mile or so south of Imbros. Withdrawing at 1130 hours, the Covering Force had now delayed the enemy for almost five hours. The Germans had, however, advanced two miles but in doing so, suffered significant casualties.

The third position occupied had been established in depth by the Royal Marine Battalion but they had already moved back as the Covering Force fell back on the main line of defence. The force occupied the positions hidden on a rocky slope beyond a sharp bend. Sergeant Trethowan described the results of this ambush:

The enemy came into range with troops in trucks followed by walking personnel. They were an easy target, and the first column when fired upon scampered for cover while their trucks tore down the road and gained cover. The enemy began a searching fire with mortars and machine guns but failed to locate us. A column of marching troops came into range on the road soon after and we dealt with them in a similar manner.

The Covering Force at one point staged a feigned withdrawal and having lured the enemy into the open, 'they were dealt with' by the tanks and carriers that returned to occupy their positions after ten minutes. They estimated that they had killed or wounded around forty or fifty of the enemy. The July 41 Report, however, stated that:

The trick did not work a second time, and the Germans brought an A/T gun to bear from the high ground to the left. The last demolition was blown at about 1320 hrs and the tanks and carriers retired to the next bend.

The *Gerbirgsjäger* were now even more cautious and started to move

Gerbirgsjäger of *1/100 GJR* attempt a flanking move around the blocking position.

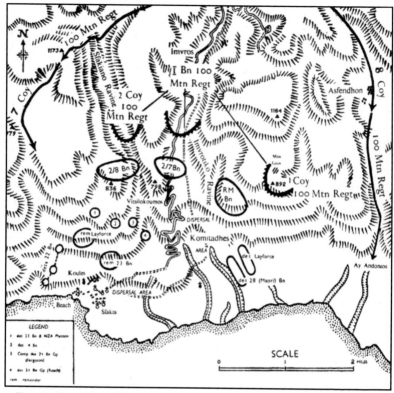

The situation at Hora Safakion 31 May.

around the precipitous slopes to outflank the Covering Force, who claim to
have been 'driven back, chiefly by mortar fire, from one bend to another,
until they reached the main infantry position (2/7 Australian Battalion) at
about 1700 hours'. The damaged Light Tanks finally broke down. The
report continued:

> By this time the last two tanks were finished; they had steering, brake,
> engine and clutch troubles, so they were wrecked and abandoned on the road
> blocks which had been erected and the crews proceeded to the beach, where
> they arrived at 1845 hours.

The carriers were able to press on until the rough dirt and stone road
finally ran out where the mountains dropped down to the narrow coastal
plain. Here they too were destroyed, having provided excellent service
with the covering force, delaying the enemy for over seventeen hours. The
enemy was however, just three miles from the sea. 'The Germans came on
and made contact with Brigadier Vasey's main rearguard position but did
not press their attack.' *Oberst* Utz sent messengers (he had out-run his

Inside the Creforce HQ Cave.

radio communications) with requests for close air support but it was too close to darkness for a response from the *Luftwaffe* and the artillery were too far down the mountain to help without time consuming moves. Consequently, he despatched companies to the flanks to find the extent of the Commonwealth rearguard's positions.

During the evening of the 30th a patrol of eleven *Gerbirgsjäger* managed to slip around the rearguard, through the Safakio Gorge to the west of the road and had to be driven off from the vicinity of the HQ CREFORCE cave. A New Zealand Platoon killed all eleven men and took their weapons, including a *Spandau*, into use.

In another action in the Safakio Gorge, Colonel Kippenberger tangled with one of the companies dispatched to the flanks by *Oberst* Utz. He sent the remains of two companies of 20 NZ Battalion including Lieutenant Upham to block their progress down the gorge. Colonel Kippenberger recorded the destruction of a part of the enemy force:

> … *Upham's platoon was slowly climbing up the steep 600-foot hill west of the ravine. The men were weak and very weary but they kept slowly going, and we could see that Upham was working round above the Germans still in the bottom of the ravine and pinned down by Washbourn's company and by fire from the eastern bank. Two hours after they had started the climb there was another sharp outburst of firing. It lasted about a minute, there were then some single shots, and then silence. A little later Upham's platoon started to come back and then a message came that all twenty-two of the enemy party had been killed, completely helpless under his plunging fire.*

253

That night, 30/31 May, Naval Force D evacuated 1,500 men from the port just three miles behind the rearguard's main position. Amongst those ordered out by Cairo that night were General Freyberg, Group Captain Beamish and Brigadier Stewart. Approaching 2300 hours, they were walking down to the Sunderland flying boats waiting just off the harbour. Encountering Brigadier Inglis *en route*, Freyberg ordered him to join the party. Inglis demurred and was in his turn 'sharply overruled'. General Freyberg wrote of his departure:

> *My feelings can be imagined better than described. I was handing over a difficult situation with the enemy through in one place almost to the beaches from which we were to make our last attempt to get away the remnants of the fighting force that still held out, tired, hungry, and thirsty on the heights above.*

Major General Weston was now in overall command.

The Evacuation

While the rearguard action was being fought at Megala Khoratia by the Commandos and Maoris on 28 May, the first 700 men were being evacuated from Hora Safakion and about 4,000 members of the Iraklio garrison escaped from the Island. The risks that the Royal Navy took to bring ships to Crete to rescue the Army, when they had already been driven from the seas north of Crete, were considerable. The destroyers and cruisers of Forces B (Iraklio) and C and D (Safakion) lost a further three ships, with six being damaged. The principal evacuation took place from Hora Safakion on the nights of 29, 30 and 31 May and 1 June. Ships could only approach to within *Luftwaffe* range of Crete once it was dark and had to be well to the south by dawn. This gave a very short window between 2300 and 0300 hours in which to load the ships, which had to be by small boats ferrying troops out to the ships.

Ashore, the *ad hoc* arrangements for the evacuation were always under pressure, with up to 9,000 men awaiting evacuation lying up by day in cover at the foot of the dry Imbros Gorge, or around Komitades, where both water and food were in short supply. A full water bottle of potable water a day was a luxury but there was even less chance of a full belly. Commando Arthur Swinburn describes a meal that he had on arrival at Hora Safakion:

> *Twenty-seven men into one tin of sausages (one tin contains thirteen) so each man had half a sausage leaving the 27th man, poor blighter, with the tin, some fat and the smell of what was once there!*
>
> *As the senior in each case had to distribute the ration, imagine how unlucky I was! But I did better on potatoes. Nine into a tin of potatoes left one over for me. Army biscuits were distributed 1 biscuit per man. This was the first food we had had for a very long time.*

Safaklon in the 1940s and right, present-day.

Selection of troops for evacuation was a tricky and political business. Correct proportions of New Zealand, Australian and British troops had to be allocated to the ever changing number of ships expected on a particular night. The principle that combat troops would be evacuated as a priority was more or less maintained but HQs were prime units that had a political significance of their own and they too were evacuated with a high priority. Brigadier Hargest personally filled the last of his quota by looking at a man, if he had a rifle, he stood a chance of selection but 'If they came without rifles I turned them down cold – they were stragglers'.

To ensure discipline and security of the beach and village, a cordon was maintained by the Royal Marines and other troops of the MNBDO. A crowd of men milled around awaiting their opportunity but no one could get through the cordon without the correct written authority and those who tried to bluff their way through 'found themselves on their backs, no matter what their rank!' Unit nominal rolls were compiled and at check points on the route to the beach they were checked and rechecked. 'Extras' were ruthlessly weeded out. In most cases, with fewer places on the ships than men waiting, selection for evacuation was principally based on the need to regenerate the unit once back in Egypt.

Nominated for evacuation, Captain Baker of A Company 28 Maori Battalion recalled the instinctive soldierly preparation of his men:

> ... on the morning of the 30th, by a pooling of resources the personnel of my Company Headquarters numbering, I think, seven, had all managed to change. One man had managed to locate a safety razor with an ancient well-used blade, another had sufficient water in his water-bottle, a third provided a brush, while my steel helmet was used as the shaving mug. It had been hard work as none of us had shaved for some few days and I think we all balked when it came to shaving the upper lip. The proportion of moustaches in the Battalion was high when we eventually reached Egypt.

The final evacuation took place on the night of 31 May / 1 June. Those who were serving with the infantry stood the highest chance of evacuation aboard the King's ships, based on the natural assumption that they had done most of the fighting. For those among the gunners, drivers and Petrol Company soldiers who had fought exceptionally well at Galatas, 'This was perhaps unfair'. On the afternoon of 31 May, an officer called a conference of his hundred men.

> Two things could be done: either the men could make an illegal trip to the beach that night and try to gatecrash a boat, or they could wait their turn, staying put until officially told to move. Veale said: 'If you do go down to the beaches tonight, other fighting troops will miss out. Make up your own minds. If you decide to go, I'll help all I can. If you stay, I'll stay.' The RMT decided to wait another night.

In the morning the Germans came down to the coatal plain.

Amongst Australian and New Zealand veterans there is an abiding suspicion that during the final scramble for the ships, the 'Johnny come latelies' or the 'one battle wonders' of Layforce jumped the queues for evacuation. However, detailed post war explanations of orders given, times and locations would seem to put the issue to rest. But, technically available since the mid-seventies, though misfiled, the Layforce War Diary for 31 May contains a seeming smoking gun:

> 2200 hrs. On finding that entire staff of CREFORCE had embarked, in view of the fact that all fighting forces were now in position for embarkation and that there was no enemy contact, Col LAYCOCK on own authority, issued orders to Lt Col YOUNG to lead troops to SFAKION by a route avoiding the crowded main approach to town and to use his own personality to obtain priority laid down in Div orders.

> LAYFORCE reached SFAKION outskirts in good time for boats but were unable to penetrate the rabble [the cordon with strict orders]; flank detachments were able to reach beach but main body remained ashore.

Col LAYCOCK, accompanied by Brigade Major and Intelligence Officer embarked HMS KIMBERLY. Total numbers of LAYFORCE evacuated 23 Officers, 186 ORs.

Typically fifty percent of combat contingents escaped capture or death on Crete. Only twenty-five percent of Layforce were evacuated and the fact that most of 2/7 Australian Battalion was left behind, is only indirectly connected to Layforce.

Major General Weston left Crete with the final evacuation leaving orders to surrender.

Surrender

With the final departure of the ships well before dawn, the remaining 9,000 soldiers waited in their caves and patches of shade, having been ordered to surrender to the first Germans they saw. Most of the infantry had come down from the hills and down the gorges and the Germans ready to renew the battle found the rearguard that had held them back the previous day gone. The German view of the situation:

What a sight is presented by our Gerbirgsjäger. Sun-tanned and parched, our uniforms in rags, caps flattened and caked with sweat and mud. Our mountaineering boots are patched up with insulating tape and leather straps, soles worn through, nails torn out from jumping and falling. Arms and legs are grazed. Every group has its wounded and yet we carry on with unheard of élan. We no longer feel the heat and have overcome extreme exhaustion ... Below us is the sea and the port of Safakion with the white cubes of its serried buildings. The rugged mountains drop steeply to the ground below. Crete's southern coast towers over the blue waters of the Mediterranean.

Moving cautiously down the track from the mountain, the Germans could see men flying white flags on the beach below. Down below, as senior officer remaining, Colonel Walker was handed Major General Weston's order to surrender. 'He decided that resistance was hopeless.' He gave instruction the men to destroy such equipment as they had, but despite the white flags, they were machine-gunned by *Luftwaffe* aircraft.

Colonel Walker returned back up to Komitadhes at the foot of the Imbros Gorge, where he formally surrendered the remains of the force to an Austrian officer. Back down at the beach, the transport drivers were waiting:

Orders to show anything white were ignored by the RMT party of a hundred which watched in dour silence a blond Bavarian hastily stumbling down the rocks, towing a huge swastika flag to call off the dive-bombers.

Driver Cumming, ordered out of his gully by the *Gerbirgsjäger* recalled:

It was funny even then to watch some chaps raise their arms above their heads while others raised them, and then lowered them, hesitant about being

shot or looking silly. However, the Jerries were also glad it was all over, and patting us on the back made signs we could drop our arms. We were a motley looking crew then.

The war was over; drab prison camps lay ahead for the Division's crack drivers.

Conclusion

While Student's *Fallschirmjäger* and *Gerbirgsjäger* won a remarkable victory over the Commonwealth Armies in Crete, they suffered heavy losses in capturing an island that never delivered its supposed advantage of extending Germany's air umbrella. Events in Russia (Operation BARBAROSSA), restored Allied naval superiority in the Mediterranean and steadily increasing air power, marginalised Crete. Worse, the partisan war waged by the fearsome Cretans in the island's mountains represented a running sore and a drain on scarce German resources.

Student's dream of a new form of warfare based on his airborne forces was over. The level of casualties, hitherto not experienced by Germany, led Hitler to conclude that 'The day of the *Fallschirmjäger* is past'. When OKW would no longer consider accepting the risks inherent in mounting large-scale airborne operations, General Student referred to Crete as 'the grave of German airborne forces'. In contrast, the Allies were developing their own airborne capability, and when at the outset of MARKET GARDEN no less than three airborne divisions passed over his HQ in Holland during September 1944, Student mused 'If ever I had such powerful means'. The lessons of Crete had not been lost on the Allies. Accounts of the battle and conclusions were all carefully studied.

Even though the Germans continued to train and equip *Fallschirmjäger*, they were never used in any significant operational level airborne operation, with the arguable exception of *FJR 3*'s drop into blocking positions on Sicily. Successful smaller scale parachute operations were mounted, including special operations, such as the rescue of Mussolini. The *Fallschirmjäger*, however, continued to be used as elite infantry, earning a fearsome reputation in battles such as Monte Cassino where the Division fought with distinction. The *Gebirgsjäger* never received their full measure of credit for their part in the Cretan Campaign but continued to be employed as high quality infantry.

What of the Commonwealth Allies? The New Zealand and Australian battalions were reconstituted and commanders progressed up the ranks as the war progressed. Freyberg became a Lieutenant General, commanding the New Zealand Corps at Cassino. Kippenberger, unsurprisingly rose to command the New Zealand Division but lost a foot when he stepped on a mine on the rocky slopes on Monte Trocchio in Italy, while preparing to battle his old adversary *FJR 3* at Cassino. Brigadier Hargest who, though much criticised at Maleme, won admiration during the withdrawal across the mountains for his leadership and physical presence that did so much to keep his men going. He served as New Zealand's observer in North-west Europe.

Let, however, an ordinary soldier, Private Diamond of 23 NZ Battalion, have the final word:

> *I long for the day when we can match the Germans in the sky, 'plane for plane'. When that day dawns, Germany is beaten. We know by experience that we can whack his land forces, tanks included, any day of the week.*

German cuff title for Crete celebrating victory, however, the *Führer* had decided that parachuting troops into battle had proved too expensive in casualties.

Chapter Twelve

THE ABDUCTION OF GENERAL KREIPE

The aftermath of the invasion of Crete was bloody. The Cretans, who had spontaneously joined the fighting and had given little quarter to the enemy, were the first invaded people to actively resist the Germans. Retribution was severe from the outset. This was justified in their eyes, by accusations of atrocities.

Crete has a long tradition of resistance and guerrilla warfare in the rugged terrain of the island's mountains. Old weapons came out of hiding, soon to be supplemented by drops of modern equipment and ammunition, organised by SOE agents who were sent anywhere where they could ferment or enhance resistance to the Germans. The enemy responded with the full panoply of Nazi retribution; torture, executions, destruction of villages and mass murder. By 1944, the cycle of attack and response was following its familiar pattern. SOE sought to raise the stakes by abducting

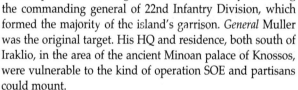

the commanding general of 22nd Infantry Division, which formed the majority of the island's garrison. *General* Muller was the original target. His HQ and residence, both south of Iraklio, in the area of the ancient Minoan palace of Knossos, were vulnerable to the kind of operation SOE and partisans could mount.

On 4 February 1944 Major Patrick Leigh-Fermor, Captain Bill Moss and two Cretan SOE agents, Manoli Paterakis and George Tirakis planned to jump into the island, contact partisans and set-up the abduction but the weather was poor and only Major Leigh-Fermor was able to drop in a fleeting gap in the clouds. The other three made fourteen attempts to

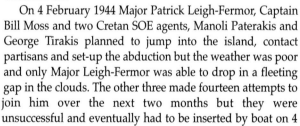

General Heinrich Kreipe.

join him over the next two months but they were unsuccessful and eventually had to be inserted by boat on 4 April. However, by this time, *General* Muller had been replaced by *General* Heinrich Kreipe, who had been transferred to a 'quiet post' from the Eastern Front.

Landing on a remote beach on the south coast the party made their way by night across the island to the target area south of Iraklio, using a combination of safe houses and caves to lie up by day. The Germans, alerted to the presence of what they erroneously calculated, from the aircraft noise of the abortive attempts to drop Bill Moss and the two Cretan agents, to be forty parachutists, were actively hunting British agents.

Despite the threat, *General* Kreipe kept to his routine of travelling to and from his divisional headquarters in the village of Archanes to Villa Ariadne at Knoossos. It was this predictable routine that Major Leigh-Fermor and his group planned to exploit. Observing his routine the partisans worked out that he would travel unescorted by car to his HQ at around 0900 hours and return to his villa for lunch at 1300 hours. At 1600 hours the General would be driven to his HQ and return to the villa around 2000 hours for dinner. However, occasionally he played bridge at his HQ Mess until late in the evening, which was the only regular variable to his routine.

With sunset at 1945 hours during April, his normal return journey would be in the gathering gloom and this would be the ideal time to ambush his car. It was also reasoned that his house staff at the Villa Ariadne, would assume that the *General* had stayed at the Mess for dinner and a game of bridge, and would not raise the alarm if he were late.

While awaiting the arrival of the rest of the team Major Leigh-Fermor identified the ideal spot for the abduction on the route between HQ and residence; a T-junction where the *General's* road from Archanes joins the Iraklio to Peza road near the village of Patsides. Here with a slope down to the main road, a car would have to slow down to make the turn and would consequently be easy to stop and the banks and ditches on either side would give cover for the waiting men.

One of the local partisans, Ellias, spent days spotting the *General's* Opel staff car, complete with its pennant, so that he could positively identify it as it approached in the dark. He would alert the ambush that the *General* was on his way by means of a simple switch, battery, 300 metres of cable and buzzer system. As recalled by Bill Moss:

Bill Moss and Patrick Leigh-Fermor disguised as German military police corporals.

… we thought it advisable to detail somebody to the specific job of "buzzer man", who would listen for the signal and at the critical moment flash a torch at Paddy and me, who would be standing by in a ditch.

Patrick Leigh-Fermor and Bill Moss were to stop the car by pretending to be a German check-point. For this they needed uniforms, which were procured by the partisans from Iraklio, without the bloodstains being too obvious. The other SOE agents and the partisans would be deployed in the ditches on both sides of the road, all with specific tasks such as holding up any other traffic. Bill Moss recorded in his personal diary the detail of the plan:

In the guise of German police

262

corporals, equipped with red lamps and traffic signals, Paddy and I were going to stand in the centre of the road as the car approached and signal it to stop. We would then walk towards it, Paddy on the left side and myself on the right and make certain that the General was inside; then, on a given word, we would rip open the doors, Paddy hauling out the General while I dealt with the chauffeur. Eiles had told us that the General usually sat in the front seat of the car beside the chauffeur, so we felt safe in basing our plan of action on this supposition.

On 26 April 1944 the plan was ready for execution and at 2000 hours, the group was in position. During the hour's wait, there were five false alarms as German trucks and motorcycles passed. Bill Moss commented that the German figures 'were silhouetted against the night sky. It was a strange feeling to be crouching so close to them … while they drove past with no idea that nine pairs of eyes were so fixedly watching them'.

An hour after the *General's* normal time for making his return journey, the group were begging to wonder where he was. Shivering with cold, Bill Moss continued:

> *I remember Paddy's asking me the time. I looked at my watch and saw that the hands were pointing close to half-past nine. And at that moment Mitso's torch blinked.*
>
> *'Here we go.'*

Scrambling out of the ditch on to the road, Major Leigh-Fermor switched on the red lamp and Moss held up a traffic signal, and together they confidently stood in the centre of the road. 'In a moment – far sooner than we had expected – the powerful headlamps of the *General's* Opel swept round the bend and we found ourselves floodlit.' The driver, as predicted, was already slowing down as he approached the junction. **See page 274**

According to *General* Kreipe, who wrote well after the event:

> *…in the afternoon I was at Divisional HQ at Archanes. I spent the evening in the officers' mess and at 9 o'clock I drove home. There was a machine pistol in the car and my driver was armed with a pistol. We were alone… Suddenly a red light appeared in the darkness in front of us, approximately on the bend. The driver asked 'Shall I stop?' We were accustomed to traffic control points, and I answered 'Stop'. As the car drew to a halt two Germans in the uniforms of Oberschütze stepped forward. The older one, Leigh-Fermor, demanded to see my travel document. As I did not have one – it was not normally required – I said 'Don't know about that.' 'In that case the password please.' Then I did something foolish. I got out of the car and said "What unit are you? Don't you know your General?" Leigh-Fermor in his German soldier's disguise, said 'General, you are a prisoner of war in British hands.'*

Bill Moss took on the driver. His account written up the following day:

> *As we came level with the doors of the car Paddy asked, Ist dies das*

General's Wagen?

There came a muffled Ja,ja from inside.

Then everything happened very quickly. There was a rush from all sides. We tore open our respective doors, and our torches illuminated the interior of the car – the bewildered face of the General, the chauffeur's terrified eyes, the rear seats empty. With his right hand the chauffeur was reaching for his automatic, so I hit him across the head with my cosh. He fell forward, and George, who had come up behind me, heaved him out of the driving-seat and dumped him on the road. I jumped in behind the steering-wheel, and at the same moment saw Paddy and Manoli dragging the General out of the opposite door. The old man was struggling with fury, lashing out with his arms and legs. He obviously thought that he was going to be killed, and started shouting every curse under the sun at the top of his voice.

The engine of the car was still ticking over, the hand-brake was on, everything was perfect. To one side, in a pool of torchlight in the centre of the road, Paddy and Manoli were trying to quieten the General, who was still cursing and struggling. On the other side George and Andoni were trying to pull the chauffeur to his feet, but the man's head was pouring with blood, and I think he must have been unconscious, because every time they lifted him up he simply collapsed to the ground again.

Fortunately at this critical moment, no other traffic came along the road and Major Leigh-Fermor, Manoli, Nikko, and Stratis carried the *General* towards the car and bundled him into the back seat. The three Cretans, 'one of the three holding a knife to the *General's* throat to stop him shouting' handled the *General* roughly. Kreipe claims that he was beaten to the ground:

I was belaboured with gun-butts, tied up and gagged and I am afraid, called 'you damned German pig'. I was thrown into the car and two partisans lay on top of me, threatening me with a dagger. 'If you move we will kill you!'

In front sat the two 'Oberschütze', that is to say the British officers.

Bill Mose's version is:

Paddy jumped into the front seat beside me. The General kept imploring, Where is my hat? Where is my hat? The hat, of course, was on Paddy's head.

We were now ready to move. Suddenly everyone started kissing and congratulating everybody else; and Micky, having first embraced Paddy and me, started screaming at the General with all the pent-up hatred he held for the Germans. We had to push him away and tell him to shut up. Andoni, Grigori, Nikko, and Wallace Beery were standing at the roadside, propping up the chauffeur between them, they waved us good-bye and turned away and started off on their long trek to the rendezvous on Mount Ida.

The car was a brand new Opel, and the tank was full. They had been driving for a minute when they passed a convoy of German infantry travelling in the opposite direction. They 'thanked our stars that it had not come this way a couple of minutes sooner'. When the convoy had passed Major Leigh-Fermor 'told the *General* that the two of us were British officers and that we would treat him as an honourable prisoner of war'. The *General*, unsurprisingly, 'seemed mightily relieved to hear this'. His chief concern apparently was the whereabouts of his medal.

The first opportunity for the enemy to realise that something was wrong, was when rather than turning into the gates of the Villa Ariadne, the car accelerated along the road past the Villa's gate and the in surprised sentries. This either didn't excite suspicion or the passage of information was too slow to alert the check points in the area. It was not long before they saw a red flashing lamp of the first of the military check posts through which they would have to pass. Expecting this, 'the plan had contained alternative actions which we had hoped would suit any situation, because we knew that our route led us through the centre of Iraklio...'

A German sentry was standing in the middle of the road. As we approached him, slowing down the while, he moved to one side, presumably thinking that we were going to stop. However, as soon as we drew level with him – still going very slowly, so as to give him an opportunity of seeing the General's pennants on the wings of the car – I began to accelerate again, and on we went. For several seconds after we had passed the sentry we were all apprehension, fully expecting to hear a rifle-shot in our wake; but a moment later we had rounded a bend in the road and knew that the danger was temporarily past. Our chief concern now was whether or not the guard at the post behind us would telephone ahead to the next one, and it was with our fingers crossed that we approached the red lamp of the second control post a few minutes later. But we need not have had any fears, for the sentry behaved in exactly the same manner as the first had done, and we drove on feeling rather pleased with ourselves.

It was a similar drill as they passed through no less than twenty-two such checkpoints announcing themselves as '*General's wagen*' and cheekily offering '*Gute Nacht*' as they accelerated away. One of the tenser moments, however, was when in the centre of Iraklio they drove through a crowd of Germans leaving a cinema. They had the satisfaction of sending them running for safety, no doubt cursing senior officers and their drivers!

Near a beach, widely known to be used in the past by British submarines, they abandoned the car to begin their long journey over the mountains to the south coast, leaving a message designed to throw the Germans off the scent and to avoid bringing reprisals down on the local population.

TO THE GERMAN AUTHORITIES IN CRETE
April 23, 1944

General Kreipe with his SOE captors in the Cretan mountains.

GENTLEMEN

Your divisional Commander General Kreipe was captured a short time ago by a BRITISH raiding force under our command. By the time you read this both he and we will be on our way to CAIRO.

We would like to point out most emphatically that this operation has been carried out without the help of CRETANS or CRETAN partisans and the only guides used were serving soldiers of HIS HELLENIC MAJESTY'S FORCES in the Middle East, who came with us.

Your General is an honourable prisoner of war, and will be treated with all the consideration owing to his rank.

Sufbaldiges Wiedersehen!

PS. We are very sorry to have to leave this beautiful car behind.

The latter was added to give the message that inescapably British authenticity. Even so threats of 'the severest measures of reprisal', scattered by air dropped leaflet, were made to the populace. The Germans must have doubted Cretan involvement, as they were not carried out. Also arranged was a radio broadcast along the same lines, with the addition of a phrase in the report that the General was 'already in Cairo' but when it was read the wording had been changed to 'is on his way to Cairo'. Heading across the mountains, the group, with their prisoner riding much of the way on a donkey, only evaded capture by dint of luck, resourcefulness, skill and tenacity. In an epic seventeen-day march, they crossed Mount Ida and narrowly avoided disaster several times, before reaching their beach on the south coast, from which they were picked up on 14 May 1944, successfully ending one of the most audacious SOE operations of the war.

Chapter Thirteen

THE AIRBORNE INVASION TOURS

The tours of the Airborne Invasion battlefields are thoroughly worthwhile, despite the spread of development, holiday sprawl and an EU subsidy-driven proliferation of olive trees. The six tours in this chapter start from an obvious point in the nearest town. Hire car is the normal means of transport for the battlefield visitor but the excellent Cretan bus service can be used to get to the main tour area and the hardy can walk the tours – except the withdrawal, which would take three days to complete on foot!

Currently available 100K maps are not particularly accurate or complete. Consequently, the use of signs in these directions (in a fast developing area!) and the various photographs will enable the visitor to navigate around the battlefield. However, larger maps and air photographs not suitable for inclusion in this book are available for download at www.galahadhistory.com.

Please be warned that as the long-standing regional difficulties are liable to come to the boil at any time, the military on Crete maintain a high state of security. Taking photographs of military bases and airfields, even if there are no visible signs banning photography, is asking for trouble!

Many readers will be expecting to visit the German *Fallschirmjäger* memorial on the outskirts of Hania during the tours in this book. However, despite attempts to represent the memorial as being to all nations' airborne forces, the monument fell into increasing disrepair and with mounting vandalism, it has been removed. There are no firm plans to relocate the memorial but some hope that it will be incorporated into the Cemetery Hill museum/memorial complex, when it is built.

The highly controversial and detested *Fallschirmjäger* memorial. Even with the swastika deleted from the claws it has attracted the attention of vandals over the years. It has now been removed and may appear in a more secure location – or not.

Preliminary Visits
If travelling to Crete via Greece it is worth visiting the following places on a stop-over:

Hotel Grande Bretagne The hotel taken over as the HQ of *Luftflotte 4* and that of *Fliegerkorps VIII* and *XII* is located in central Athens on Syntagma Square, just north of the National Garden. The Grande Bretagne is a 5 Star establishment and while enjoying a cup of Greek coffee in the hotel's halls, it is easy to imagine the bustle of *Luftwaffe* officers coming and going as tensions mounted.

The Corinth Canal The Bridge over the Corinth Canal that was the objective of *Fallschirmjäger Regiment 2*'s Operation HANNIBAL is only an hour east of Athens and is worth a visit.

Tour 1 – The Maleme Area

Leave Hania, following signs to Kastelli. You can either take the Old Coast Road through Platanias, which takes about thirty minutes through tourist sprawl or the National Road, which takes only fifteen minutes and provides a good view of the ground slightly inland. If taking this route, look out for the Tavronitis exit, turn left at the foot of the ramp and turn right in the village on to the Old Coast Road, heading east. The old iron bridge is to the left of the modern concrete bridge.

If taking the Old Coast Road through Platanias, after Maleme Village the development gives way to more rural country. Here the road goes between the Maleme airfield to the right and a Hellenic Army Barracks (RAF camp) on the left.

The Tavronitis Bridge The old steel bridge over the Tavronitis River (dry in most summers) that carries the Old Coast Road is to the seaward side of its modern equivalent. Once across the bridge turn right and park by a C1943 German bunker and *Tobruckstand.* Walk down to the bridge and look for the battle damage to the steel structure. Looking due east along the bridge is the area of the RAF Camp. On the low ground to the left was 22 NZ Infantry Battalion's C Company position and to the right, on the forward slope of Hill 107 was D Company's position.

The RAF 30 and 33 Squadron Memorial Crossing the new Tavronitis Bridge there is a large gravel open area. Hidden amongst the Cypress trees at the far side behind a chain link fence is a stone memorial built by the modern RAF successors to the two squadrons. It is located on the forward edge of the RAF Camp area in full view of the Tavronitis Bridge. Biannually, the RAF fly out to take part in the commemorations on and around 20 May. There are plans to put up a sign, which will help locate this memorial.

Drive back past the RAF Camp, now the barracks of a Greek parachute battalion, towards Maleme. The airfield is to the left – note the 'no photography' signs on the fence.

The German Cemetery In the outskirts of Maleme, after the second filling station, look out for a blue sign to the right, with a white square and the words *Deutscher Soldatenfriedhof and Vlacheronitissa 4 Kms*. Driving up a narrow road, take the signed right turn, following a sinuous route up hill and park at the cemetery. Toilets and a café are available here. See Appendix 2 for a description of the Cemetery.

Lieutenant Colonel Andrews' HQ was just beyond the top gate at the left corner of the cemetery; beyond lies the ridge of Hill 107 running due south.

Hill 107 There are two ways of reaching the crest of Hill 107, which has a traditional white chapel and memorial cross on its highest point.

Approach A. Step over the gate at the top left corner of the cemetery and follow the track through the vines and olives. It is about a ten minute walk.

Approach B. Leave the cemetery and drive down the approach road tuning right at the T-junction and follow the winding road and fork right just before the bridge over the National Road. This metalled road eventually becomes a track after the hairpin bend but the white painted chapel can be seen several hundred yards ahead.

Up here, it is easy to visualise the fighting amongst the olive groves and vines, both individual engagements, such as that of Helmut Wenzel and the organised probes by

II/LLSR through the gap where the National Road now runs.

Go down to the open area below the chapel, to the north-east the view is down onto 22 NZ Battalion's HQ Company positions and further inland are those of 21 and 23 Battalions, with 28 Maori battalion beyond.

There is also a post invasion German bunker and gun pit built on the crest of the hill used to protect the *Luftwaffe* anti-aircraft gunners, who took over a 3-inch anti-aircraft troop's gun pits for their own defence of the airfield both during the battle and up to the island's eventual liberation in 1945.

German Cemetery after the war with veterans visiting the last resting place of their fallen comrades. Present-day German Cemetery.

To the south of Hill 107, on a site that is today occupied by modern antennas, was a pair of forty foot high radar masts, a part of the old Air Ministry Experimental Site. This was a part of the chain of such radar stations deployed to Crete to give the Commonwealth forces warning of the approach of aircraft.

From the Cemetery or the chapel continue towards Vlacheronitissa. Drive through this traditional Cretan village and park near the T-junction. This is where Strentzler led *6 Kompanie* through the hills using the broken low ground.

Turn right. The detached platoon from 21 NZ Battalion were on the high ground to your right. After going through an underpass under the National Road bridge, you will be driving along the front of D Company's position. Entering the open area of the RAF Memorial at the junction, the Tavronitis Bridge is to your left. You will have now completed a circuit of Hill 107.

Maleme/Pygi Turn right and drive into Maleme/Pygi, where a sharp eye will spot older buildings, amongst the modern developments, complete with bullet holes in the walls. Turn left just after the Hotel EL-KI and the supermarket IN.KA. Drive down to the beach and turn left along the old beach road and park where the road peters out. The beach was used to crash land Ju 52s, initially those that had been badly hit by anti-aircraft and New Zealand small-arms fire and subsequently as a deliberate but desperate measure to reinforce the *Fallschirmjäger*. The beach also marks the right flank of the counter-attack mounted on the night of 21/22 May by 20 NZ Inf Bn, the tanks of 3 Hussars on the Maleme/Tavronitis road and 28 Maori NZ Battalion to the south of the road. The restaurants here provide a welcome chance of a drink and a meal.

Tour 2 – The Galatas Area

To reach the LZs and DZs of *Gruppe Mitt*, drive through Maleme, Girani and into Platanias. When nearly through Platanias turn right at the 24-Hour Bank opposite Café Bamboo. Annoyingly the turning is only signed Galatas from the east, so if you miss the turning (and you probably will), use the BP garage just beyond the Daratos sign, to turn around and have a second attempt.

At the next major crossroads go straight across following the sign to Daratos. After a hundred yards take an uphill right fork. Follow the road. Galatas is to your right. When you come to a Cemetery turn off the road to the left and make your way up to the top of Cemetery Hill. From here you will have an unrivalled view of Prison Valley and the

Galatas then and now.

neighbouring Pink Hill. You will not be able to locate the lake/reservoir to the west as it has been drained.

Leave Cemetery Hill and head down into Prison Valley. Turn right and at the second crossroads, turn left. Reaching the main Hania-Aghia road, turn right and drive past the prison. This was HQ *FJR 3*, with the Prison being used as the aid post.

Galatas   Drive into the centre of the village and park in the square opposite the church.

Lygides   From the Prison Valley Road, heading towards Hania, turn right, signed to Lygides. At the centre of the village, go straight on up a narrow road (to the left of a taverna). Stop at the T-junction. This is the area where von der Hydtes' *I Battalion* fought. Across the valley to your front are the 19 Australian Brigade positions.

Galaria   Leave Prison Valley Road by turning first right after the Vamvakopoulo sign. Drive through olive groves and park at the crossroads. This is the centre of 19 Australian Brigade's position.

Force Reserve Positions Heading east towards Hania, drive under the National Highway. On the left is a sports complex with lights. Turn left uphill after the sports field and follow the road. Park at the end of the road and walk around the far side of the sports pitches up onto the high ground. The centre of 1 Welch's position was up here. The Rangers and Northumberland Hussars were down in the area of the road and the last stand took place in the area of the underpass.

42nd Street This is on the south-eastern outskirts of Hania. From the city centre follow the signs to Souda. As you leave the city, the density of houses, factories and car dealerships start to thin, look out for a sign to Tsikalaria on the right. To confirm that you are on the correct road look out for the small street sign Chickalarion Street. This is 42nd Street. Drive several hundred yards and park by an old olive grove. It is through these old trees that the Australians and New Zealanders delivered their momentous charge on 27 May 1941.

Souda Bay Commonwealth War Graves Commission Cemetery
Take the same route out of Hania, past 42nd Street. Follow signs for Souda and go straight across a large, open and complicated junction, ignoring the New Road signs. Just before the set of traffic lights, there is a green and white CWGC sign to the Cemetery indicating that you should turn left at the traffic lights. After the lights, follow the road around some bends and another CWGC sign indicates to the right. Park by the Cemetery gates. A description of the Cemetery is to be found in Appendix 2.

The Maritime Museum of Crete This Museum at the western end of the Venetian Harbour in Hania, is well worth a visit in its own right but also has a large display dedicated to the invasion on its upper floor. There are photographs rarely seen outside Crete and a collection of Commonwealth and German artefacts.

Souda Bay Cemetery.

Tour 3 – Rethymno

Hill B From Platanias take a right turn signed to Marbulas. Go under the National Highway, ignore the next sign to Marbulas and go straight on Hill Brises in front of you. Turn left up a rough track opposite an EKO filling station. After 200 yards you will reach a T-junction; turn left and then next right. This will take you to an open area on Hill B, the position of 2/11 Australian Infantry.

Hill A Return to the filling station junction, continue east and turn left to Adele. In the village turn left towards Kambos. The feature on your right is Hill A and the valley between the road and hill is Wadi Pigi. Continue down the road where the road bears left and goes parallel to the National Highway; follow. Go straight under the bridge to return to Platanias and turn left or take the unsigned ramp up to the National Highway before the bridge to rejoin the Highway eastbound.

Tour 4 – Iraklio

WARNING Do not take photographs of the airfield, barracks or the 'Golf Ball' their perimeters or facilities. The area doubles as an active Hellenic air base and the consequences of, no matter how innocently compromising security, are severe for the unwise. It has been pointed out to me regularly that Greece is potentially 'just fifteen minutes from war'.

Take the airport spur off the New Road. Approaching the airport terminal's concourse, turn left and follow the road. After the hire car lots, on your left, is a Hellenic Army barracks; both this and the airfield were a part of 1 Black Watch's area of responsibility. When entering the built up area look out for a sign Agios Nikolaos Old Road to the left. Take this road, which was the boundary between the Black Watch and 2/4 Australian Infantry Battalion. 2 Leicesters were beyond them and further still to the west were 2 York & Lancs.

East Ridge Continue on towards Agios Nikolaos, following the road around to the left before the new road. The airfield perimeter is on your left and you will go under an underpass. Take the first right and then follow the road to the left (No through road sign) and take the first non-gated left turn. This will take you behind a waste disposal processing site. Park and in front of you is East Ridge, held by a platoon of Black Watch.

Tour 5 – The Withdrawal to Hora Safakion

This tour will take a whole day, including a late and leisurely lunch at Hora Safakion. From Hania to the south coast the total driving time is about 1 hour 30 minutes. Set your distance measurer to zero on turning off the Coast Road.

Megala Khorafia (Beritiana Junction) Heading east from Hania and Souda, turn off main Coast Road, signed Megala Khorafia. Cross the bridge and follow the road up the zigzag (the new post-war route) into village. Park by a shop on the outskirts and take a small made-up road behind the shop to where you can get a view of the valley. This is where a part of the Maori force was located during the battle on 28 May. Deep in the valley below is the unenviable position occupied by the commandos. The enemy approached via the coast road and over the hills opposite.

Continue south through the village towards Vyres. Vyres is one of the points en route where dumps and transit camps were established. These camps were welcome sources of supply and rest but were only partly successful in organising the mass of withdrawing troops. Continue through the village south towards Stylos.

Stylos (Km 5.5) Halt by the bridge over the defile short of the village. This is the area where 23 NZ Battalion deployed on the morning of 28 May, covering the bridge and the high ground to the south-west, where they were nearly surprised by *GBR 85*.

Agh Pandes (Km 11) Stop on a zigzag short of the village. Up on the ridge, looking north, was the right flank of Layforce, who were deployed in blocking positions. Across the road, to the west, through the low ground to the left were another two companies. Behind you, towards Agh Pandes were the scant reserves and the tanks. The enemy's main attack came through the low ground having been rebuffed on the higher ground.

Vryses (Km 17) This small town was one of the stopping, rest and collection points en route to Hora Safakion. Just a few miles south the road up to the mountain pass starts to rise steeply. A good place to stop.

The Saucer (Km 34) As the green Askifou plain comes into sight, stop. From this area it is possible to see the course of the old road.

The War Museum, Kares, Askifou This is the hospitable Hatzidakis family's private collection of items collected from across the island. Pieces of Ju 52 lie alongside British petrol tins, helmets and the remains of a Bren gun. Not a conventional museum but charming and a useful illustration of many of the things mentioned earlier in this book. A visit is also an opportunity to see an old style Cretan house and have a cup of Greek coffee in the simple village store, well off the beaten tourist track.

While coming down into the Saucer, look out for hand painted 'Military Museum' signs, in yellow at the time of writing, off the modern highway to the left. Drive down into the village following the signs.

Blocking Position 1 (Km 36) Leaving the saucer one passes the area of the first of the covering force's positions. It is easy to envisage the fight back to the village of Imbros and the Second blocking position.

The Imbros Gorge   (Km 41) At five miles this spectacular gorge is less than half the length of the Samaria Gorge and walking down it takes about 1 hour 30 minutes and is worthwhile in its own right, as well as and to follow in the footsteps of the withdrawing Commonwealth force. Purchase a ticket at one of the cafés at the top and walk down to the ticket office. **Water, good footwear for rough terrain and cover from the sun are essential. Please be aware that there is no easy evacuation from the Gorge, which should not be attempted by the unfit or those who are less than fully healthy.** Buses and taxis are readily available to take you back up to the valley.

Blocking Position 3   (Km 53) The ridges and bends in the road were used by the tanks and carriers to block the German advance.

Komitades Off the modern highway, at the foot of the Imbros Gorge, the caves and the gullies provided shelter for men before making the last leg of the journey to the port and the hope of evacuation. This is where the final surrennder took place.

Hora Safakion This attractive and, despite the portside restaurants, unspoiled village was where the ships' boats came in. Most troops were, however, evacuated from the beach through the houses just to the west. Immediately above the village is St Peter's

Cave which was where the regulating HQ was located. Hora Safakion itself was, of course, surrounded by a security cordon of Royal Marine infantry.

Tour 6 – The Abduction of *General* Kreipe

This very short tour is best done in conjunction with the obligatory visit to Knossos. The site of the abduction is six and a half kilometres south of the palace complex. Drive through Agh Irine and stop at the junction signed Archanes.

Spila Junction The road junction was the scene of the abduction. Even though there have been changes to the layout since 1942, the excellence of the site chosen can be fully appreciated.

Villa Ariadne The villa long described as 'the most beautiful in Crete', was built by Sir Arthur Evans during his excavations at Knossos. It was a natural choice for the German *General's* residence, being between his HQ in Archanes and the largest town on the island, Iraklio. The villa was used as a field Hospital during Operation MERKUR and, after being used as the German Commander's quarters, was were the Germans signed their surrender on 9 May 1945. It is located about 100 yards north of Knossos and although it is not open to the public, if you ask nicely it is usually possible to enter the grounds.

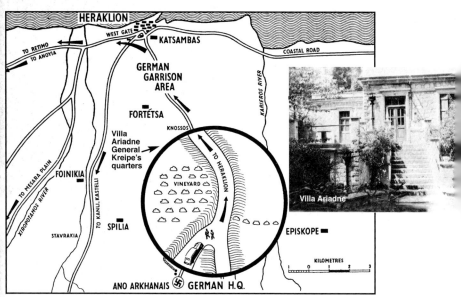

Villa Ariadne

Appendix I

VICTORIA CROSS CITATIONS

Second-Lieutenant Upham VC and Bar

Charles Hazlitt Upham won the Victoria Cross in Crete in May 1941 and again at Ruweisat Ridge in Egypt's Western Desert during the equally dark days of July 1942. He was only the third person to receive the VC and Bar, the only man to do so during the Second World War and the only combat soldier to receive the award twice. The others are Captains Arthur Martin-Leake and Noel Chavasse, both of the Royal Army Medical Corps in the Boer War/Great War.

Charles Upham was born in Christchurch, New Zealand on September 21 1908. He was educated at Christ's College, Canterbury and Canterbury Agricultural College where he earned a diploma in agriculture. He worked first as a sheep farmer, later as manager, and then as farm valuer for the New Zealand Government.

On the outbreak of war, Upham volunteered for service, saying he 'wanted to fight for justice'. He enlisted in the 20th NZ Battalion and left for Egypt with the advance party of the 2nd NZEF in December 1939 in the rank of sergeant. He was commissioned in November 1940.

8077 SECOND-LIEUTENANT CHARLES HAZLITT UPHAM

During the operations in Crete this officer performed a series of remarkable exploits, showing outstanding leadership, tactical skill and utter indifference to danger. He commanded a forward platoon in the attack on Maleme on May 22 and fought his way forward for over 3000 yards unsupported by any other arms and against a defence strongly organised in

275

depth. During this operation his platoon destroyed numerous enemy posts but on three occasions sections were temporarily held up.

In the first case, under a heavy fire from an MG nest he advanced to close quarters with pistol and grenades, so demoralising the occupants that his section was able to 'mop up' with ease. Another of his sections was then held up by two MGs in a house. He went in and placed a grenade through a window, destroying the crew of one MG and several others, the other MG being silenced by the fire of his sections. In the third case he crawled to within 15 yards of an MG post and killed the gunners with a grenade.

When his Company withdrew from Maleme he helped to carry a wounded man out under fire, and together with another officer rallied more men together to carry other wounded men out. He was then sent to bring in a Company which had become isolated. With a corporal he went through enemy territory over 600 yards, killing two Germans on the way, found the Company, and brought it back to the Battalion's new position. But for this action it would have been completely cut off.

During the following two days his platoon occupied an exposed position on forward slopes and was continuously under fire. 2/Lieut. Upham was blown over by one mortar shell and painfully wounded by a piece of shrapnel behind the left shoulder by another. He disregarded this wound and remained on duty. He also received a bullet in the foot which he later removed in Egypt.

At Galatos on May 25 his platoon was heavily engaged when troops in front gave way and came under severe Mortar and MG fire. While his platoon stopped under cover of a ridge 2/Lieut. Upham went forward, observed the enemy and brought the platoon forward when the Germans advanced. They killed over 40 with fire and grenades and forced the remainder to fall back.

When his platoon was ordered to retire he sent it back under the platoon Sjt and he went back to warn other troops that they were being cut off. When he came out himself he was fired on by two Germans. He fell and shammed dead, then crawled into a position and having the use of only one arm he rested his rifle in the fork of a tree and as the Germans came forward he killed them both. The second to fall actually hit the muzzle of the rifle as he fell.

On 30th May at Sphakia his platoon was ordered to deal with a party of the enemy which had advanced down a ravine to near Force Headquarters. Though in an exhausted condition he climbed the steep hill to the west of the ravine, placed his men in positions on the slope overlooking the ravine and himself went to the top with a Bren Gun and two riflemen. By clever tactics he induced the enemy party to expose itself and then at a range of 500 yards shot 22 and caused the remainder to disperse in panic.

During the whole of the operations he suffered from diarrhoea and was able to eat very little, in addition to being wounded and bruised.

He showed superb coolness, great skill and dash and complete disregard of danger. His conduct and leadership inspired his whole platoon to fight magnificently throughout, and in fact was an inspiration to the battalion.

276

Sergeant Alfred Hulme VC

In 1941 Alfred Clive Hulme was a 30-year-old Provost Sergeant in 23 NZ Battalion (The Canterbury Regiment), detatched to the Force Punishment Centre. During the period 20/28 May 1941, Sergeant Hulme displayed outstanding leadership and courage. At Maleme he led a party of soldiers under sentence against the *Fallschirmjäger* who had landed in the force Punishment Centre's area. Later, at Galatas, he drove the enemy away from a school building with hand grenades. At Souda Bay he killed five snipers and at Stylos he wiped out a mortar crew and accounted for three more snipers.

In 2006, law professor Bill Hodge argued that one of Hulme's actions was a *'prima facie* war crime', having broken the rules of war by wearing German uniform when hunting snipers. The battalion history describes Hulme's actions:

Most of his outstanding efforts were made alone or with small patrols and did not fit into any unit action. They were typical of this man who sought so frequently to fight a one-man war. Hulme was the battalion Provost Sergeant from early 1940 onwards. In his official capacity he was assisting Lieutenant Roach of 21 Battalion to run a Field Punishment Centre east of the 23rd's area and south-west of Platanias when the Germans began to land on 20 May.

At first Hulme and the other members of the Field Punishment Centre were busy dealing with the parachutists dropping in their area. Later, Lieutenant Roach reported that the Germans gave some trouble but 'Sgt. Hulme got cracking – very aggressively. He stood in full view of any German and fired bursts into any suspected places and that closed up the odd burst of fire'. Sometimes alone and sometimes with another – for example, on two occasions he had Private Shatford with him – Hulme went out and dealt with enemy riflemen. Stalking them carefully, he almost invariably got his man. Roach's report shows how much one determined infantryman could dominate an area when it says: 'Hulme used to wander about a lot – from the camp to the road was all his country.' Hulme himself claimed no special credit for the manner in which the Punishment Centre men cleaned up their area but 126 German dead were counted in that general area. Reporting in to 5 Brigade Headquarters on one occasion with some marked maps, Hulme was detailed by Brigadier Hargest to deal with a sniper, whom he stalked and shot.

Hulme returned to the 23rd the day before the unit left its area near Maleme. By this time he had acquired two items from parachutists he had shot which gave him some protection on his stalking patrols and may possibly have misled the Germans. These were a camouflage suit or blouse which he wore over his battle-dress tunic and a camouflage hat, which could be worn either rolled up like a balaclava or down in a hood, with eye-slits, over the face. He killed two other Germans before the order to withdraw came. On a visit to Brigade Headquarters, he ran into a small party of New Zealand engineers held prisoner by one German sentry. Afraid to shoot for fear of hitting a New Zealander, Hulme crept up behind the sentry, jumped on him and killed him with a short German bayonet. Directed to find out how many Germans were in Pirgos, Hulme ran into two unguarded aircraft which he set on fire with German fusee matches.

After Galatas, Hulme heard that his brother, Corporal 'Blondie' Hulme, of 19 Battalion, had been killed. Determined to avenge his brother, Hulme dropped behind the withdrawing unit and, taking up a position covering a food dump, waited till the leading Germans arrived. Before this patrol pulled back, Hulme shot three of them.

During a conference of senior officers, including Australian and British, at 5 Brigade Headquarters behind 42nd Street, German snipers sent bullets whistling over. Hulme volunteered to deal with the trouble. He climbed the hillside from which the Germans were firing, came out above four Germans, and shot the leader. He was wearing his camouflage suit at the time and, when the Germans looked round to see where the shooting was coming from, Hulme also looked round, giving the impression he was one of them. When the men below him looked down again, he quickly picked off two of them and then shot the fourth as he moved up towards him. A fifth he shot as he came round the side of the hill towards him. Most of these proceedings were watched by Major Thomason through his binoculars.

Sergeant Hulme's official citation says that he 'made his score thirty-three enemy snipers stalked and shot'. It adds: 'Sergeant Hulme's Brigadier, in supporting the recommendation for the award of the Victoria Cross, states that during the whole of the fighting until he was wounded, Sergeant Hulme conducted himself with such courage that the story of his exploits was on everyone's lips.' That this was true of the commanding officer of the 23rd may be seen from Lieutenant Thomas's account of a visit from Colonel Leckie in the dressing station behind Galatas: 'Colonel Leckie limped over to see me. He stayed and talked with me for some time, speaking sadly of the Battalion's casualties and proudly of its showing throughout the fighting. He spoke at length of Sgt. Hulme who … had done wonders.'

Appendix II

THE CEMETERIES

'The soldiers' graves are the greatest preachers of peace.'
(Albert Schweitzer, Nobel Peace Prize laureate)

German Cemetery, Hill 107

In 1961, the German War Graves Commission (*Volksbund Deutsche Kriegsgaberfursorge (VBK)*) succeeded in obtaining permission from the Greek government for the recovery of German dead. Pending the ratification of the formal war graves treaty, bodies were collected and moved to the Monastery of Gonia. In the early seventies, the *VBK* were commissioned by the German Government to create a single cemetery at Maleme, on a site on Hill 107, overlooking the airfield where so many German's had died. They had to principally rely on donations, with volunteers, former comrades from the *Fallschirmjäger* and *Gerbirgjäger Division* helping with the construction.

More than 4,466 bodies, from both the invasion and occupation periods, collected from across Crete, were eventually buried in the cemetery, which was consecrated on 6 October 1974. Since then, international youth camps and small parties from the *Bundeswehr*, regularly help the *Volksbund* gardeners to maintain the cemetery.

The information area at the entrance is amongst the best to be found anywhere. The information on the cemetery, the effect of the communist East on the families' knowledge of their next of kins' fate and the extent of the current work of the *Volksbund* is outstanding. The personal stories are in many cases harrowing.

The *Volksbund* decided not to have a single architectural scheme like the British, American or the French. The style of uniform gravestone, cross of

GEFREITER
KARL-HEINZ JOHN
8.4.1921 + 23.5.1941

JÄGER
ALEXANDER HEIM
27.5.1921 + 23.5.1941

85 86

sacrifice or national flag were rejected, instead, they elected to design the gardens and memorials that blend with the natural features of the local area. The Maleme Cemetery is divided into four plots, representing the principal battle areas during the invasion; Maleme, Hania, Rethymno and Iraklio. Each grave marker bears the names of two of the German dead. In the centre of the cemetery, mounted on the walls of the terrace, are metal plaques, memorials to the missing, listing the 360 German soldiers who lost their lives on Crete and have no known grave.

Convicted as a war criminal and executed, former Military govenor of Crete Brauer was, in a magnanimous gesture by the Greek Government, allowed to be buried amongst his *Fallschirmjäger* comrades. He was held responsible for the deaths of some 3,000 persons in Crete during the German occupation, also for murders and massacres; systematic terrorism, deportations, pillage, wanton destruction and torture and ill-treatment of civilians. He was shot 20 May 1947.

CWGC Cemetery Souda Bay

The site of Souda Bay CWGC Cemetery at the end of the bay overlooking the blue water of the natural harbour was selected at the end of the war by the returning Commonwealth military. Graves were moved there from the four burial grounds that had been established by the German occupying forces at Hania, Iraklio, Rethymno and Galatas, as well as from isolated battlefield and civilian cemeteries. However, it became apparent to 21st and 22nd Australian War Graves Units who undertook the work, that the German victors took few steps to adequately record the identities of bodies or to mark the resulting graves properly. This accounts for the high proportion of unidentified graves in Souda Bay Cemetery; 778 graves out of 1,502. The special memorials commemorate men known to have been buried with other men but whose actual graves cannot be identified.

The cemetery was designed by Louis de Soissons (1890-1962), a Canadian by birth, who designed Welwyn Garden City before the war and was the Commission's architect for all Second World War cemeteries and memorials in Italy, Greece and Australia. The forecourt is paved with rosso di Verona marble and travertine limestone. Around and between the stone, pebbles are set in decorative patterns. Inside the cemetery, on the left, is a shelter with walls of the same travertine stone, in alternate dark and light bands, and with a roof of red Roman tiles. The register, visitors' book and the historical notice are located in the shelter. The planting around the cemetery includes shrubs from New Zealand and Australia, reflecting their leading contribution to the island's defence.

Those Commonwealth servicemen who died ashore on Crete and who have no known grave are commemorated by name on the Athens Memorial, which is in Phaleron cemetery, at Athens. There are also 19 First World War graves and 37

The CWGC Cemetery at the eastern end of Souda Bay.

other graves that were moved from Souda Bay Consular cemetery in 1963. These include graves of civilians, seamen and the military particularly the Seaforth Highlanders.

There are three Special Boat Service/1st Special Air Service Regiment graves dating from late 1944 and 1945, prior to the liberation of the island. They are Captain Charles Maurice CLYNES MC attached from the Royal Irish Fusiliers (16.A.20), Craftsman Leslie CORNTHWAITE attached from the Royal Electrical & Mechanical Engineers (16.B.1), Lieutenant Kenneth Butler LAMONBY, Suffolk Regiment (13.E.12) and Private Thomas MORRIS Royal Army Service Corps (16.B.2).

Amongst those buried in the British cemeteries at Souda Bay, there are three Germans. The *Volksbund* explained that buried in Souda bay are:

> *...two civilians as well as Alfred Hamann, whose rank was that of a corporal. The fact that he is buried in Souda Bay is the result of a mistake. His mortal remains were discovered near Maleme in 1956 while building work was being carried out. At the request of the local*

281

*police chief, his identity tag was removed from the body, and his remains were
again buried provisionally in a garden in Maleme.*

In 1960 his remains were recovered by the re-burial service of the *Volksbund*. The
only thing that was found on him was a watch which had been made in England.
For this reason, the body was held to be that of a fallen British soldier and was
handed over to the British War Graves Commission, which had the remains
buried in Souda Bay.

Only later was it discovered from his ID disks that it was in fact *Oberjager*
Alfred Hamann, of *10 Kompanie Luftlande Sturm Regiment* who was killed in
action on 20 May 1941. The *Volksbund* continue:

> *Following an agreement reached between the Commonwealth War Grave
> Commission and the* Volksbund, *a decision was taken not to transfer the
> remains again from Souda Bay to the Maleme cemetery. The two German
> civilians - Carl Wagner and Johann Troyer - were buried in Souda Bay as a
> result of a mistake made by CWGC staff. After details of their nationality
> were clarified, their mortal remains were left in the British cemetery.*

ORDERS OF BATTLE

Particularly in the case of CREFORCE the size of unit or sub-unit, its equipment and capability should be treated with caution in the list below. Greek 'Regiments' were mostly of battalion strength and organisation.

RM = Royal Marines, RA = Royal Artillery, RHA = Royal Horse Artillery, RE = Royal Engineers

CREFORCE

SUDA-HANIA SECTOR

Mobile Naval Base Defence Organisation 1, Royal Marines

Artillery

Z Coast Battery, RM

15th Coast Regiment, RA (-)

Y Battery

'S' Group Heavy Anti-aircraft

HQ 2nd Heavy Anti-aircraft Regiment, RM

A Heavy Anti-aircraft Battery, RM

C Heavy Anti-aircraft Battery (-), RM

234th Heavy Anti-aircraft Battery, RA

23rd Light Anti-aircraft Battery (-), RM

304th Searchlight Battery, RA

'M' Light Anti-aircraft Group

HQ 52nd Light Anti-aircraft Regiment, RA

151st Heavy Anti-aircraft Battery (-)

129th Light Anti-aircraft Battery

156th Light Anti-aircraft Battery (-)

Troop and section, 7th Royal Australian Light Anti-aircraft Battery

Engineers

Crete Composite Company, RE

42nd Field Company (-), RE

5th Field Park Company, Royal New Zealand Engineers

Infantry

9th Battalion, The King's Royal Rifle Corps (The Rangers)

106th (Lancashire Hussars) Light Anti-aircraft Regiment RHA (-) (Infantry role)

102nd (Northumberland Hussars) Anti-tank Regiment, RA (Infantry role)

S Battery, 11th Searchlight Regiment, Royal Marines (Infantry role)

211th Medium Battery, RA (Infantry role)

122nd Light Anti-aircraft Battery, RA (Infantry role)

16th Australian Composite Battalion (2/2nd and 2/3rd Bns)

17th Australian Composite Battalion (2/5th and 2/6th Bns)

2/3rd Field Regiment, Royal Australian Artillery (Infantry role)

2/2nd Field Regiment, Royal Australian Artillery

The Royal Perivolians (assorted British sub-units)

2nd Greek Regiment

CREFORCE Reserve

Squadron (-), 3rd King's Own Hussars

1st Battalion, The Welch Regiment

MALEME SECTOR

2 New Zealand Infantry Division

4 New Zealand Infantry Brigade

18th New Zealand Battalion

19th New Zealand Battalion

20th New Zealand Battalion

Company, 27th New Zealand Machine Gun Battalion

5 New Zealand Infantry Brigade

Section B Squadron, 7th Royal Tank Regiment (two Matilda Tanks)

21st New Zealand Battalion

22nd New Zealand Battalion

23rd New Zealand Battalion

28th (Maori) New Zealand Battalion

19th Army Troops Company, Royal New Zealand Engineers (infantry role)

7th Field Company, Royal New Zealand Engineers (infantry role)

1st Greek Regiment

Company, 27th New Zealand Machine Gun Battalion

10 New Zealand Infantry Brigade

New Zealand Divisional Cavalry Regiment

Composite Battalion (Infantry Role)

4th NZ Field Regt part of 5th NZ Field Regt

Detachment 7th NZ Anti-Tank Regiment

4th Reserve Mechanical Transport Company

Elements 5th NZ Field Company RNZASC
(Petrol Company)
6th Greek Regiment
8th Greek Regiment
Company, 27th New Zealand Machine Gun
Battalion

Divisional Troops

Artillery
Z Coast Battery, Royal Marines
Detachment, 15th Coast Regiment, RA
Troop, 151st Heavy Anti-aircraft Battery, RA
5th New Zealand Field Regiment
27th Battery (in support of 5 NZ Bde)
28th Battery (in support of 10 NZ Bde)
Troop, C Heavy Anti-aircraft Battery, Royal
Marines
23rd Light Anti-aircraft Battery, RM (two
troops)
156th Light Anti-aircraft Battery, RA
7th Light Anti-aircraft Battery, Royal
Australian Artillery

IRAKLIO SECTOR
14 Infantry Brigade

Airfield Area
Troop B Squadron, 7th Royal Tank Regiment
2nd Battalion, The York & Lancaster
Regiment
2nd Battalion, The Black Watch
2nd Battalion, The Leicestershire Regiment
2/4th Australian Battalion

Iraklio Town and Area
Greek Garrison Battalion
7th Medium Regiment, RA (infantry role)
3rd Greek Regiment
7th Greek Regiment

Troop, 3rd King's Own Hussars
Artillery
Detachment, 15th Coast Regiment, RA
Troop, C Heavy Anti-aircraft Battery,
Royal Marines
7th Light Anti-aircraft Battery (-) Royal
Australian Artillery
Troop, 156th Light Anti-aircraft Battery
Section, 23rd Light Anti-aircraft Battery,
Royal Marines
234th Medium Battery, RA

Engineers
Section, 42nd Field Company, RE

RETHYMNO-GEORGEOUPOLIS SECTOR
19 Australian Infantry Brigade
Greek Gendarmerie

Rethymno Area
Section, B Squadron, 7th Royal Tank Regt
2/1st Australian Battalion
2/11th Australian Battalion
2/3rd Field Regiment (-), Royal Australian
Artillery
4th Greek Regiment
5th Greek Regiment
Company, 2/1st Australian Machine Gun
Battalion

Georgioupolis Area
2/7th Australian Battalion
2/8th Australian Battalion
X Coast Battery, RM
Battery, 2/3rd Field Regiment, Royal
Australian Artillery
Section, 106th (Lancashire Hussars) Light
Anti-aircraft Regiment, RHA
2/8th Field Company, Royal Australian
Engineers

Tymbaki Area
1 Battalion Argyll and Sutherland Highlanders
7th Royal Tank Regiment (3 Matildas)

LAYFORCE

A Battalion, Layforce Commando
D Battalion, Layforce Commando

XI FLIEGERKORPS
7 *Flieger Division*

Gruppe West
Luftlande Sturm Regiment
  I Battalion (- 2 companies)
  II Battalion
  III Battalion
  IV Battalion (support Weapons)
3 Kompanie FJ MG Battalion 7 (-)
1 Kompanie FJ Artillery Battalion 7

Gruppe Mitt
Galatas Sector:
Fallschirmjäger Regiment 3
  I Battalion
  II Battalion
  III Battalion
2 companies Luftlande Sturm Regiment
Detachment 3 Kompanie FJ MG Battalion 7
Fallschirmjäger Pioneer Battalion 7
1 Kompanie Fallschirmjäger Medical
Battalion

Rethymno Sector:
Fallschirmjäger Regiment 2
  I Battalion
  III Battalion
2 Kompanie FJ Artillery Battalion 7
1 and 2 Kompanie FJ MG Battalion 7

Gruppe Ost
Fallschirmjäger Regiment 1
  I Battalion
  II Battalion
  III Battalion
Fallschirmjäger Regiment 2
  II Battalion
2 Kompanie Fallschirmjäger Medical
Battalion

INDEX

287